How to W
(And T

Robert Graham

How to Write a Short Story (And Think About It)

2nd edition

First published 2006 by Palgrave Macmillan
Second edition published 2017 by
PALGRAVE

Palgrave in the UK is an imprint of Macmillan Publishers Limited, registered in England, company number 785998, of 4 Crinan Street, London, N1 9XW.

Palgrave® and Macmillan® are registered trademarks in the United States, the United Kingdom, Europe and other countries.

ISBN 978–1–137–51705–0 hardback
ISBN 978–1–137–51706–7 paperback

A catalogue record for this book is available from the British Library.

A catalog record for this book is available from the Library of Congress.

Contents

Contributors

James Friel's most recent novel is *The Posthumous Affair*. His other novels include *The Higher Realm, Left of North, Taking the Veil* and *Careless Talk*. He is programme leader for the MA in Writing at Liverpool John Moores University.

Rodge Glass is the author of the novels *No Fireworks* (Faber, 2005), *Hope for Newborns* (Faber, 2008) and *Bring Me the Head of Ryan Giggs* (Serpent's Tail, 2012); also the graphic novel *Dougie's War* (Freight, 2010, with Dave Turbitt), *LoveSexTravelMusik: Stories for the EasyJet Generation* (Freight, 2013) and *Alasdair Gray: A Secretary's Biography* (Bloomsbury, 2008), which won a Somerset Maugham Award in 2009. His work has been nominated for multiple awards, and been translated into Danish, Hebrew, Italian, Serbian, Spanish and Slovenian. He is currently a Reader in Literary Fiction at Edge Hill University and Co-Director of Edge Hill University Press.

Ursula Hurley teaches English and Creative Writing at the University of Salford, where she is Director of Postgraduate Research for the School of Arts and Media. Her research and teaching interests include hybrid, experimental prose practices, historical fiction and contemporary women's writing. She is a founding editorial board member of the Intellect journal, *Short Fiction in Theory and Practice*, although the day job doesn't leave a lot of time for her own practice at the moment.

Heather Leach's stories have appeared in *Salt Best British Short Stories, Mslexia, The Big Issue, City Life Book of Manchester Stories, Northern Stories, Metropolitan* and *Pool*, and on BBC Radio. Her non-fiction has been published in *Dedal-Lit, Mslexia*, the *Times Higher Education Supplement* and others. She is co-editor of *Everything You Need to Know About Creative Writing* (Continuum, 2007) and *The Road to Somewhere* (Palgrave Macmillan, 2014, 2nd edn). She has won a number of literary prizes.

Helen Newall is a Professor of Theatre Praxis, and a Research Impact Fellow at Edge Hill University. She has written for companies such as the Nuffield Theatre, Southampton; Action Transport; Chester Gateway Theatre; HTV West Television Workshop; the Royal Liverpool Philharmonic Orchestra; and Quays Culture, Salford. She is a writer-in-residence with award-winning company Theatre in the Quarter, for whom she has written several plays, including the acclaimed *Over by Christmas*, which toured railway stations in 2014 to audiences of over 20,000. She is a co-editor and contributor to *The Road to Somewhere: A Creative Writing Companion* (Palgrave Macmillan, 2014, 2nd edn).

Jenny Newman has written two novels, *Going In* (Penguin) and *Life Class* (Chatto & Windus), and *A Novel in Nine Steps* (Mslexia). She is a co-writer of *The Lille Diaries: A Writers' Group Weekend* (Hawkins & Quiggin), editor of *The Faber Book of Seductions*, and co-editor of *Women Talk Sex: Autobiographical Writing on Sex, Sexuality and Sexual Identity* (Scarlet Press), *British and Irish Novelists: An Introduction Through Interviews* (Arnold) and *The Writer's Workbook* (Arnold). Her short fiction has been widely published, and she has contributed to many books on contemporary writing. She was formerly Head of the Centre for Writing at Liverpool John Moores University.

James Rice is a writer from Liverpool. His debut novel *Alice and the Fly* was published in the UK in 2015 by Hodder and Stoughton, and has since been published in the United States, Mexico, Turkey and Sweden. He also writes short stories, several of which have been published, and writes songs with his friend Josh, which he sings in a very high-pitched voice people have charitably referred to as 'unique'. He occasionally teaches creative writing at Liverpool John Moores University and is currently working on his second novel.

Tom Vowler is the author of two novels and two short story collections, and his essays and stories have appeared widely. He is an associate lecturer at Plymouth University, where he completed his PhD. Tom is editor of the literary journal *Short Fiction*, and occasional all-rounder for the Authors XI.

Acknowledgements

This isn't the first time I'll say this, but I'd like to express my gratitude to HTWSS's guest contributors. Apart from writing terrific chapters, they have also suggested titles for 'Stories and Resources to Read (And Think About)', which you can find at the end of the book.

It was characteristically kind of Angi Holden and Jo Selley to allow me to quote from some of their reflective writing. Thanks, both.

I want to thank my editor, Rachel Bridgewater, for her insights, guidance and patience; Clarissa Sutherland and Vidya Venkiteshwaran Iyer, who were kind and generous as they guided me through the production process; Graham Hughes for eagle-eyed copy editing; and my family, for being more or less willing to live with a writer.

Introduction

George Saunders' collection *Tenth of December* debuted at number 3 in the *New York Times* fiction bestseller list, and the same newspaper called it 'The best book you'll read this year'. At one time, a short story collection was a novelist's whim, an indulgence publishers would grant, as long as the novels sold in great quantities, but Alice Munro, the most acclaimed English language short story writer of the past fifty years, has published nothing but short story collections, and in 2013 she won the Nobel Prize for Literature. Short Stops, one of many online short story forums, lists 206 UK and Irish literary magazines that currently publish stories. As lit mags accepting stories also exist in, for instance, Canada, Australia and the US, it's reasonable to assume that there are hundreds of online and print magazines in the English-speaking world – maybe even a thousand or two.

Authors of short stories don't lack outlets for their work, and magazines are not the only market. Thresholds, another online story forum, lists twenty-six UK publishers (majors and independents) who regularly release short story collections. Themed anthologies (Christmas, Birds, Transgender, Ghost, Horror, Boxing, World War I – you name it) abound, as do annual round-ups such as Houghton Mifflin's long-established *Best American Short Stories* and its more recent transatlantic equivalent, Salt Publishing's *Best British Short Stories*. These are further indications of a growing interest in the form. Any way you care to look at it, the short story is no longer fiction's poor relation. It's a celebrated, popular and, it appears, commercially viable form. Maybe nobody writing now will earn the $120,000 a year (in today's money) that F. Scott Fitzgerald in his prime made from his stories, but in the twenty-first century the short story is flourishing.

According to Lorrie Moore, 'A short story is a love affair; a novel is a marriage. A short story is a photograph; a novel is a film.' Leaner and more distilled, a story is said to be less like a novel, more like a poem. It can take all kinds of shapes, too. It may have a beginning, middle and end; or omit the beginning and end; or consist of an interior monologue; or come in the form of an instruction manual, or a list, or a series of post-card messages. Et cetera.

In terms of length, nobody can say for sure when a flash fiction becomes a short story, or when a story becomes a novella, but there is broad agreement that short stories are short. Possibly. Edgar Allan Poe's much-quoted definition – a short story is a fiction that can be read in one sitting – isn't entirely accurate. A short story may be long, a good bit longer than you might think. Ten-thousand-word Alice Munro stories are common, but 10,000 words isn't as long as a story can get. In his introduction to *The Granta Book of the American Long Story*, Richard Ford suggested a point where a work of fiction ceases to be a short story and becomes a novella. 'When a writer approaches the 20,000-word mark, he knows he's edging out of the country of the short story.'[1]

Stories may be tauter, arguably purer and possibly more elegant, but certainly more distilled than novels. Since it may not take as long to write, and since completing one might not drain your energy and emotions as much, you might think the short story is less demanding than long-form fiction. Not so. Hemingway was once asked to explain what it was that led to him writing thirty-nine drafts of *A Farewell to Arms*. 'Getting the words right,' he replied. If it's difficult to do that when writing a novel, how much more will that be the case when writing a story? You won't be able to conceal it if you fall short of Hemingway's objective. Readers will be more likely to notice it when you use an inexact word or place the right word in the wrong place. And getting the words right is only one of the problems facing you, as I hope you'll see while going through the book you're now holding in your hands.

So. Nobody knows for sure what a short story is, or how long it ought to be, and whatever it is and whatever its length, you may already have come to understand that writing one is difficult. Nonetheless, for all kinds of reasons, writers want to tackle the form – which is why you're reading this book.

How to Write a Short Story (And Think About It) – let's call it *HTWSS* – is divided into five parts. The design of Parts III to V ought to be clear when you glance at the contents pages, but let me unpack the first two parts a little. Part I, 'How A Writer Works', introduces you to some primary writer's disciplines: reading as a writer, writing practice and using a writer's journal, for example. Through studying examples of good practice and practising the craft of fiction yourself, Part II, 'How to Write a Short Story', examines some of the elements of craft that writers of fiction use. To illustrate, when we come to look at dialogue, you will be offered suggestions about what makes for good dialogue. You will have the chance to analyse its use in Elizabeth McCracken's story 'It's Bad Luck to Die'. Along the way, you will be given writing exercises in which you will practise writing dialogue yourself, and perhaps emulate what you have learned from looking at the suggested theory and good practice. Broadly speaking, that's the approach in each chapter: theory of the element of craft; analysis of its use in a particular story; and relevant writing exercises. In this way, over time, my hope is that *HTWSS* will help you acquire a portfolio of skills and techniques – a writer's toolbox, if you like. (It's sometimes repetitive, which I hope is not a bad thing.)

The bracketed part of the book's title indicates the centrality to writing of reflective learning. In thinking about your work, you will become more real to yourself as a writer, which is important. Reflection will help you develop the habit of examining the creative processes involved in your work and the reading that informs it. Reflective writing leads to a growing understanding of the kind of writer you are and the literary context to which you belong, an awareness that's essential to any creative writer.

After studying a craft text like this, it's possible to feel daunted when you sit down to write, to feel weighed down by all the craft you think you're supposed to have learned. Don't be. When you come to redraft, you might wish to consult a particular chapter to overcome a specific problem, but at first draft stage just trust your unconscious mind. Everything you need to have learned from this book will be lodged safely there, and will emerge as you fill the empty page.

Writer-teachers who more than cover my blind spots have greatly enhanced *HTWSS*. James Friel, Heather Leach, Helen Newall and Ursula Hurley have generously revised the already sharp and informed chapters they wrote for the first edition, and Rodge Glass, Jenny Newman, James Rice and Tom Vowler have written new, equally insightful chapters for this one. I'm very grateful to them, and I'd urge you to seek out and enjoy their fiction.

Most of what I know about writing short stories I've learned from teaching writing, so I'd like to thank my students for what we've learned together. In researching and writing my chapters for this book and studying my guest contributors', I've learned more about how to write a short story. I hope you will, too. Your future, you can be certain, is going to consist of years and years of honing your writing and studying the craft of other practitioners; years of reading and writing, reading and writing, reading and writing. If the study of craft texts such as this one is important, reading and studying short stories is essential. *HTWSS* uses extracts from many. It wouldn't do you any harm to go off and read the stories from which they are derived – and seeking out the collections and anthologies recommended at the back of this book, in 'Stories and Resources to Read (And Think About)', would be a good idea, too.

Wherever it takes you, enjoy your reading and your writing. It may be the most fun you can have with your clothes on.

Note

1   In his introduction to *The Granta Book of the American Long Story* (London: Granta Books, 1998).

Part I

How a Writer Works

1

How a Writer Works

Many people believe that our creative practice divides into two categories, however we label those categories. It has been suggested that producing great writing was 99 per cent perspiration and 1 per cent inspiration, but this is the division of creativity we're talking about: between the work that the imagination produces and the labour that goes into producing the finished whole. Oscar Wilde argued that genius was an infinite capacity for detail, which, like the inspiration/perspiration proverb, suggests that the balance lies firmly on the side of effort. Most informed opinion, however, indicates a more even split between inspiration and perspiration – that creativity involves both stages. The process is one of having an idea and then fashioning it into shape. In writing fiction, the first stage is the imagining. This comes from the same place as your dreams: the unconscious mind.

Unconscious Mind

Think for a moment: when did you last have a light bulb moment? You know, that feeling when a cartoon light bulb appears above your head because, in a flash, you've just had a great idea? Suddenly it has occurred to you that the new Bowie compilation is the perfect birthday present for your brother. Or it comes to you with a shock of recognition how you can afford to go to Australia *and* pay your tuition fees.

Think of a recent light bulb moment of your own and try to remember what you were doing at the time. Most likely you were engaged in something repetitive and tedious, something hypnotically dull. Driving at a steady 70 mph on a quiet motorway. Ironing shirts. Walking the dog.

Here's another form of light bulb moment: you wake in the night for the toilet and while you're there calmly doing your business it occurs to you with brutal clarity that you should visit your parents more often, that in fact you weren't that nice to your dad the last time you did visit them. Or another: you wake up ten minutes before the alarm and while you're lying there crawling towards consciousness you all of a sudden see the solution to a conflict between two of your close co-workers. Or another: you dream a perfect narrative, what feels like an infinitely more realised, more compelling, more delightful story than you could ever conceive of awake. What do these light bulb moments have in common? You've probably got there way before me. Apart from the perfect story in a dream, when you obviously *were* unconscious, in all of these examples, you were either entering or leaving your unconscious mind. Waking in the morning or getting up in the night, obviously you were just coming out of unconsciousness. In all the other examples, your mind was being nudged towards it – put into neutral gear, you might say – by repetitive, tedious conditions. In other words, good ideas emerge from the unconscious mind. Sometimes they may arrive fully formed. John Lennon differentiated between songs that appeared in a handful of minutes, which he regarded as inspired, and songs that he had to chip away at over time, which he saw as of inferior quality because he had fashioned them with the craft he had built up over years. Sometimes the unconscious may throw up an idea ready to go.

Many writers eschew plotting; setting off with only a vague idea of where they are heading, they write to discover. Pat Barker argues that the narrative structure 'is the gift of the unconscious' and Barbara Trapido speaks of a story 'lying under the surface, and you're trying to dredge it up'. Guy Claxton, a professor of psychology, corroborates this:

Even scientists themselves, or at least the more creative of them, admit that their genius comes to them from layers of mind over which they have little or no control (and they may even feel somehow fraudulent for taking personal credit for insights that simply 'occurred to them').[1]

Dorothea Brande, too, is adamant that it isn't by labouring, whittling, revising or restructuring 'that an excellent piece of art is born. It takes shape and has its origin outside the region of the conscious intellect.'[2] You could see the flash of inspiration as a postcard from your unconscious that invites you to come and visit and discover the whole of what that inspired moment intimates.

One way in which you may tap into the fully realised form of the inspired idea is in the writing itself. We've seen that inspiration may arrive when the mind has been stilled by monotonous, rhythmic activity, but isn't the act of writing itself, whether on a keyboard or with pen and paper, rhythmic and monotonous? In both instances – the arrival of the inspiration and the production of the first draft – aren't you experiencing something similar to being hypnotised by the proverbial pocket watch swinging back and forth before your eyes? 'The process of imagination that underlies creative writing,' says Madison Smartt Bell, 'what happens just as or just before you are putting the words down on the page, must inevitably involve a process of autohypnosis.'[3]

Throughout her classic book *Becoming a Writer*, Dorothea Brande approaches the functions of the unconscious from a variety of angles and suggests that the unconscious mind is not just where ideas come from, but also a facility for developing those ideas until they reach their final, fully realised form:

> Every author, in some way which he has come on by luck or long search, puts himself in a very light state of hypnosis ... Far behind the mind's surface, so deep that he is seldom aware (unless at last observation of himself has taught him) that any activity is going forward, his story is being fused and welded into an integrated work.[4]

Brande not only argues that knowing when our unconscious mind is in the ascendant will benefit the writer, but also that 'it is possible to learn to tap it at will, and even to direct it'. At an advanced stage in a story's gestation, during the work that leads to completing it, she talks of inducing 'the artistic coma', of pausing the mind in order to mine the unconscious. 'Learn to hold your mind as still as your body,' she tells us[5] and puts forward a model that amounts, really, to meditation: stilling the mind by focusing on a word or an object. Brande recommends holding a rubber ball and focusing on it until the chattering monkey of the conscious mind is silenced. When we achieve this state – to do so, Brande recommends a walk followed by a bath *and* focusing in a meditative fashion on a rubber ball – we may escape into the unconscious mind. For Natalie Goldberg, one of the contemporary gurus of Creative Writing, this term is too limiting; for her, that creative part of the mind is *wild mind*. Here, in her book of the same name, she recommends that we

> let everything run through us and grab as much as we can of it with pen and paper. Let yourself live in something that is already rightfully yours – your own wild mind … This is all about loss of control … Can you do this? Lose control and let wild mind take over? It is the best way to write.[6]

Writers need solitude and headspace, time for idling and daydreaming. In this respect, being a writer is time-costly; a frenetic, jam-packed life doesn't lend itself to creative endeavour. You will need the time and the space to stare out of the window, to muck about, to *play*. In learning to maximise your access to your unconscious mind, you could do worse than think of the novelist William Boyd's working day, as he outlined it in a British newspaper feature. He has a fairly leisurely start to the day with breakfast at about nine or nine thirty. After pottering about, looking at the papers and so on, he leaves the house around eleven and walks for miles around his neighbourhood, maybe stopping for a coffee in an agreeable café bar or to flip through CDs in his favourite record shop. He gets home in time for lunch about two and shortly after that, when he's feeling more like having a nap than working, he settles at the keyboard and works until around six, when he stops to cook for himself and his wife, have drinks and dinner, a bit of chat with maybe a few more drinks and then bedtime. At first glance, not a heavy day's work, but isn't half of Boyd's work, possibly the most important half, done during the hours he spends walking?

My experience is that the ideas that come when I'm out on a walk are more insightful, more inspired, than those I get when I'm at my desk, trying hard to develop a story. After two or three hours' work, I take a couple of questions about the story out for a walk. What happens next is unfailingly the case: after thirty-five to forty minutes' walking, pithy, creative, helpful ideas begin to flow. I record them, and when I look at them back at my desk, all are relevant, some more so than others. At that point, all I have to do is sift through them to see which insights I will apply to the ongoing work, which ideas are the solutions to the problems I took out for a walk. Brande writes about it, and here I am testifying about my experience. Walking works, every time.

Conscious Mind

Understanding the unconscious and learning to manage it is something we have to learn (or relearn) in adult life. Western education prioritises conscious mind functions from the start. Schools, colleges and universities depend on order, judging, analysis, logic and rationality. Even before we reach nursery school, the order and logic of language is being imposed on our young, chaotically creative minds. I see this every autumn when the new first year arrives. In each workshop there will be an academic student, very diligent, reliable and organised, probably with great A level results, who in an English Literature class can analyse the life out of a text, squeezing every last drop of meaning from it in an accomplished, literate fashion. He may have been head boy at school and the linchpin of the debating society. He has probably spent the past two years being his local Tesco's most reliable Saturday worker. But this same student won't know where to start with filling a blank page with original writing. In fact, this student lives so much in his conscious mind that he is paralysed by the very idea of having to put even one letter on the blank page; he will be worrying about the syntax, the punctuation and whether or not he could ever come up with an original thought of his own. When we move on to reading as a writer, or learning to show rather than tell, this same student will make a pig's ear of it; not only that, but he lives so much in his conscious mind, organising his life, analysing and criticising whatever is put in front of him, that he will find it almost impossible to be inspired to understand *why* he is making a pig's ear of it.

In the same class, there will be a chaotic freewheeler, the kid with tattered T-shirt and limited personal organisation who attends haphazardly, and this one will fill a page without stopping to think about it, fill it with good stuff, too. Maybe she's doing Drama alongside Creative Writing, so she's used to improvising, I don't know, but she's already got the hardest part under her belt: she knows how to use her unconscious mind – and she probably doesn't even know she knows it.

Most of us spend far too much of our lives living in the conscious mind. It's how we pass the exams that get us into university and on in life, but it isn't, at the core, how a writer works.

Balancing Unconscious and Conscious

Throughout *Becoming a Writer*, Dorothea Brande puts the case for the existence of these two sides of the mind, the unconscious and the conscious. She goes as far as recommending that we consider them not just as separate functions of the same mind but almost 'as separate personalities' and argues that, with discipline, we may learn to balance our use of these two distinct personalities. Yes, you have to train yourself to give rein to or hold in check both your inner Tie-dyed Truant *and* your inner Head Boy. 'The composition of fiction can, at least theoretically, be broken into two stages,' Madison Smartt Bell says. 'First, and most important, comes imagination. Next is rendering.'[7] You need to be able to turn on both your playful, imaginative attributes and your critical, reflective, analytic gifts, and you need to be able to switch between the two modes at will. Guy Claxton devotes a good deal of energy in *Hare Brain, Tortoise Mind* to examining how we may move backwards and forwards between unconscious and conscious mind, how we may close the gap between the two. Here Dorothea Brande proposes a way in which they may be used to complement one another:

> The unconscious must flow freely and richly, bringing at demand all the treasures of memory, all the emotions, incidents, scenes, intimations of character and relationship which it has stored away in its depths; the

conscious mind must control, combine, and discriminate between these materials without hampering the unconscious flow.[8]

When you write a story, this has several implications. I've already gone into some detail about what our unconscious is capable of, so let's look very briefly at the conscious mind. Its functions will include reading as a writer (see Part I, Chapter 5: 'How to Read as a Writer') and everything we learn about craft, in and out of the workshop, through looking at how published fiction writers achieve their effects. They will include emulating tricks you see your favourite author pull off. Conscious mind functions also include theories about certain elements of craft (characterisation, dramatisation or transitions, for instance) that you study in your workshops or in texts like this.

If you understand the functions of the two parts of the mind and when to prioritise the one or the other, you've begun to understand how a writer works. And then you'll be on your way.

Notes

1   Guy Claxton, *Hare Brain, Tortoise Mind: Why Intelligence Increases When You Think Less* (London: 4th Estate, 1998), p 3.
2   Dorothea Brande, *Becoming a Writer* (New York: Jeremy P. Tarcher, 1999), p 149.
3   Madison Smartt Bell, *Narrative Design: A Writer's Guide to Structure* (New York: W.W. Norton, 1997), p 14.
4   Brande, *Becoming a Writer*, pp 159–60.
5   Brande, *Becoming a Writer*, p 164.
6   Natalie Goldberg, *Wild Mind* (London: Rider, 1991), pp 32–3.
7   Smartt Bell, p 15.
8   Brande, *Becoming a Writer*, pp 45–6.

2

Writers' Habits

In the forthcoming chapters, I'm going to be looking at some essential disciplines – notebooks and journals, reading as a writer, reflection, etc. – but first I want to examine writers' habits. The distinction between a discipline and a habit may be too subtle; perhaps what I mean by habits are just disciplines that I want to be emphatic about. You can decide. The fundamental writers' habits are reading and writing, so let's start there.

Reading

Stephen King's opinion on the importance of reading and writing is often quoted, which is probably a good enough reason to quote it again: 'If you want to be a writer, you must do two things above all others: read a lot and write a lot. There's no way around these two things that I'm aware of, no shortcut.'[1]

Many, many writers have articulated the reasons why writers must read. For Joyce Carol Oates, reading is an essential part of any writer's apprenticeship: 'Even before we know we will be writers, our reading is a part of our preparation for writing … Every book, every story, every sentence we read is a part of our preparation for our own writing.'[2]

This is corroborated by research into how we read. Jonathan Franzen interviewed an expert in the subject, Shirley Brice Heath, Professor of English and Linguistics at Stanford University.

> There's a second kind of reader. There's the social isolate – the child who from an early age felt very different from everyone around him … What happens is you take that sense of being different into an imaginary world. But that world, then, is a world you can't share with the people around you – because it's imaginary. And so the important dialogue in your life is with the *authors* of the books you read. Though they aren't present, they become your community.[3]

John Gardner uses the stick rather than the carrot: 'No ignoramus – no writer who has kept himself innocent of education – has ever produced great art.'[4]

You already know you're a compulsive reader, and you empathise with anyone who advocates reading as much as you can, reading like your life depended on it. Lesley Glaister has said that if it came to a choice between reading and eating, as long there was no question of dying from the decision, she would always opt for reading. You can never read too much. You write because you read and you read because you write. You won't be doing badly if, in years to come, you manage to acquire the breadth of Hemingway's influences:

> Mark Twain, Flaubert, Stendhal, Bach, Turgenev, Tolstoy, Dostoevsky, Chekhov, Andrew Marvell, John Donne, Maupassant, the good Kipling, Thoreau, Captain Marryat, Shakespeare, Mozart, Quevedo, Dante, Virgil, Tintoretto, Hieronymus Bosch, Brueghel, Patinir, Goya, Giotto, Cezanne, van Gogh, Gauguin, San Juan de la Cruz, Gongora – it would take a day to remember everyone. Then it would sound as though I were claiming an erudition I did not possess instead of trying to remember all the people who have been an influence on my life and work.[5]

When it comes to reading, quality counts as much as quantity. Your reading is what shapes your writing; it's your diet. Good nutrition makes for a healthy writer. I remember once hearing the notion expounded that what you focus on is what you image – or put more simply, what you concentrate on is what you will come to resemble. This is one of the reasons Stephen King insists that 'reading is the creative centre of the writer's life'.[6] Writers read.

Writing Exercise: The Reading Log

You're not going to benefit as much as you might from your reading if you don't create a means of digesting your intake. A reading log is one way to do it. Buy yourself a notebook that you will enjoy writing in, something that looks attractive and feels agreeable. Now keep it adjacent to wherever you do most of your reading: on the bedside table if you read in bed, on an occasional table if you read on the sofa in your living room. The kinds of entries you make in your reading log are up to you, but here, to get you started, are a few suggestions.

- Make notes on passages you especially admire. An example: I was reading Yiyun Li's story 'Immortality' (in her collection, *A Thousand Years of Good Prayers*), and I made some notes in my reading log on her confident use of narration.
- Reading fiction will inspire you. Art often inspires further art, in ways that have nothing to do with plagiarism or *homage*; you just get excited by the imagination of the writer you're reading, and that fires your own imagination. Have your reading log ready for such occasions.
- Sometimes your entries will be variations on the previous Writing Exercise: you will be looking at the use of a particular technique in the novel or story you're reading and making notes in your reading log.
- Then, when you finish what you're reading, you will want to see what you thought of it, which will be more fruitful if you write some concluding notes on it in your reading log. You'll be saying why this novel or story worked for you, or, to the extent that it didn't, saying why this was so.

Of course, keeping a reading log isn't a writing exercise at all; it's a way of life.

Natalie Goldberg commends the idea of *writing practice* (Chapter 1: 'How a Writer Works'), a discipline writers need in the same way as musicians need to practise their instrument or athletes to train each day. If you want to produce material you might use, first you have to write in order to teach yourself to say everything and anything in writing. You write to exercise your writing muscles, to train yourself to use all of the vocabulary you have somewhere inside your mind, to develop your style and your voice, to exercise your pen and your imagination. Nick Hornby once said that before he got going he had wanted in a vague way to be a writer. His turning point was when he realised that writers write.

Rules of Writing Practice[7]

1. Keep your hand moving
2. Lose control
3. Be specific
4. Don't think
5. Worry about punctuation & grammar later
6. You are free to write the worst junk
7. Go for the jugular

Dorothea Brande's *Becoming a Writer* suggests writing each day to develop the habit of opening up a channel to the unconscious mind, harvesting our own creativity. (See Chapter 1, 'How a Writer Works'.) Julia Cameron, author of *The Artist's Way*, calls this *Morning Pages*. She recommends three pages of longhand, stream-of-consciousness writing each morning. 'They are about anything and everything that crosses your mind – and they are for your eyes only. Morning Pages provoke, clarify, comfort, cajole ... Do not over-think Morning Pages; just put three pages of anything on the page ... and then do three more pages tomorrow.'[8]

Writers write. However, writers also study writing – you are, right this moment – and that can make producing a first draft feel daunting.

The Problem of Craft Consciousness

When you sit down to write, you – all of us – may be faced with a problem: the more you know from reading as a writer and studying your craft, the harder it is not to feel inhibited – as Madison Smartt Bell says here:

> So you go home from class with your pumped-up craft consciousness sitting on your shoulder ... When you sit down to write, you are stuck in yourself, paralysed by self-consciousness, unable to separate yourself, unable to relax your mind, unable to pass through the auto-hypnotic gate

into the realm where the narrative you are working with becomes true and alive to you. Whatever you write falls dead on the page.[9]

What do you do? How do you put pen to paper when you have the whole weight on your shoulders not only of world literature but also of your growing craft consciousness, built up over months and years of studying to be a writer? Well, you turn again to Natalie Goldberg's Rules of Writing Practice, specifically to rules 1, 2, 4, 5 and 6. And you forget about everything except, as Raymond Carver once memorably remarked, getting one word down after the other, one sentence down after the other. After that, you have all the time in the world to worry about whether or not it's any good. Writer first, editor second. I'll be saying that again. And when you turn to the task of reading your work critically, you'll know what to do because you'll have acquired the habit of reading all the fiction you can and constantly studying craft.

Free writing is one way of liberating yourself from the problem of craft consciousness.

Writing Bursts

Every class I teach begins with a ten-minute writing exercise I call a *writing burst*. I give a stimulus and ask the class to start writing and keep writing for ten minutes, and I encourage them not to stop to worry for one second about the quality of the work appearing on the paper.

This is good practice, and it ought to become a habit for you. Many of my students' writing bursts end up as the starting point for a short story or become scenes in finished short stories. In module evaluations, one of the things students consistently enthuse about is the writing burst. It makes you write, instils the discipline of writing without stopping to criticise and shows you how much may be achieved in only a short period of time. Producing 200 words in ten minutes isn't difficult. We all live lives that are too packed with activity, too full of online distractions, so discovering that ten minutes is a valuable amount of time to spend writing is an eye-opener and an encouragement.

This book is liberally sprinkled with writing bursts. The stimulus in most is an opening line or a topic, but I've also included visual and aural prompts. (You can also find all of the writing bursts collected at the end of the book.)

Each time you come to one in a chapter, I suggest you pause and write for ten minutes. After you've tried it a few times, you may find you want to make the practice of short writing bursts part of your daily routine. Try this:

Writing Burst
- 'This isn't what it looks like.'

Routine and Rituals

Writing fiction requires a routine. It's difficult to keep a piece of fiction at the centre of your consciousness if you aren't spending time with it, and it's impossible to keep your fiction-writing muscle working if you don't exercise it. When you're writing a story, you will need to spend at least an hour and ideally a morning working on it three, four, five or six days a week. (I'd recommend resting your work at least one day a week; breaks refresh you.)

As important as a routine is a rhythm. Nature isn't always active; sometimes it's dormant. In spring, summer and autumn the natural world is in different ways alive. In autumn nature pauses and then breaks off for the winter. As a writer, you too will have rhythms. You won't always be producing stories, but when you are writing, you will develop a ritual. All writers have their personal preferences when it comes to rituals and routines. These range from what makes practical sense through to quirky little habits and outright superstitions. Toni Morrison always gets up, makes a cup of coffee and watches the light come. Haruki Murakami rises at 4:00am and works for five to six hours. In the afternoon he exercises, runs errands and reads. In the evening, he listens to music before going to bed early. Stephen King always sits down at the same time, takes his vitamin pill, sits in the same seat, with his papers all arranged in the same places on his desk.

You'll know some of your own approaches to writing and you will already have made your choice about many of the following options.

It's possible, though, that one or two of them will present you with a choice you didn't know you had.

How, When, Where

Working late at night	Working early in the morning
Writing at home	Writing out in the world – in a café, in a park, in your local library, on a train
Maintaining a strict routine (same place, same times, same everything)	Working in various places and at different times, maybe even tackling the writing differently each time you go to compose
At a desk (even if it's the kitchen table), a desk where you sit or an upright desk or, in the case of Hemingway, standing up at a lectern	Lying down or even, like Truman Capote, writing in bed. Take encouragement from Anne Hartigan's lovely poem, *Heirloom*:
	My father said It's always good weather In bed.
Needing to be strictly alone	Working equally comfortably in the presence or absence of others
Beginning with a ritual, perhaps a superstitious act (Hemingway sharpened 20 pencils and Beethoven ground 60 coffee beans)	Starting in without ritual, without superstition
With a view out of a window	Avoiding a view, facing a wall
With music	Without music
With music that has lyrics or a libretto	With purely instrumental music
Writing	Dictating, to a secretary or an audio recorder
In longhand	Straight to the screen
With a quota (1,000 words a day etc.)	Without a target quota (Do you assess your success by quantity or by quality?)
Quickly	Slowly
Polishing as you go	Pressing through to the end of a first draft before beginning to redraft
Without ever moving except to eat or sleep	Getting up and walking round at regular intervals
Planning on paper or on-screen	Planning through the use of index cards, A1 sheets, or long scrolls spread out across the floor

If you want to know more about other writers' habits, you'll find any amount of material online. At the time of writing, *The Guardian* has been running a series on writers' working days: www.theguardian.com/books/series/my-writing-day. Naturally, these short features make for fascinating reading. 'Certain physical rituals help both the good days and the bad,' Rose Tremain says. 'A lettuce-enhanced cold lunch usually makes the afternoon writing stint feel possible.' Deborah Moggach mentions distractions, how she tries 'not to look at property porn, but the flesh is weak'.

You could also go the *Paris Review*'s site and dip into its vast reservoir of interviews with writers: www.theparisreview.org/interviews/. Here you can eat your fill of writers on writing. You will discover that Marilynne Robinson claims that while writing she dresses like a bum. 'John Cheever', she says, 'would wear a suit and a hat and go down from his apartment to the basement of his building with an attaché case. But that's not me.' Joan Didion needs 'an hour alone before dinner, with a drink, to go over what I've done that day. I can't do it late in the afternoon because I'm too close to it. Also, the drink helps. It removes me from the pages.'

If you're fascinated by the habits of other writers – and I'd guess that most of us are – you'll enjoy Mason Correy's *Daily Rituals*.[10]

Notes

1   Stephen King, *On Writing* (London: Hodder and Stoughton, 2000), p 164.

2   Joyce Carol Oates, *Telling Stories* (New York: W.W. Norton, 1997), p xv.

3   'Why Bother?' from Jonathan Franzen, *How to Be Alone* (London: 4th Estate, 2002), p 74.

4   John Gardner, *The Art of Fiction: Notes on Craft for Young Writers* (New York: Vintage, 1991), p 10.

5   Ernest Hemingway, quoted in George Plimpton (ed.), *The Writer's Chapbook* (New York: Penguin Books, 1992), p 12.

6   King, *On Writing*, p 173.

7   Goldberg, *Wild Mind*, pp 1–4.

8   Julia Cameron, 'Morning Pages', The Artist's Way, juliacameronlive.com/basic-tools/morning-pages (accessed 7 July 2016).

9   Bell, *Narrative Design*, p 15.

10   Mason Correy, *Daily Rituals* (London: Picador, 2014).

3

Making Notes

Why do 100-metre sprinters train? In part to keep fit, but perhaps mainly so that they are prepared for the events in which they will compete. Same deal with concert pianists: they practise in order to perfect their technique, to keep their fingers supple, to learn to keep in time, and it's all preparation for the occasions when they will perform. Every time you sit down to write fiction you are giving a performance. If you want to perform to the best of your ability, you need to practise, practise, practise – which is certainly part of what writers use notebooks for. John Fowles says, 'I am a great believer in diaries, if only in the sense that bar exercises are good for ballet dancers.'[1]

Writing Burst
- She didn't want to go to London.

The Present Moment

Throughout her books for writers, Natalie Goldberg talks about the importance of practice, and she is an enthusiastic advocate of writing in cafés. In the following extract, she recommends one way in which you may use your notebooks to keep writing fit:

There are two tall glass salt-and-pepper shakers on my wooden table, a pottery bowl full of white packages of sugar. Three pats of butter sit in a white dish, and my favourite pen, that one that Pueblo Runner Printing hands out freely and generously, is lying on the table pointing to the big white plate with only one slice of French bread left and a slice of tomato lying on a piece of lettuce. These are the original details. This is what is on the table. Now if you learn this deeply – what is in the present moment – you can transport it.[2]

Writing Exercise: The Present Moment

Take pen and notebook to a café where you know you're not too likely to be disturbed. Begin writing. Describe your surroundings in clean, clear language, working from the tabletop outwards. Stick with what's there. Occupy the moment fully. If you can do this to your own satisfaction, you will have increased your ability to express yourself in writing, to write descriptively and to record the world you live in, which is an important part of what writers do: hold up a mirror to the world, and some day others may read it and say, *Yes, that was my experience too. That was just how it seemed to me.*

Retaining Your Ideas

Artists maintain sketchbooks, which they carry about their person so that they may record stimuli as they find them, so that they may break off at various points in the day and, wherever they are, sit down and draw. What's good for Turner and Hockney is good for you, too: it's hard to be a writer, perhaps impossible, if you don't develop the habit of keeping a notebook on you at all times.

There are several reasons for learning this discipline. For one, without your notebook you run the risk of losing your ideas. Joseph Heller, the author of *Catch 22*, once remarked, 'I don't get my best ideas while actually writing.'[3] Your ideas for and about stories will come while you are mooching in shops, while you are unable to sleep in the middle of the night, while you are putting up shelves – mostly at times when you aren't at your keyboard working on your fiction. Carry a notebook.

How It Felt to Be You

Amongst the many further reasons for using notebooks is Joan Didion's in this extract from her essay 'On Keeping a Notebook':

> See enough and write it down, I tell myself, and then some morning when the world seems drained of wonder, some day when I am only going through the motions of doing what I am supposed to do, which is write – on that bankrupt morning I will simply open my notebook and there it will all be, a forgotten account with accumulated interest, paid passage back to the world out there: dialogue overheard in hotels and elevators and at the hatcheck counter ... *How it felt to me:* that is getting closer to the truth about a notebook ... *Remember what it was to be me:* that is always the point.[4]

As well as observing the present moment, as well as recording your ideas, your notebook may allow you to make a deposit in some metaphorical bank account, one from which you will withdraw in the future, and your withdrawal may be more than just the record of what you witnessed, more than just story material; it could be worthwhile as a record of how you were in the moments you were writing up what you saw, a record of how it felt to be you.

Maybe you think you know how it feels to be you. Writing about your observations and experiences in your notebooks would still be a good idea, though, because you may never be in that café, that situation, that city, that country, that moment again. And for sure, as time moves on, you will have forgotten what you saw and who you were. Look at this, which I came across recently:

> We've just come back from a short holiday at Glenwherry. Uncle Billy was cutting, 'tedding', turning and baling hay while we were there, so I saw plenty of the sun. The weather has been scorching for these last few days and it's just as warm here at the foot of Craigantlet. Jock, needless to say, is running about with his tongue hanging out. (Running is not quite the right word for it, though; slouching would fit better.) All the roses are out at the moment and there is a great variety of shades. One of the nicest is a beautiful maroon colour.

I have a whole stack of short stories, essays, poems, drawings and cartoons home with me which I am trying to edit into next term's school magazine, which we call *OINK*. This is a new idea which a few of us started last term. We have an editorial committee and each member of it takes a turn as editor. David Lloyd was editor of the first issue, which came out last term. I am the editor of issue two, which will come out at the beginning of next term. We sold about 250–300 copies at 6p each of the last one.

I know plenty about how it feels to be me now, but maybe not so much about how it felt to be that sixteen-year-old kid in 1972. All my adult life I've thought of myself as a person who hates rose bushes; here's the evidence that I once admired them. In 1972 I bought most of the attitudes I had been brought up with wholesale. Nowadays I haven't that many of them left. And so on. By the time you reach mid-life, you have been a lot of people. Use your notebook to record who you are while you are that person, and how it feels to be that person at that time. In due course, you will become somebody different, and the person you were may be lost. Why is this important? Because you can use these records in, or to inspire, your stories.

For Your Own Joy

In a list he made of attitudes and practices necessary to Jack Kerouac, the beat generation novelist, he notes the pleasure of having a place you can go to and write whatever you want. Number one on his list of thirty points was this: 'Scribbled secret notebooks, and wild typewritten pages, for your own joy.'[5]

Writing Exercise: The Joy of Notebooks

Get yourself a notebook to set aside as your den, your secret place, the snug you go to say everything you want to about everything that matters to you, everything that doesn't matter to anyone and all points in between. Keep this notebook for the sheer pleasure of pouring out your thoughts and feelings about your life, about you. Nobody ever has to see this; it's for you alone. It's your Batcave, your Fortress of Solitude, and what you do there will help you to be the superhero you are when you go to write a short story.

Paying Close Attention

The Greek word *skopos* means look out for or pay close attention. In English, we form the words 'telescope' and 'microscope' from *skopos*. This is instructive. We use a telescope to see things that are some distance away, and we use a microscope to see things so small we would otherwise miss them. You understand what I'm saying.

I went to Glasgow with a friend once and the first thing we did was take an underground train. On it, my friend took the only free seat and I hung on a strap. One of the nearby seats contained what seemed to be an old-fashioned hotel commissioner. He was wearing a dark blue uniform lavishly covered with brass buttons, gold braid and yellow and blue epaulettes. He was sporting mutton chops and holding an imperious looking hat. As I was drinking in every detail of this peacock, something caught my eye and I noticed that my friend was watching me study him and grinning her head off. I mouthed *What?* at her and she smiled and shook her head, as much as to say, *Never mind*. Afterwards, she told me that what she'd been laughing at was my habit of people-watching.

One of the writer's disciplines is paying close attention to the world you live in. My guess is you already study your surroundings. You'll know what it's like then to hoover up every detail of wherever you happen to be. It's watchfulness. It's being aware of your surroundings, of the people in them. It's noticing what goes on, what people look like, sound like. It's paying attention to the ways in which they interact. You're part anthropologist and part spy. Maybe you haven't been conscious until now that this is something you do; maybe you have. Either way, it's a tendency you might think of developing; it's a trait that you can easily turn into a discipline.

Writing Burst
- The next day was better.

Watching, Listening

Years ago, when I was in my twenties and, of course, arrogant, I remember feeling critical of an acquaintance that I considered boring and thinking to myself *I could write a more interesting character.* I was wrong. One thing to get straight as we start to look at the whole business of observing and writing stories is that life is invariably more interesting and more complex than fiction. Truth, the old saw goes, is stranger than fiction. You bet it is. The most seemingly uncomplicated person you know is infinitely more multi-faceted than any character you will ever create. Wilde said that drama is life with the dull parts left out, but there's no reason to conclude that life itself is universally dull. It's richly, abundantly of interest, and every time you leave your keyboard and venture into the thick of it, you'll be able to harvest all kinds of data, detail, characters, settings and narratives. All you have to do is be alert to what's around you.

Public places are full of stimulus for the writer. As you stand in the checkout queue at Tesco, you'll be able to read people by what they say to the staff scanning their purchases and by the contents of their shopping trolley. Last week as I was looking for a bottle of wine in Morrisons, I witnessed a micro-story. A guy in his late thirties was berating a member of staff, a calm woman who was biting her tongue and offering no resistance to his complaints. His problem was that the price of a pack of Heineken had been confusingly displayed. 'You've done this before,' he was saying. 'It's deceitful, it's a deliberate racket.' The assistant wasn't engaging with him, but was apologising if the signage had been misleading. She said she would report it. The angry guy wasn't satisfied, though, and turned on his heel to leave, shouting behind him that Morrisons had lost a customer.

There are two characters here, each distinct. One is angry for little reason; the other is calm and forbearing. If you were a writer taking all of this in, you would have the makings of a scene here: characters, conflict, setting. You might, as I did, conclude that this guy had had a bad day, that he was transferring anger about something else onto this trivial irritation. Maybe he had been angry since childhood. Maybe he didn't have all that much to put up with – not when you compared him with the assistant, who might be a single mother of three children, living in cramped conditions with a parent suffering from Alzheimer's. And so on.

Watching and listening are part of your job. Smelling, touching and tasting, too. What does the supermarket fresh produce aisle smell of?

Railway stations and airports are good places to observe and eavesdrop, too. Why? Because many people gather in these places and they are all interesting and all of them are in the middle of the thousands of stories that make up their lives. Public transport is a gift to the writer. There's nothing like sitting on a bus, a tram or a train and soaking it all up. Mobile phones have enhanced that. If, as I was, you were born in the middle of the last century, you will probably still be amazed at how naked people are prepared to allow their phones to leave them when they are travelling. On crowded trains, I've heard people discussing their sex lives on the phone. Mobile phones are pure gold for the writer. Join me on the train from Manchester to London and you'll see what I mean.

I'm sitting there, doing a bit of work, and I can't help but overhear the calls the guy in front of me is making. I can see through the gap between the two seats before me that he has a laptop on which he's working on spreadsheets between calls. From time to time, he scribbles on the screen of his smartphone with a little plastic stylus. He calls his secretary and asks her to book a restaurant for him in Berlin. His hi-spec gear suggests that he's a corporate high-flyer and he's definitely a bit of a thruster, very in control, taking care of business. But basically he sounds like an okay guy. Once we're past Watford, he kicks back, puts on headphones and watches an episode of *Mad Men*.

Then he makes a different kind of call. His tone is defensive now, not empowered. 'I just want what's best for you,' he's saying. 'I just want to make a good settlement for you and the kids. That's all.' He has to do a lot of listening during this call. At one point he refers to somebody who seems to be his lawyer. Finally, he's talking about a woman. 'You'd like her,' he says. 'I want you to meet her some time. I think you'd get on.' Then he makes a lot of short, defensive replies – 'Yes … yes … all right … yes' – and reiterates that he just wants 'what's best for you and the kids'.

We're on the slow roll into Euston when he packs up, puts his raincoat on and moves diagonally across the carriage to the table near the door. He wants to get off the train as soon as it pulls up at the platform. I can see his face now. He doesn't look like his high-flying lifestyle is doing him much good. There are shadows under his eyes and he looks careworn and beaten.

Now I'm not claiming to be good at this, but if you think about my people-watching anecdote, you may see that a surface reading of the guy in front of me on the train to London would have been that he was your average corporate executive, doing battle in the world of modern business. Doing pretty well at it, too, to go by the technological paraphernalia and the restaurant booking in Berlin. But if you were able to hang round long enough, as I was, and observe closely enough, another tale emerges. Now he's a nice guy whose family has been broken apart, possibly by the stresses of his job. On the face of it, a player, but under the surface, a victim.

Writing Exercises: Paying Close Attention

Many novelists have backgrounds in journalism, and one of the things a fiction writer and a reporter have in common is that both are reporting. Your job, like the reporter's, is to find out about the world and report back on what your research has thrown up. All you need to do is watch and listen. You need to look at the world around you and penetrate the surface of things. Listening will be as important as being watchful. More important than any of these disciplines is the need to record in writing what you pay close attention to; you see and hear the world all your waking hours, but you haven't processed the data until you have passed it through your own thoughts and feelings, until you have written it down.

Eavesdrop as you move from one place to the next. Picking up snippets of dialogue from people who have passed out of earshot before you hear the end of their sentence can be a spur to the imagination. As I was walking between classes, I once heard one passing student say to another, 'Five points, right …', which gave me a whole scenario with which to conjure.

Pay attention in lifts. Here you are enclosed in a space with strangers, who if they are alone like you are probably trying to pretend that nobody else in the lift is actually there. If they're with people, they will be talking about something for which you will have to deduce the context. This is fruitful for writers.

When you're watching people, look for the telling physical detail. Everyone's face and body will have a few defining details. Or perhaps it's a run of phrase that is characteristic of the person. A friend of mine often used to begin her anecdotes with, *And by all accounts* … We all have stock phrases that we use too much. As with telling physical detail, look for them and record them.

In *Something Happened*, Joseph Heller analyses office politics entertainingly. He does a wry breakdown of the pecking order in the workplace of his protagonist. The way Heller expresses the power structure here is in terms of who *has the whammy on* whom. Write an analysis of who has the whammy on whom in your workplace and note the difference between official and actual positions.

Research

Be specific comes number three in Natalie Goldberg's Rules of Writing Practice,[6] and just about any book on craft you care to pick up will endorse this advice. (This one does. See Chapter 6: 'Research'.) For one thing, it's about precision. If I write *I noticed the vase of flowers as soon as I entered the room* it tells you a little, but not as much as *I noticed the vase of carnations as soon as I entered the room.* In fiction, you are trying to build a believable world in the mind of the reader. Each detail you can specify within that picture becomes a little jewel that decorates the fabric and enhances the imagined world. Generalities won't do that, so you should avoid them.

The best advice on researched detail I've come across is in a book on writer's craft by George V. Higgins, the American crime writer:

> Solid reportage is interesting precisely because the reporter has gone to the trouble of acquiring information about his or her subject, and then has carefully organised it, so that the reader completing the text knows something that he or she did not know before. James Reston, reflecting on his long and distinguished career as a reporter and commentator on national politics for *The New York Times*, concluded that any respect he deserved was probably attributable to his early experience as a sportswriter. To cover sports, he said, the reporter soon learns that he must pay attention at all times, because no one ever becomes sufficiently expert to predict unerringly the outcome of every contest ... When the reporter is promoted to writing a column about sports, it is usually with the understanding that mere opinions on the topic of the day will not suffice; those opinions will be taken seriously only if they are manifestly grounded in fact ... When [sportswriters] get it wrong, there is hell to pay ...
> The fiction writer owes the same debt of respect to the reader.[7]

What this is all about is a little more than just specifying; it's about doing the necessary research so that you are in a position to specify. The reporter has gone to the trouble of acquiring information about his or her subject, and has then carefully organised it, so that the reader completing the text knows something that he or she did not know before. If you have done the research, you will be able to give your work texture, and so make it credible. It will have the ring of authenticity that your readers require of it.

A few years back, Nicholas Royle, editor of Salt Publishing's annual *Best British Short Stories* anthologies, came to talk to a group of my students. One of the memorable things he discussed was his predilection for trespassing. He has a fascination with derelict buildings and will regularly enter one, equipped with torch, notebook and the camera app on his phone. He risks arrest, attack and, I guess, buildings falling in on him. But his readers benefit because in his work, in novels such as *First Novel* and *Antwerp,* buildings are a real presence, lending his fiction genuine atmosphere. (See Chapter 14: 'Setting'.)

To show you how your writing may benefit from researched data, look at this passage from Kate Atkinson's story 'Wedding Favours'. I very much doubt Atkinson has ever had a small business offering a particular service to couples getting married, yet, as you will see here, she appears to know all she needs to about a highly specialised enterprise. In the following extract, Maggie is the friend and potential business partner of the protagonist, Pam.

> 'They're foreign, it's a symbolic gift,' Maggie explained, her mouth full of cake. 'Each bomboniere contains five sugared almonds, five because it's a prime number that can't be divided, just like the bride and groom. Each almond symbolises something – happiness, health, wealth, fertility and long life … The nice thing, Pam, is that you can coordinate the colour of the almonds to the nets – pink, blue, lemon, etcetera. But the bombonieres are only part of it, obviously, there's all kinds of favours.' Maggie reached into her capacious bag and pulled out a cheap looking brochure. 'Look, little baskets filled with foil-wrapped chocolate hearts, miniature rolling pins decorated with bells or white heather – I'm thinking artificial – dried flower cones, clown boxes, personalised mini-hats, decorated fans (heather), decorated shoes (heather again) – and everything accessorised with little bows of tartan ribbon – dress Black Watch, I thought, because it's more sophisticated … Mini brass horseshoes, filled brandy glasses, filled flower pots, mini rugs filled with heather, mouse boxes filled with chocolates, then, of course, there are the centrepieces for the tables – pot-pourri rings filled with dried flowers, white lace crackers filled with chocolate hearts and decorated with little silver horseshoes, tartan ribbon and heather—'[8]

In order to write this piece of fiction, Atkinson had to do some research. That's lesson one. Note also how she has used this research. Not only has she given us sufficient detail to convince us that Maggie is setting up a wedding favours business, but she has also filtered the researched data through the character. We don't just learn about this arcane world; we learn about it from Maggie's perspective. There is a similarity here to what I say about using setting to enhance character (in Chapter 14: 'Setting'). You may reveal characters by showing them engaging with a particular setting, but also by the way they engage with a role or a job.

Writing Exercise: Research

Either from a text (a book, television programme or website) or through interviewing somebody, find out about a very particular profession. Piano tuning. Brain surgery. Car mechanics.

You will need to generate only one page of notes.

When you have done this, imagine the character of the person who does this job. Now write about a page of fiction, using not only data, but also some of the other craft you have acquired from studying this book, to engage the reader.

Other Purposes of Notebooks

There will be more reasons to maintain the notebook habit than those I cover in this chapter; but, beyond what I've said so far, here are some further purposes for this vital writer's tool:

* Recording overheard conversations.
* Collecting interesting words you come across.
* Noting down dreams.
* Capturing thoughts, impressions, reflections, feelings – everything that passes through your head.
* Making observations, in the manner of an anthropologist: look at human behaviour like a clinical psychologist. Chekhov brought a physician's perspective to his characters, whom he almost diagnosed like the doctor he was. Somehow, if you are studying the world to record it, you notice a great deal more.
* Making sketches in words of settings for your fiction. There's a spirit or a character to every place you go, and creating a sense of place in fiction is crucial. (Put these last two together: how do people behave

in particular places? At the airport or in a café. At motorway services or in the bank.)
* Collecting your research. This may mean taking notes from a book, a film or a TV programme.
* Making notes on the stories you read.
* Making notes on published writing about writing (see 'The Reading Log' in Chapter 5: 'How to Read as a Writer').

Writing Exercise: Test Drive a Writer's Notebook

Buy yourself a notebook that will fit in your pocket and carry it with you at all times for one whole week. As a bare minimum, set aside ten minutes to write in your notebook between getting up and lunchtime, and a second ten minutes between lunch and bedtime. (You may well end up taking the notebook out and writing more than twice a day, but keep to the commitment of at least two ten-minute slots.)

In these short slots, take yourself away from the people around you, find a quiet spot and either observe and record your surroundings or reflect on something interesting that has occurred in the previous few hours. Maybe you will write down interesting conversations you have overheard. Maybe you will have an insight about some issue or relationship in your life. Perhaps you will describe a billboard that strikes you as entertaining or resonant. You might have to express your frustration about something you've just experienced.

Maintain this twice-a-day habit for a week. At the end of the week, summarise the kinds of writing that have appeared in your notebook and assess the worth of this writer's discipline.

Notes

1   John Fowles, in Plimpton (ed.), *The Writer's Chapbook*, p 55.
2   Goldberg, *Wild Mind*, p 204.
3   Joseph Heller, in Plimpton (ed.), *The Writer's Chapbook*, p 57.
4   Joan Didion, 'On Keeping a Notebook' in *Slouching Towards Bethlehem* (London: Flamingo, 2001).
5   Jack Kerouac, 'Belief & Technique in Modern Prose', cited in Oakley Hall, *The Art and Craft of Novel Writing* (Cincinnati: Story Press, 1989), p 161.
6   Goldberg, *Wild Mind*.
7   George V. Higgins, *On Writing* (London: Bloomsbury, 1991).
8   Kate Atkinson, 'Wedding Favours' in her collection, *Not the End of the World* (London: Black Swan, 2003), pp 306–7.

4

Keeping Journals

The habit of keeping a writer's journal is another key writer's discipline. Apart from anything else, it is where you assemble the resources that will become your fiction. In *Words Fail Me,* Patricia T. O'Conner says that 'a writer with good material is one who never lets a useful nugget slip away ... A titbit doesn't have to be earth shattering to be worth saving. It only has to be useful.'[1]

Being faced with beginning to keep a writer's journal may provoke a number of questions: What does a writer's journal look like? Where do you keep it? How do you use it? How is it different from using a notebook? Before starting, though, let's get one thing out of the way: your journal and your notebook are not two separate things. Inevitably, your notebook may form part of your journal. You might organise your practice that way, or, if you're like me, there's no distinction between the two.

Writing Burst
- They went to school together, in different classes.

The Theory

Looking back on notes I made on the first book I ever read on the subject of journals, Tristine Rainer's *The New Diary*, I would say the most appealing concepts of journal writing I derived there are that it may be:

* a repository for thoughts, feelings and ideas which would otherwise be lost
* a creative project journal
* a diary (record of daily events etc.)
* a place to paste in photos, clippings, letters, quotes, drawings, doodles, dried flowers, business cards, labels
* a place for the writer to work out.

Jennifer Moon's *Learning Journals*[2] introduces other attributes of journaling – that it can enable learning from experience and increase critical reflection and, most notably, that writing is a method of thinking, and thus the journal is a place to think, and that thinking in written words slows the pace of thinking and creates time and space for reflection. Moon also suggests that the habit of keeping a journal as a place to reflect will develop self-awareness and self-confidence.

Daniel Price's *How to Make a Journal of Your Life*, a little book with a hand-made feel, includes advice that is often liberating:

> When there are no more rules about how much time you're supposed to be spending with your journal, and when you feel light-hearted and buoyant about what you want to put in, you'll find yourself enjoying the time and doing good work. Not just making it another addition to your already busy schedule.[3]

In other words, bear in mind that rather than being a chore to feel bad about when you're not keeping to some imagined schedule, journaling is best seen as an opportunity to work enjoyably, even to play.

Price has come to see journaling as at least as much a visual record of his perspective on life as a written one, so his book may introduce you to new ways of recording your life, beyond what you write. 'Always remember', he says, 'that your voice and anything you create is uniquely yours. No one else in the entire world can say things quite the way you do.'[4]

Amongst the approaches he recommends are:

* sketching what you observe alongside what you write about it
* photocopying paragraphs from books, newspapers or magazines and pasting them into your journal
* collecting flowers and seeds in the journal by attaching them to the page with clear adhesive tape
* taking a camera everywhere with you and attaching the resulting photographs to the pages of your journal. (Some or all of your journal may be on a computer, so saving digital photographs within a digital journal makes this final technique easy.)

My Writer's Journal

I used to have an unconscious view that a writer's journal looks like something, that it is something, *one* thing. I don't believe this any more. I don't think that a writer's journal is a notebook of some kind, an A5 hardback with a beautiful cover. I've kept ones like that and I still do, but a writer's journal is more than that. I wouldn't want you to labour under the illusion, as I did, that there are two physical items in a writer's armoury: a notebook and a journal. I certainly have at least one and usually two or three notebooks on the go at any time, but when it comes down to it, I have never had a single physical object that on its own could be described as my writer's journal. The writer's journal is much more diffuse than that.

Mine isn't ever in any one place; it's spread through several places, through quite a few physical locations. In electronic form, it's either inside the Mac I'm writing this chapter on or on the external hard drive just next to it. Here I can find the following:

* research notes and drafts of short stories, in various stages of completion
* a daily spiritual journal I've been keeping for over thirty years now

* a folder of song lyrics, both work in progress and completed
* research, planning, reflection
* drafts and completed scripts for the youth arts group I work with
* drafts and completed chapters for books like this one – including, in five minutes when I stop for lunch, this draft of this chapter.

Note that one of the possible uses of your journal mentioned twice in the bullet points above is *research*. Often in your fiction you will need to find out about an aspect of your story or novel of which you have inadequate prior knowledge. This is one of the functions of your journal: as a repository for research notes. And speaking of research, bear in mind that research isn't only what you find; it's also what finds you, as Bernard MacLaverty explains here:

> I attended an advertised composer's workshop at the BBC, with the Chinese composer Tan Dun. He worked on a stage with about ten music students. There were no musical instruments and he used breath and voice to compose – along with mouth pops and hand claps. He talked about pre-hearing and inner hearing. I was sitting rapt on the edge of my seat in a lecture on composition listening to people breathing. Tan Dun became the basis for the composer Huang Xiao Gang in *Grace Notes*.[5]

If I step a metre to my left, I come to a second desk in which I have stashed letters, postcards and mementoes from quite a few friends over the past forty years or so, going back as far as this 1975 letter from my girlfriend then, telling me about her Christmas holiday job delivering mail in North London:

> I made the acquaintance of a dog and a few cats – which are so cold sometimes that I ring the bell hoping they will let their cat in again.

If I move beyond the desk with the letters a further metre to the left, I come to a section of my bookshelves where I stash old notebooks. In a spiral notebook with a faded cover, which at a guess comes from 1990, I find a heading, 'SHORT STORIES', and two shorthand ideas:

John & Picasso on the beach at the Isle of Wight.

—

Paul B. stuck in Belfast harbour trying to rescue a dog from some trees. Nothing on but his underpants. A bunch of residents looking on.

Helen Newall (see Chapter 10: 'Characterisation') once told me that she recommends assiduous journal keeping because:

> When I'm having a black writing day, and can't come up with a single word, I put on some music and go trawling though old notebooks and journals and look for a starting point. I flip through old journals and if I'm lucky I may come across something where I'm excited by, for instance, a certain rhythm. Since I no longer know why I wrote the original piece, I am liberated from the original intention. Not so long ago, I managed to use this technique to produce a story, which *Mslexia* published.

And by the way, in the same conversation, Helen told me that her writer's journal, unlike mine, is always a physical object, an attractively bound book with unlined pages. 'I like to have at least one journal for each writing project,' she said. 'For one thing, it means you have more chance of finding what you're looking for when you want to turn up the crucial notes you made on, say, eighteenth century Highland crofts.'

Writing Burst
- Put 'Henri Cartier-Bresson: Puddle' in your search engine and use the photograph as your prompt.

Your Writer's Journal

Let's try to summarise some of the key points of this chapter. Arguably, the most important uses you can put your journal to are:

- recording your experiences and perceptions
- as a place to work out, to practise writing

* as a creative nursery, a place to nurture your ideas for stories, poems, scripts, memoirs
* reflecting about your reading and writing, about your intentions as well as your achievements.

And remember that it doesn't matter whether what you call your journal is a single physical object, a stylish artefact from Paperchase, or a collection of writing spread through computer files, notebooks, letters, desk drawers, shelves, cupboards and, if you're like me, over the carpet. Your writer's journal may take the form that suits you best. What matters most is that you write on a daily basis. If you acquire this habit, what you are doing, according to Dorothea Brande, is 'training yourself … simply to write. It makes no difference to the success of this practice if your paragraphs are amorphous, the thought vague or extravagant, the ideas hazy.'[6]

If you're not writing every day, you won't be as competent as you need to be when you sit down to compose something you hope to polish and publish. The cellist Julian Lloyd Webber once claimed that if he didn't practise three hours a day he would notice an impaired performance at his next concert; if he only practised two hours a day, his fellow musicians would notice; and if he only practised one hour a day, the public would notice.

Of the things that matter most about acquiring the journaling habit, perhaps second on the list, is that in keeping a journal you are storing up your small precious items. As Patricia T. O'Conner has it:

> an idea in your head is merely an idle notion. But an idea written down, that's the beginning of something! Stripped to its briefs, a piece of writing is nothing more than a handful of ideas, put into words and arranged to do a job. We all get ideas – try *not* thinking in the shower. The trick is to write them down.[7]

You could think of your journal as the storehouse for all the grapes you pick at harvest time: you're collecting the resources you will need to make your very own Shiraz Cabernet (quaffable, and who knows, maybe even transcendent).

Writing Exercise: A Week with Your Journal

You should commit one week to this exercise. That way, you may experience some of the virtues of maintaining a journaling habit.

What You Will Need

Whether you use a bound book with 80 gm paper or files on your computer, you will need to create three repositories for your writing:

- a place to practise
- a place to record
- a place to reflect.

You will also need to put your writer's notebook to work during the course of each day, recording anything interesting that you think of, witness or experience. (See the end of Chapter 3, 'Making Notes'.) For this initial exercise, I'd suggest aiming to make just three entries in your notebook each day. The idea throughout this exercise is to make all of this as feasible for yourself as you can.

What You Do

First of all, *practising*. Choose a point in the day when you can spare ten minutes. Because you are closest to your unconscious when you wake, early in the morning is best, but you will have to decide yourself what's achievable. All you're committing to for those brief ten minutes is sitting down and writing the first thing that comes into your head – writing without stopping. All you have to do is keep your pen moving over the page, your fingers over the keyboard. If you find getting started difficult, why not select a Writing Burst from this book to help you begin each day?

Next, *storing*. Decide on a point in the evening when you can spare another ten minutes and copy your three notebook entries into the recording section of whatever you're using for your journal.

Finally, *reflecting*. Once you have reached the end of a week in which you have practised and recorded each day, set aside half an hour to look at what you've amassed. As Helen Newall suggests above, put on some music that will help to create a relaxed mood. Have a glass of wine, a beer, or some peppermint tea – whatever relaxes you. Do all you can to make the experience chilled and pleasurable. Having spent half an hour looking over your writing and your notes, contemplating anything that seems to have some promise, spend another half hour expressing your thoughts about what you see before you now and about the experience of this week-long exercise. When you've finished, tot up how much of your time this exercise has taken. (Not much, I'd guess.)

500-Word Story Project

Person, Place, Thing

Throughout this book you will find story projects, assignments to get you practising what you have been studying.

Your first story project is to attempt a very short story, one of only 500 words. While we're here at your first (slightly) extended fiction assignment, let me defend the discipline of word limitations. Being asked to write to a given length is very good for your development. Having limitations placed on the length of the story you write will concentrate your mind and teach you how to use language and your developing craft economically and efficiently.

As a stimulus, here's a table.

Person	Place	Problem
Nurse	Starbucks	Man she was meeting hasn't turned up
Fresher	Campus finance office	Loan hasn't come through
Shop assistant	Department store	Colleague is stealing from till

Each of these has the makings of a story, but I don't want you to do the obvious and select horizontally. Instead, take the Person from one row, but take the Place from a different row and the Problem from yet another row. In other words, if you select 'Nurse', you can't select 'Starbucks' and 'Man she was meeting hasn't turned up'. You could select 'Nurse', 'Department store' and 'Loan hasn't come through'. In selecting, you can hop around as you like, but no two items may come from the same row.

Your story doesn't need a beginning, middle and ending, but it must have a change of some kind.

Notes

1   Patricia T. O'Conner, *Words Fail Me: What Everyone Who Writes Should Know About Writing* (New York: Harcourt Brace and Company, 1999), p 19.

2 Jennifer Moon, *Learning Journals: A Handbook for Academics, Students and Professional Development* (London: Kogan Page, 1999).

3 Daniel Price, *How to Make a Journal of Your Life* (Berkeley: Ten Speed Press, 1999), p 7.

4 Price, *How to Make a Journal of Your Life*, p 9.

5 Bernard MacLaverty, interviewed by Sharon Monteith and Jenny Newman in Monteith, Newman & Wheeler (eds), *Contemporary British and Irish Fiction: An Introduction Through Interviews* (London: Arnold, 2004), p 111.

6 Brande, *Becoming a Writer*, p 73.

7 O'Conner, *Words Fail Me*, pp 18–19.

5

How to Read as a Writer

'My purpose in reading', John Updike wrote, 'has ever secretly been not to come and judge but to come and steal.'[1] This is what writers do.

Artistic practice is a matter of consumption that leads to production. Artists in any field consume their preferred examples of good practice and synthesise them into something new. David Byrne, the main songwriter in Talking Heads, talks about the process in his song 'The Good Thing', where he alludes to adapting things and making them his own. In fiction, Graham Swift modelled the structure of his Booker Prize–winning novel *Last Orders* on that of William Faulkner's *As I Lay Dying*. At the time, Swift drew a good deal of flack in the media, just as Zadie Smith did with her novel *On Beauty*, which is informed by the work of E.M. Forster. However, to anyone who ever tried to write fiction, to anyone who has engaged in any kind of creative practice, these accusations of plagiarism must have seemed wide of the mark. If we can't base what we create on previous models, how can we be expected to come up with anything at all? There's nothing new under the sun. 'All great writing is in a sense imitation of great writing,' John Gardner says. 'Writing a novel, however innovative that novel maybe, the writer struggles to achieve one specific large effect, what can only be called the effect we are used to getting from good novels.'[2]

This is how artists work. We look at the models of good practice we admire, several of them at once, and we synthesise the techniques we see here to make something new, something the world has never seen before.

Why is it new? Because each of us has different tastes and selects his or her own range of influences. Here's the American writer Rick Bass discussing one of his influences:

> I used to model a lot of stories after [Richard Ford's] *Rock Springs* collection. It's a very powerful book. I remember the end of the title story, 'Rock Springs,' where the narrator asks the reader all these questions beginning, 'Would you think ... ' I never heard of such a thing. We're always told it's bad to put rhetoric in a story. To put it at the *end* of a story, what kind of stunt is that? All of a sudden, five or six stories in a row, and he's ending them with questions. There was an opening of boundaries. Also, I like his roundabout way of telling a story, that air of relaxation mixed with immediacy. It's a fine tension, a fine ambivalence.[3]

Writing Burst
- Put 'Cy Twombly untitled peonies' in your search engine and choose one of these paintings as your prompt.

How to Read as a Writer

Heather Leach talks about learning 'to look beneath the surface of the print for traces of the *making* process, the writer at work'.[4] This is at the heart of reading as a writer (RAAW). If you study Literature at university you will be trained in the disciplines of literary criticism, taught to interpret, to look at themes, to examine meaning and literary context and often to do so with an implicit understanding of some literary theory or other. None of these things trains you to read as a writer. When you read as a writer, as Heather Leach intimates, you are trying *to find out how it was done.* Rather than interpreting the fiction, you are dismantling it to see how the end result has been achieved. You're reverse engineering. As a writer, you read each short story to see what you can take away from it, adapt and make your own.

In studying the art of writing fiction, I would argue, you are learning a craft or, to use Joyce Carol Oates' term, you are serving a writer's apprenticeship. Learning a craft, you might say. Thus, reading as a writer will involve you in discussing specific elements of craft. In this regard, some of the following will be relevant to your work:

* point of view
* characterisation
* narrative structure
* plot
* setting
* use of dialogue
* description
* plant and pay-off
* transitions
* voice
* the handling of time

Over the years, the method I've evolved for students preparing reading as a writer essays is to combine a response to the text they are dismantling with an understanding of some of the relevant works that theorise the specific element of craft they happen to be considering. So, if you happen to be examining Margaret Atwood's use of dialogue, you will of course analyse it in context, within the story in question. You'll also compare her practice with the various theories of dialogue writing articulated by fiction writers and authors of craft texts; you'll turn, perhaps, to Gardner or Burroway, but also to the wisdom of the authors themselves. You'll trawl through the *Paris Review* interviews to find observations that this or that author has made about writing dialogue. You'll go, too, to one of the increasing number of texts by authors about their craft – Stephen King's, for instance, Kate Grenville's, Graham Swift's – or indeed Atwood's. In this way, you might begin your analysis by summarising some contemporary theories about what makes for good dialogue and relating that to the particular use of dialogue you are examining. This will lead to an examination of the effect on the reader of this particular passage of dialogue.

RAAW in a Nutshell

This is terribly reductive, but when I'm trying to help my students get their head around reading as a writer I suggest what I hope is an easy way of ensuring that they are RAAW as they look at a particular element of craft in a particular story.

* Include a short, relevant quote from a craft text that theorises the technique you're focusing on.
* Include a short, relevant quote from the story in question that exemplifies the theory you have just cited.
* Analyse the effect on the reader.

Which brings me on to the relationship between writer and reader.

Much of the focus of reading as a writer is on the reader's response to the text. The notion of affecting the reader, of putting the reader's mind and heart to work, is crucial for the fiction writer. You want to keep readers' minds active; you want readers to be constantly caught up in the story. You want to generate suspense, and, to my mind, creating an emotional effect is key to achieving it. Whether you agree with me on this particular emphasis or not, I hope you'll accept that fiction which doesn't at all times engage either the mind or the heart of the reader, and ideally both, will not be effective. Much of the focus of your work as a fiction writer will be devoted to intriguing readers, to creating questions in their minds. *Who did it? What is going to happen to this beleaguered protagonist? Is this character going to get away with it? Are this man and this woman going to end up together?*

When you read as a writer, working out how the story affects the heart and mind of the reader is your central focus.

Writing Burst
* Things were dead, but now they're picking up.

Let's practise reading as a writer on an extract from James Salter's story
'Last Night'. It focuses on a middle-aged couple, Walter and Marit, and
a family friend, Susanna; Marit has terminal cancer. In this scene, they
are in a restaurant.

> They were all feeling better. They sat for a while and finally made their way
> out. The bar was still noisy.
> Marit stared out the window as they drove. She was tired. They were
> going home now. The wind was moving in the tops of the shadowy trees.
> In the night sky there were brilliant clouds, shining as if in daylight.
> - It's very beautiful tonight, isn't it? Marit said. I'm struck by that. Am
> I mistaken?
> - No. Walter cleared his throat. It is beautiful.
> - Have you noticed it? she asked Susanna. I'm sure you have. How old
> are you? I forget.
> - Twenty-nine.
> - Twenty-nine, Marit said. She was silent. We never had children, she
> said. Do you wish you had children?
> - Oh, sometimes, I suppose. I haven't thought about it too much. It's
> one of those things you have to be married to think about.
> - You'll be married.
> - Yes, perhaps.
> - You could be married in a minute.
> She was tired when they reached the house. They sat together in the
> living room as if they had come from a big party but were not quite ready
> for bed. Walter was thinking of what lay ahead, the light that would come
> on in the refrigerator when the door was opened. The needle of the syringe
> was sharp, the stainless steel point cut at an angle and like a razor.

Writing Exercise: Reading as a Writer

Tom Bailey refers to 'a sort of demon-driven reading ... at the heart of
learning for a writer'.[5] If you're going to learn from reading fiction as a
writer, you need to be to some extent like a dog with a bone.
So here's your first reading as a writer exercise.
Since I used it to illustrate what an element of craft might be just now,
let's begin with dialogue.

Most pundits agree that good dialogue will create and maintain tension. How does the dialogue in this passage achieve that?

Next, dialogue is a particularly potent means of revealing character. From this short excerpt, you ought to be able to tell a few things about the personalities involved. What can you deduce about the characters of Walter, Marit and Susanna, and how has James Salter conveyed this information to you?

I alluded earlier to intriguing the reader. This is a formidable device for creating narrative tension. Intrigue usually boils down to creating questions in the mind of the reader. What questions does this passage raise for you?

It's quite likely you will have some hint of how these questions might be answered later in the narrative. What do you think will happen next?

When you're a writer, you read fiction in a different way. You study the theory and practice of a particular element of craft and your focus is on how the story engages the mind and affects the emotions of the reader. Why? To learn how to write better fiction. So you work out how the author has achieved a particular effect and you go off and apply what you've learned to the story you're working on.

Reading as a writer isn't just something you do in the abstract, though – an exercise you complete to train yourself as a writer. It's not a matter of studying Joyce's use of epiphany in 'The Dead' and coming away more informed and better equipped to create an epiphany yourself, should the opportunity ever arise. That's wonderful and marvellous, but sometimes you'll face a challenge in a story you're writing and need help dealing with it right there and then, in mid-production. Maybe you're not sure your ending strikes the bittersweet note you intended it to. You've done a few drafts, but you're still not happy with it. What do you do? You think back to stories you've read that end on something like the note you hope for, and you dig them out and analyse them to see how the author pulled off the desired effect. You follow in the footsteps of Updike (and any other writer you like to name); you come and steal.

Notes

1   John Updike, *More Matter: Essays and Criticism* (New York: Fawcett Books, 2000), p 418.

2 Gardner, *The Art of Fiction*, p 10.

3 From an interview in Bonnie Lyons & Bill Oliver (eds), *Passion and Craft: Conversations with Notable Writers* (Chicago: University of Illinois Press, 1998), pp 76–7.

4 Heather Leach, 'Reading as a Writer' in Graham et al., *The Road to Somewhere: A Creative Writing Companion* (Basingstoke: Palgrave Macmillan, 2013), p 74.

5 Tom Bailey, *A Short Story Writer's Companion* (New York: Oxford University Press, 2001), p 109.

6

Research

James Rice

Occasionally people ask me what it's like to be a writer and the only honest answer I can give is that being a writer is like constantly having homework to do. In exam season. While everyone else has broken up for the summer. Because as a writer you are never off duty, you are always looking for inspiration. You are always researching.

A writer is a researcher of all human life. Your job is to observe the world around you, to reflect upon it from your own unique perspective. You are there to look for those details that nobody else has noticed (you are like a stand-up comic in that way: seeking out and recording life's little idiosyncrasies). Each person you meet becomes a potential character, each place a potential setting, each anecdote you hear (no matter how embarrassing or tragic for those involved) becomes fair game, up for grabs; often resulting in an internal battle over the ethics of *stealing it*. The more fiction you write, the more life seems to transform into one big research project, with the sole purpose of fuelling your art.

And this works both ways. Even when you're not researching, you'll find that life feeds into your writing. Writers don't exist in a vacuum. All fiction is a result of research (whether you're aware of it or not). Although you may like to think that your imagination is limitless – that you can create entire worlds, people and their stories from nothing – the truth is that anything you create is a product of your experiences. Writing is a reflective process. We have to experience things before we can reflect upon them.

As the late James Salter once wrote: 'Life passes into pages if it passes into anything.'[1]

Why Research?

I'm sure you've come across the term 'write what you know' – we're all given this piece of advice at some point in our writing lives. In my opinion there are two ways to interpret this. The first is that you should stick to autobiography, write only about characters from a similar background as you, in settings that you know well. Write what you are qualified to, stay inside your comfort zone. And this makes sense, right? It's certainly easier than stressing over the thoughts and feelings of a Syrian refugee, or the harsh conditions of the snowy peaks of Mount Everest. As a writer you should stay true to who you are – your own voice and experiences.

But then what if you're life isn't very exciting? Most writers spend their time sat at their desks, not exactly material for a bestseller. What if Aldous Huxley or J.K. Rowling or George R.R. Martin had only written what they know? What about imagination? Creation? The sheer joy of *making something up*?

The other interpretation is that, if you do step outside your comfort zone, then you have to do your research, and do it thoroughly! Do whatever it takes to make yourself an expert on a subject before attempting to write about it. Approach every story as informed as you can possibly be. Otherwise, what gives you the authority to write it?

I would agree with both of these statements, to an extent. Staying true to your voice is important, and, even if it takes a bit of the fun away, you have a responsibility to your reader to be an informed writer, to do your research. But also as an act of self-preservation: there will always be someone out there who knows more than you about any given subject. Someone who can call you out on any mistakes you've made. Try your utmost not to give them the opportunity, otherwise it could come back to bite you. In an interview with the *Paris Review*, Hilary Mantel, twice Booker Prize–winning author of *Wolf Hall*, said: 'Once you know that you are working with historians in that way, then you have to raise your game. You have a responsibility to make your research good.'[2]

How Much Research?

It's impossible to give a definitive one-size-fits-all research plan. Each writing project you undertake will be unique and will require different amounts, and types, of research.

Historical fiction, for example, can require a lot of prior knowledge. Not only of historical events and figures, but also of the nitty-gritty: names, occupations, speech patterns; the details that make up people's everyday lives. This is all achievable. The exact setting of your story may no longer exist, but some rough approximation of it will, somewhere. Find it, use it. Check the archives, dig out old newspapers, use case histories, go to stately homes or museums, or even just go to a field and close your eyes and pretend it's 1807. Or, if it's more recent history you're after, see if you can find somebody to give you the details you need, a grandparent who can tell you about their own parents' lives, or how different the world was during their childhood.

Another example: science fiction. If you're creating a future world, research what that future may be. What are the emerging technologies that will influence it? Also remember that, as with historical fiction, a good way to give us the future is to steal from the present. Ridley Scott credits his design ideas for *Blade Runner* as being a mixture of Edward Hopper's *Nighthawks*, the French science fiction comic magazine *Métal Hurlant*, and a combination of the industrial landscape of his one-time home in north-east England, fused with modern Hong Kong. He stole from a host of different artworks and settings to create an authentic-feeling future. So can you. Think about it: what can you take from our existing world to create a whole new one?

But a word of warning: be careful not to get waylaid by your research. Research is enjoyable and immersive and time-consuming, and it can be much easier than the hard graft of writing. At some point you have to stop and actually put pen to paper (or fingers to keyboard). In an interview for Waterstones, crime writer Harlan Coben had this to say on the subject:

> I think research is tremendously overrated. And in fact, if you're a new writer, I'm going to recommend to you that you do no research, or as little as humanly possible ... Researching is more fun than writing, so you use it as an excuse not to write. It'll be like, 'I'm going to write a scene in Piccadilly Circus. Oh, but first I'd better go to Piccadilly Circus and watch the people ...' No, no, no. You know what it's like, you've been there. Write the scene right now![3]

While I wouldn't agree with his recommendation of doing no research at all, it's certainly worth bearing this advice in mind. Always remember you're a writer, first and foremost. You need to actually *write*!

Where to Research?

The Internet

Recently I asked a class of students what their most common research tool was. The first answer I was given was 'the library'. I didn't believe them (and didn't dare enquire as to how many of them have actually set foot in a library recently). Another suggestion: 'the streets'. Not one of them said 'the internet', which I assumed would be a no-brainer. When I suggested it as a tool for research, they admitted that it was often their go-to resource, though they kept their heads bowed in shame all the same.

Should we be ashamed of the internet? The romantic view is researcher as adventurer, off exploring the Amazon rainforest. Or an academic, scouring dusty tomes, alone in some grand city library at 2:30am. The reality is much less exciting, much less Indiana Jones. A writer's research is more likely to consist of hours Googling street names, or brands of 1980s washing-up detergent.

But the internet is an amazing tool. You have a device in your pocket with the power to access all of earth's combined knowledge. Plus, it's so easy to use – the perfect resource to have handy while you write. No need to scrawl through indexes in reference books any more, just type in a few keywords and you have the answer to any question in seconds. Shouldn't you be making the most of that?

Recently I had to fit a new set of headlights in my car. A few years ago when I attempted this I had to remove the entire fuse box to get to the back of the lights – it was a nightmare. This time round I simply typed my make and model and the words 'fit headlights' into Google and instantly a YouTube video popped up, showing me a much simpler way of doing it (turns out you just unclip them at the front).

How is this useful to your writing? Well, say you had a scene in which your protagonist was a plumber, fixing a toilet. You know nothing about plumbing (I assume) and have no interest in it beyond the writing of this scene (again, I assume) and no desire to go fiddling around in your own toilet (feeling confident in these assumptions by now). But, Google 'How to fix a blocked cistern', and you'll immediately find a YouTube video with enough of the actions and terminology to get you through the scene.

And the internet's a godsend for settings too. You can Google Map your way almost anywhere in the world now. You can wander down streets on the other side of the world, without ever leaving your bedroom. A friend of mine who went to New York recently wanted to know how to get from the airport to the city by train and he found there were YouTube videos of that journey. People had filmed it all, in real time, so he could do a few practice runs at home first. What a great resource for a writer! To be transported across the globe with the click of a mouse!

But, it's important to remember that the internet can only ever give us an approximation of the experiences. If you can, don't *just* use the internet. It can be a helpful quick fix, but it doesn't give you a fully rounded experience. It shouldn't be seen as a substitute for reality and the experiences that can be gained from actually venturing into the world. A huge part of research is as simple as that: just being awake and aware in our everyday lives. So often we pass through the world without experiencing it. We don't really take in our surroundings. (We're too busy using the internet on our phones!)

So, basically: if you get the train home tonight, spend the whole journey with your iPod in, and then have to look at a YouTube video of a train journey to help you write a train journey scene in a short story, then you're doing it wrong.

Places

If you can go to the places where your writing is set, then you should. This isn't always easy – it often depends on logistics and money – but it's a worthwhile activity, and something all new writers should do, a sort of rite of passage.

I've just spent a long time advocating the internet and how it can be helpful with regard to this – but again, it's an approximation of the experience. Take my friend, the one that went to New York. When he actually got there he realised just how different the real-life experience was, that nothing could have prepared him for it. The YouTube video didn't capture the electric atmosphere of the place. The smell, the sounds, the chaos of the city. Nor did it capture the shirtless man who got on a few stops in and started saying he was going to 'take a dump' on the train. It didn't capture the smell of him (a smell which my friend could only describe as 'garbage' – the smell was uniquely American in a way that allowed it only an American description). It didn't give him the swaying of the carriage or the feel of the seats or the feeling of awe as he stepped out from the subway into the vastness of the city and its skyscrapers.

Often it's useful to know your setting. In an article for *The Guardian* on this issue, David Nicholls writes:

> Many years ago, while writing my first novel, I took a train to find the house where my fictional character lived. I brought with me a notebook, pen and camera and walked the streets from the station down to the sea, found a spot that felt right and took a great many photographs of quite staggering dullness. In retrospect, the expedition was probably little more than an exercise in procrastination ... But if the expedition was a little foolish and pretentious, it still felt important to go, because wasn't this what proper writers were meant to do?[4]

He returns to this idea when talking about writing his bestselling novel *One Day*:

> While there's clearly no agreed method for an author to acquire a sense of place, I've always wanted to know a location at first hand, and have always been able not only to place a pin in the map but also to specify a date and time, so that the flat on Rankeillor Street in Edinburgh where Emma Morley and Dexter Mayhew wake on 15 July 1988 is the same sublet flat that I shared with 15 other students during that summer's fringe festival. This is not to say that the events are autobiographical – that's rarely the case – but experience provides a sort of sense-memory, an authenticity that hopefully finds its way on to the page, because if the background is tangible and real, then hopefully events in the foreground will seem more plausible, too.[5]

So, even if this research is all for the writer, it's still an important part of the process. It still finds its way onto the page. Nicholls needs to know that the settings of his stories are real to give him the confidence to convince his reader they are real. This can be really useful. My debut novel, *Alice and the Fly*,[6] was set in a fictional town, but it was really the town in which I lived, given a fictional name. It wasn't until I drew a map of the town and hung it on my wall that I realised how close the resemblance was. But even without this map, all of my friends who've read the book have recognised these places immediately (even though I tend to avoid descriptions of the settings). And for me that's what researching your setting allows; a sense of authority that's hard to define, but exists nonetheless. Even those readers who aren't my friends and don't recognise the locations still get a sense that this place is *real* and that's what matters.

It's like David Nicholls says, about knowing the house where it's set. It's often good practice to base your fictional homes on a real house that you know well. Then you can hold it in your imagination – the logistics of it. You won't accidentally have someone entering the kitchen from the living room, whereas before they've entered from the hallway. You can also avoid having to over-describe settings (which a lot of us do) to make the world real to yourself, before you can give it to the reader. Bear in mind that when we read we often have our own go-to templates in terms of settings. Whether it be a church or a farm or a grandparent's house – everybody's imagination has these stock locations already.

People

People can be fantastic resources for your writing. Family, friends, neighbours, people who talk to you at bus stops – basically anyone who can give you a fresh perspective. The main plot of my debut novel is pure fiction, but in terms of the characters and the world I created I stole a lot from life. Not always *my* life, some of it was my friends, or friends of friends, urban legends from our school.

I remember when I was first writing *Alice and the Fly*, my friends and I had no money, so a typical night out for us was that we'd drive to the beach and eat fast food in the car and talk. And often we'd reminisce about school. And this is where I got a lot of the material for *Alice* ... from these anecdotes we'd tell, from our shared memories (a lot of which were probably exaggerated beyond recognition). I'd get home and write them all down, pick the ones that fitted into the story, rewrite them into fiction.

Other Fiction

This may seem obvious, but the best source of research you have, as a writer, is fiction. There was a definite turning point in my development as a writer and it was when I started working at a bookshop and began what I now call my 'excessive reading' stage. You too may be an excessive reader, but I know writers who aren't (especially students), and so it's worth flagging up how important this is.

I'm comfortable to admit now that back in university I didn't read enough. My fellow students and I claimed it was too much hard work, we didn't think it was important, we didn't have time to read because we were 'too busy writing' (that was the classic excuse), or we thought reading a lot would pollute our writing, have too much of an influence on our 'style'. I had a student say something similar to me recently: that they heard somewhere that to be a good writer, you should either read everything, or read nothing. And that he'd decided to read nothing, because that seemed the easier option, fitted more into his schedule.

But reading is what made me a writer. Those mornings I'd spend in the garden with Steinbeck, the days sat in coffee shops trying to decipher David Foster Wallace, the nights sat on the roof with a beer and a cigarette, reading Bukowski and thinking I was a badass – these were what gave me the passion, and the patience, to dedicate so much of my life to constructing well-written prose.

Also, guess what – it's your job. I remember one day a student came into the bookshop where I worked and asked for a recommendation. He said he wanted to be a novelist but had never actually read a full novel. He wanted me to recommend a novel to him that would sum up all novels, that would teach him how to write one. I was stumped – not only because of how obvious it was that such a novel could never exist, but also because, if you've never read a novel, why on earth would you want to write one?

But I was also a little angry. Because, if you've never read a novel, why do you think you're in any way *qualified* to write one? It's such an obnoxious thing to just think you can do. It's like me sitting down to play a guitar and just assuming I can do it, without ever even having heard a *full song*.

Writing Burst
- It could all have been very different.

A Final Note

Research is always going to be your best ally in producing good fiction. Because one of the most important aspects of writing is specificity. *Be specific* comes number three in Natalie Goldberg's Rules of Writing Practice,[7] and just about any book on craft you care to pick up will endorse this advice. Specificity is the key to making your writing real, bringing it to life. Robert McKee says: 'Do research. Feed your talent. Research not only wins the war on cliché, it's the key to victory over fear and its cousin, depression.'[8]

But research is more than just finding the details to make pretty prose. It's also a huge part of a writer's life. I'm going to finish by returning to this concept that life is the great research project that informs your fiction. It's a useful philosophy that has often helped me.

Because the truth is that life is hard, especially if you're a writer. In general we don't bring home much in terms of annual salary and often have to work jobs we'd rather not to fund our fiction writing. But this is good. This is your real education: life. Think of it as research – it at least makes it bearable.

While writing *Alice and the Fly* I worked as a cleaner in a butcher's. And thinking this way was what got me through the day. Each time I scrubbed hardened blood from the walls, or emptied the fat from the chicken oven, or unclogged the mincer with my bare hands, I told myself it was research. And it was – I used all of those details in the novel.

And this goes for all of life's trials and tribulations. Joy, heartache, love, sorrow; anything you feel – use it. Write about it. Even if it's just for you. The reflective nature of writing is therapeutic in itself. But also all of these things are what make up life. And they are also the foundations for well-written fiction.

Notes

1   James Salter, *Burning the Days* (London: Vintage, 2003).
2   Hilary Mantel, Art of Fiction No. 226, *Paris Review* (2015), www.theparisreview.org/interviews/6360/art-of-fiction-no-226-hilary-mantel (accessed 19 May 2016).
3   Waterstones, 'Crime authors answer your questions – How much research do you do?' (2012), www.youtube.com/watch?v=W7HMqzy6x0Q (accessed 19 May 2016).
4   David Nicholls, 'David Nicholls: Google v Old-Fashioned Legwork – How to Research a Novel' (2015), *The Guardian*, www.theguardian.com/books/2015/may/23/david-nicholls-one-day-us-google-street-view-novels-location (accessed 19 May 2016).
5   Nicholls, 'Google v Old-Fashioned Legwork'.
6   James Rice, *Alice and the Fly* (London: Hodder and Stoughton, 2015).
7   Goldberg, *Wild Mind*.
8   Robert McKee, *Story: Substance, Structure, Style, and the Principles of Screenwriting* (London: Methuen Publishing, 1999).

7

Reflection

The part of the title of this book that's in parentheses hopefully suggests the importance to writers of reflection. The ethos and methodology of *HTWSS* has to do with thinking about the way you read and write in order to help you write better stories. It's hard to overstate the importance of reflection: you will grow much faster as a writer if you regularly examine your own and others' work. You will develop more quickly if you're able to articulate your creative processes and if you learn to become self-aware and self-critical. You'll benefit from habitually examining your growing understanding of the kind of writer you are. As well as reflecting on your own developing craft, you need to be able to analyse the craft of those you aspire to emulate. You also need to begin to be able to analyse the literary context you wish to be a part of and to articulate your own intentions.

Your reflection, whichever form it takes, must be in writing. If you don't write down your thoughts, they are never more than half-formed. Get in the habit of reflecting on paper, not just in your head; acquire the discipline of thinking in writing about what you read and write. Fundamental to the discipline of keeping notebooks and journals is the notion that if you do not record them, your ideas will be lost. A similar rationale underlies the equally essential discipline of reflection: just as you will always be having ideas for your work, so too you will always be having thoughts about your work. You will, for instance, be thinking about how to develop the story you are working on. If you don't record it, you will lose it. Reflection is a way of thinking on paper so that you can see your thoughts, organise them and decide what you want to do with them. Seen in one light, reflection is simply a particular mode of journal writing.

Seeing What You Say

Let's make this more concrete. In the past week, I've had a couple of ideas about the characters in a story I'm working on. One was that I might like to try using the epistolary form with Barbara, one of the principal characters. If I record this possibility in my journal, it has the status of a reminder of a new approach that I might take. But as I make this entry in my journal – *Maybe use epistolary form with B?* – perhaps I get caught up with the idea and begin to tease it out:

> At the moment, B is very important to the story's central character, E, but so far we always see her from the point of view of another character – E's. However, the more time I live with this story, the more intrigued and charmed by B I am. Also, the few people who have read drafts have commented favourably on her. If I were to give her the status of viewpoint character, it might extend the range of the story. It would mean that it became dual viewpoint, but if the strand in her viewpoint were to be in the form of letters, it would lend the story a greater variety of narrative technique. It would also give the readers a direct insight into the consciousness of B, one which they are not afforded at the moment.

Here I'm doing more than recording an idea: I'm thinking about it, putting my thoughts into writing, and as they appear before me on the page, they are formed. Unless and until I try to articulate these thoughts in writing, they are vague and unformed; they are only embryonic. But when I put them in writing, I find out what I am thinking. Thoughts are of limited use until they have been articulated. As E.M. Forster famously said, 'How do I know what I think until I see what I say?' Perhaps thoughts are to dough what articulation is to bread; in other words, thoughts have not been baked. Lesson one in reflection: your thinking about your work has little or no value until you have made it concrete in the form of words on a page. I recommend that you acquire the habit of reflecting in writing during and after each story you produce. You will reap the benefits.

How to Reflect on Your Own Work

In a piece of reflective writing, you may discuss the influences you had for a short story: any fiction that has fed into your fiction. Say you were trying to learn from the conflict between character and setting in Z.Z. Packer's 'Every Tongue Shall Confess' (in her collection *Drinking Coffee Elsewhere*). You might examine the ways she uses this tension to create character and then write reflectively about how you applied what you learned to your story.

In reflective writing, you might also consider the elements of craft you have used in this story. Transitions? Fragmented narrative? Which books on craft had you been looking at? Which particular theories about, say, characterisation, were you picking up on? How successfully? In a reflection, you might want to say something about your developing philosophy of writing. Are you a naturalist or a magic realist? What are your priorities when you sit down to write a story: the style, the plot or the emotional experience you want your readers to have?

In evaluating your work, you might deal with problems encountered and the ways in which they have been overcome (or not). When you came to a dead end with your plot and could see no way out, what were your strategies for overcoming this obstacle?

Writing reflections will lead to you making changes to your story; it will be a redrafting tool. However, the major benefit of writing reflections is that it will make you a self-conscious, self-critical writer, somebody who knows what you're doing, and if you can train yourself always to know what you're doing it's inevitable that you will learn to do it better.

To summarise: an important function of reflective writing is to produce writers who are more self-conscious, more self-critical, and have a better understanding of the kind of writing they are attempting.

> **Writing Burst**
> - Put 'To Kill a Mockingbird clip Boo is a hero' in your search engine and use the film clip as your prompt.

What Students Write About in Reflections

I thought it might be helpful to give you some examples of reflective writing. Two former students, Angi Holden and Jo Selley, have kindly agreed to have their work quoted. The reflection extracts below were written to complement creative work they did during their first year as undergraduates. I've organised the quotations to try to illustrate the range of subject matter that may occur in reflective writing. They come in no particular order and the sub-headings are mine.

Inspiration

My inspiration for the piece initially came from two delivery men who delivered a lounge suite to me a couple of weeks ago. It was very obvious that one was the boss, a bit of a wide-boy, and did all the talking and I got to wondering about their relationship and what conflict could follow these two throughout the day.

Working Methods

Instead of starting with the story, this time I started with the characters. This was as a result of reading 'How I Wrote the Moth Essay' by Annie Dillard in which she says start by describing something, be precise about things. So I drew up a character sketch for each person and from this various other ideas flowed.

Redrafting

During the redrafting process I decided to delete a few large scenes which took place with the people they were delivering to. By incorporating a few more lines into the main character's dialogue it was possible to exclude these scenes altogether without losing the fact that they had made the deliveries.

Process Log

When I had finished the first draft of the story, I considered rewriting it to include direct speech. In the end I felt that this would be a mistake; the tone is one of reminiscence and the introduction of dialogue would be artificial.

Genesis of the Work

When I was a teenager growing up in West London, there was a significant level of racial prejudice and homeowners expressed concern that the property values would plummet if a non-white family moved in nearby. Southall was held up as an example; experiencing an influx of Indian and Pakistani families, it had acquired the nickname Little Asia. This became the background for my story.

Reading Which Informed the Work

Around this time I picked up a book by Preethi Nair in my local library, a romantic novel with a plot pretty typical of the genre – boy meets girl, boy loses girl, boy wins girl back again. What made it a particularly enjoyable read was the setting of New Delhi and the expatriate Indian community in Cairo.

Reflecting About Craft

Sharples, in *Writing as Design,* mentions a 'primary generator', which is something that sets an idea off and that for it to be effective it should 'provoke rather than answer questions'.

Examining the Creative Process

Dorothea Brande, in *Becoming a Writer*, recommends writing as soon as you wake up, while the 'unconscious is in the ascendant'. In 'Deconstructing Creativity' Debbie Taylor quotes writers who talk about submitting to their unconscious, allowing the structure to develop while they write. My unconscious mind obviously takes over at some stage, as I never have any preconceived idea of how the story will end.

Discussing Intention

I tried to create an impending sense of foreboding by using the weather to build tension, which I think adds to the overall feel of the story: 'Cold wind blew down the back of her neck, icy fingers dancing down her spine.'

Thinking About Literary Context

I'm also starting to discover what style of writing I prefer: MacLaverty's straightforwardness and simplicity to Virginia Woolf's stream of consciousness and Faulks' emotion and realism to Carver's minimalism. This will help me develop my own voice.

I hope that will give you some possible directions as you begin to develop the habit of reflective writing. A reflection forms the next Writing Exercise, but that's only the beginning: from this point on, I would like you to produce one for each story project that follows. (They're distributed throughout the book.) It will help your work grow more quickly and it will give you an understanding of your craft and a strong sense of yourself as a fiction writer. The value of reflection cannot be overstated.

Writing Exercise: A Reflection

Once you have completed the 1,000-word story exercise that comes at the end of this section, write a 250-word piece of reflective writing about it. Here are some areas you may include in it:

Discuss the influences you had in writing this story.

Examine any techniques you've been trying to emulate. Look at the way a favourite author has used, say, dialogue, and then look at how you have tried to learn from this.

Consider any theories about writing fiction you may have studied to produce this particular piece of creative work. You can make it easy on yourself for now and perhaps discuss your attempt to apply some of the suggestions about craft in this book. For instance, was there anything in 'Living Elsewhere: Plot' that influenced your writing in this story?

What kind of writing is this? For example, has your story been an attempt to write dramatic fiction? Or have you, like Chekhov, been aiming to reveal character?

What kinds of effect were you aiming to have on the reader?

Specify which effect at which particular point in the story.

Which problems have you encountered in writing this piece?

What were your strategies for overcoming these problems?

It's good to look back on what you have studied, so for your own records include a bibliography of any texts that have informed the creative work.

Writing Burst
- It made me smile when the others began to believe that she had done it.

Broader Reflection

Whereas we have just been looking at reflection about a particular piece of work, if you are to understand the kind of writer you are and thus continue to develop, you will need to acquire the habit of reflection in a broader sense of the term. This kind of reflection is something I think we all regularly do with regard to our own lives. When you go away for the weekend, because of the perspective that's permitted by standing apart from the thick of your day-to-day life, don't you sometimes find yourself contemplating what you're doing with your life? The same is true, perhaps to an even greater extent, when you take a week's or a fortnight's holiday. Being away from your routine existence allows you to stop and consider where you're up to now and where you might perhaps be going. This kind of self-examination has to do with putting some distance between yourself and the woods so that you can see the trees.

Let's try to turn that into some useful advice for writers. Reflection involves the perspective that distance from your work offers. It will sometimes mean looking back and thinking about where you are now so that you can make decisions about where you want to go next. Note also that the purpose implicit in this examination of your work is to improve it, and, more than that, to grow as a writer. Reflection for writers is just as much about self-development as improving the story.

You should already have acquired the habit of reflection in a few different forms. You know the value of keeping a journal and using it, for instance, as a nursery for your creative work. This involves reflective thinking. (*What if, in the middle of their wedding preparations, Sarah's dad is rushed to hospital for a heart bypass operation? How will Jacob – whose own father died of a heart attack when he was twelve and who has come to regard Sarah's dad as a father – deal with this?*) You are also aware of the way keeping a reading log enhances your growth as a writer, and you have begun to learn how to evaluate your own work. In other words, you have already become familiar with a number of different forms of reflective writing.

Writing Burst

- A situation: your protagonist is entering a room and meant to be giving a speech to a large crowd. He hasn't a single idea about what to say.

The idea of writing reflections for story projects in *HTWSS* is to encourage you in the habit of reflective writing. This will inevitably lead, at points when you stand back from your work, to, for instance, writing longer pieces of reflection. These can be about your writing in general. You can reflect about the kind of writer you think you are and the kind of writer you would like to be. You can look at what you are able to do well and what you struggle to do in your writing. You can examine your intentions for a piece of work and the differences between that intention and the result. You can discuss inspiration, technique, drafting, where characters come from. You can endlessly think about why you write – Jonathan Coe's reason, hard to beat, is that he is unhappy when he doesn't – or about why you *keep* writing, as Thom Jones does here, at a time when he was feeling like giving up:

Then one day, watching television, I saw Wile E. Coyote chasing the Road Runner across a cartoon desert. Cartoon New Mexico, I figure. I was hoping that he would catch the stupid annoying bird and rip its head off. But then, in the middle of the chase, the coyote came to a screeching halt, stepped out of the cartoon, and walked toward the audience with a wry, self-satisfied grin on his face. His footfalls ka-flop ka-flop ka-flop, cartoon style. No big hurry here. He acted like he had all the time in the world. When he was finally in place, he pulled his shoulders back, looked into the camera, and said, just as cool as you please, 'Allow me to introduce myself. Wile E. Coyote … *genius.*'

'Genius,' he said. Genniiee-us. *Genieuz.* Maybe that's just another word for perseverance. Wile E. Coyote, no matter what else you might say about him, was not a quitter. I mean, if you keep plugging at it, you *might* get it. If you quit – pow, it's over.[1]

Eventually, the practice of reflecting about your work before you begin it, while you're doing it and after you have completed it should become second nature to you. That's the way writers work. Like an iceberg, the story readers see represents only the tip of what we write.

Note

1   Thom Jones, 'I Am a … Genius!' in Will Blythe (ed.), *Why I Write: Thoughts on the Craft of Fiction* (London: Little, Brown and Company, 1998), p 32.

Part II

How to Write a Short Story

8

What Is a Short Story?

Tom Vowler

It's perhaps easier to declare what a short story isn't: it's not an abridged version of the novel; nor is it a prose poem, though it can share aspects of these forms – a distant cousin to both, if you like, a younger, often brash and indecorous one. Let's start then by terming the story a compressed narrative, irreducible and intense, a piece of fiction designed to move, delight, provoke, amuse or shock – all in a single sitting.

Barbara Kingsolver remarked that stories are the successful execution of large truths delivered in tight spaces. Flannery O'Connor, too, evoked this aspect, claiming certain truths exist that can only be told through the short story.

Although assimilating elements of early forms of storytelling (fables, myths, sagas, parables, folk tales, ballads), the short story as we know it today is little more than two centuries old. The author Philip Ó Ceallaigh suggests that after food and shelter, stories are the thing we need most to sustain us. Certainly storytellers have been revered throughout history; in the gulags, for example, those who told stories were often bestowed higher status. The form, then, has its roots within the tradition of oral storytelling, where travellers would earn their supper or a bed in exchange for the narrating of an entertaining and compelling tale.

From Hawthorne and Poe to Chekhov and Joyce, right up to Carver and Munro, the short story's emergence has been universal in appeal, adapting itself to disparate cultures and genres. Yet what we regard as the modern short story is the youngest of the literary forms, hardly out of short trousers. It is the precocious child, refusing to conform, to be predictable or well behaved. Yes, it has learned from what's passed before, but it wants to push into new territory, mould the literary landscape to its own will, break free of traditional shackles.

From the earliest writings, and set down by Aristotle, we have a preconceived idea of what the important elements of drama and fiction are: the beginning, middle and end, the what happens, the sequence of exposition of character and setting, the rising action, the drama and conflict, and finally the resolution. In Maupassant's stories, and in other nineteenth-century exemplars, the emphasis was still on plot, with the narrative closed tightly at the end: stories were hewn to a formula, designed to entertain, to satisfy.

But now we expect plot to arise directly from character, if indeed it arises at all. Authors such as Chekhov and Turgenev began to spurn plot, sacrificing it for deeper characterisation and atmosphere. Conflict in their stories increasingly took place internally, the character(s) wrestling with turmoil or dilemma. Stories such as Mansfield's 'Bliss' and Chekhov's 'The Lady with the Dog' were patterned by internal emotion, mood and atmosphere rather than by external action. The traditional 'twist' ending fell out of fashion, replaced with something more resonant and true to life. Irresolution became an important aspect of the story, beginnings and endings lopped off, leaving only 'middles'.

Later still, modernism yielded authors such as Conrad, Woolf and Joyce, who injected the short story with such tropes as unreliable narrators, absurdism and a stream-of-consciousness narration. Meanwhile, in the Spanish-speaking countries of South America, there emerged a strong tradition of magical realism in the short story, one that thrives to this day.

And with postmodernism, stories became even more playful, subversive and untailored, often reluctant to reveal their meaning, the neat narrative conclusion of traditional short stories spurned for this irresolution. Metafiction and experiment dominated the form.

The modern short story is happy to find fertile material in the trivial, the seemingly mundane qualities of human behaviour, the small but devastating moments, the moments that change a life. And some might say that behind this seemingly trivial detail, short stories tap into something else. For Charles E. May it is something spiritual, something beyond the everyday realm.

> Moreover, the fact that a good short story communicates by a delicate and tightly organized pattern of language – not by argument, direct statement, temporal plot, or moral cliché – means that what the short story strives to communicate is too subtle, too ambiguous, too complex, too inchoate, to be communicated by those rhetorical means by which nonfiction and long fiction often communicate.[1]

Other short stories are interested in the weird, the unusual, the macabre. The strange, the terrible, the extreme. Often they are peopled with characters who aren't conventional heroes. Frank O'Connor calls the solitary outsider in short stories 'the little man' of literature, a trope to first appear in Gogol's 'The Overcoat', the story's protagonist an exemplar of this. Everything about the character Akaky Akakievich is absurd and mediocre, but he is transformed by Gogol imposing the image of the crucified Jesus. But Akaky is not a character the reader identifies with. For O'Connor, in reading a novel there is some kind of identification between the reader and one of the characters. The short story, though, is without a traditional notion of a 'hero' (as are many modern novels). Instead short stories are populated with what O'Connor calls a 'submerged population group'. These have been 'Gogol's officials, Turgenev's serfs, Maupassant's prostitutes, Chekhov's doctors and teachers, Sherwood Anderson's provincials, always dreaming of escape'. And so the short story seems particularly adept at shining light on the marginalised, the voiceless.

Perhaps Cortázar captures it when he says: 'A story is meaningful when it ruptures its own limits with an explosion of spiritual energy which suddenly illuminates something far beyond that small and sometimes sordid anecdote which is being told.'[2]

Certainly the stories that resonate the loudest build quietly and expertly towards some devastating (though often underplayed) reveal or epiphany, as Joyce termed it, which is somehow anticipated yet never wholly expected – surprising yet inevitable. But of course the form is a dynamic, versatile one, and stories that shun epiphanies have a delight all of their own.

Yet none of this is easily achieved. Brevity should not be mistaken for simplicity. The short form demands much, not only from the reader, but from those composing the stories.

Qualities

I've argued that the form is dynamic, fluid, versatile: a story can manifest as a list, a series of tweets, a piece of parental advice, a series of diary entries. It can personify a tree for the purpose of narration, purport to do one thing and then, mischievously, do another. It can be quiet and smouldering, grandiose and extravagant. It can be a few hundred or ten thousand words. Its first half might cover five minutes of narrative time, the second half several years. There are, simply, very few rules – well, perhaps two, which I'll come to.

To borrow from Kafka, a story must be 'the axe to break up the frozen sea within us', or from Poe: 'an exaltation of the soul which cannot be long sustained'. It must be compacted, that is, each and every word must do more than its fair share. It should shun neat narrative conclusions, its meaning ambiguous, perhaps layered deep within the text. It should have a subtext, one that is perhaps only glimpsed, obliquely referred to, as with the poem: more felt than known.

It may appear mundane, but never is. It absolutely must leave space for the reader to occupy, for them to become an active participant rather than a passive observer; there are no free rides with the short story. It must possess voltage, 'kick or bite' as the author Alison MacLeod terms it. Michèle Roberts regards the story as 'unfurling like a Japanese paper flower on water'. Every word must bear the weight of the story, every sentence should be scrutinised by a hanging judge.

Narrative Voice

Beyond a title, the first sense we get of a story – before character, plot, setting, theme – is the voice, which should entice us into the piece and is our first connection with it. Voice is a nebulous creature, often difficult to pin down, to define, yet easy to spot when done either well or badly. I'm not talking about the writer's style, which may or may not have its unique timbre and nuance; it's the specific qualities of the narrator we're interested in here, which of course vary from story to story. It's the fulcrum the piece turns on, the idea and purpose that controls how you set about saying what you say. Voice is prose that's in utter control, exerting a quiet authority and persuasion, allowing the reader to fully engage with and trust the story. It's the sum of syntax, grammar, tone and vocabulary, all woven together so that the story sings with its own effortless wonder. Most of all, it must be consistent. The surest way to break the fictive spell is with a slip in voice.

When done effectively, voice is probably the single quality that allows someone to forget they're reading, to immerse themselves in the words, confident at being left in the writer's safe hands. A strong, compelling and consistent voice is one of the best ways to not only draw your reader in, but to keep them there. It's the essence that breathes life into the story, giving the impression to the reader that composition was a seamless, almost ethereal process. Which, of course, it never is. Voice done well allows the reader's resistance to fall away, allowing them into the story, to believe it.

One of the best ways to appraise a story's voice is to read it aloud, to really listen to the rhythm of the piece, looking out for phrases that jar, that sound clunky or overwritten. The voice may slip at times, becoming inconsistent or implausible – a sure way to lose the reader, to break the spell. Consistency of voice brings about verisimilitude. This consistency might be about use of language, register, syntax or sentence structure. It might be about style or tone. Perhaps the narrator is a colloquial first-person narrator or a sparse, closely focalised third person. But the voice of the story will have its own unique qualities.

Crucially, you need to establish in your own mind how close the reader is to be to the story/text/narrator – all of which will be determined by voice. Very few modern short stories adopt a wholly god-like, omniscient third-person point of view, with all characters treated objectively and equally. There might be an implied first person to the narration, often courtesy of a free indirect voice. John Gardner, in his excellent book *The Art of Fiction*, refers to the psychic distance created by the author, which determines the proximity the reader feels between themselves and the story. Careless shifts in this distance disrupt the story's flow.

Whose point of view you decide to narrate from, and how closely you do this, will affect levels of immersion, but will also shape your story thematically. An omniscient viewpoint offers the benefits of multiple speakers but, for example, doesn't offer the opportunity of an idiosyncratic voice or deep insight into character. Perhaps your story will be well served by exploiting both: multiple narrators, separated by sections, playing with how the same event is interpreted differently, to great comic or terrible effect. Experiment with viewpoints: try a first-person narrator who is detached from the story; or narrate in the second person using the pronoun 'you'. Employ a stream of consciousness. Whatever you choose, there must be a motive for this: perhaps the narrator has crucial information for the story, a unique insight. Perhaps they are unreliable, forcing the reader to question what they are being told.

Character

For the modern short story, character has subverted plot in its importance, so time spent thinking about your main character(s) is rarely wasted, even in short fiction. The iceberg metaphor works well here, with, most likely, only the tip being necessary to reveal in the story (after all, you only have room to paint people with a few deft strokes), yet much of what's below informs this, giving the characters substance, soul. If voice is our first sense of the story, whose story it is follows on closely.

While reading a novel, the reader develops a relationship with a character, whereas the short story is more like meeting someone in a bar or having a one-night stand; you don't find out everything about the character. The short story is necessarily partial; it approaches character in a different way. In a novel, characters develop over time, but in a story, character pivots on a defining moment and this is often, though it doesn't have to be, one of change or revelation (some great short stories are about characters NOT learning or seeing things differently, as in Flannery O'Connor's work).

Creating Plausible Characters

Think about the central character(s) in your stories. Have you created an everyman/woman, a dull cipher of little originality? Worse still: a stereotype, a cliché? We all know them in real life, but they rarely belong in fiction: the grumpy, misunderstood teenager who stays in his room, hates the world, plays his records backwards; the camp hairdresser; the drunken old man, boring folk as he topples from his barstool; the serial killer who tortured animals as a child and can't relate to women; the abusive priest; the prudish spinster and her cat; the New Age vegetable grower who knits jumpers. Yes, these people exist, but dig deeper and you will find other qualities, hypocritical ones, nuances, idiosyncrasies, quirks, qualities nobody else sees. As a writer it's your job to reveal the essence that makes people unique and interesting. Think about someone who doesn't cry at a parent's funeral. Someone who buys the same novel from every bookshop she enters, but never reads it. A man who only opens his post with gloves on. Something more interesting begins to emerge.

Look at how your characters behave. Can we predict it too easily? Have you truly brought them to life, so they live not just on the page but in your readers' minds? Are they balanced? (Nobody is wholly good or bad, weak or strong, happy or sad; blur their boundaries.) Create multi-faceted, complex characters: unpredictable, inconsistent, confused and flawed – just like you and me.

Never describe a character as average height, or as having average-length hair. This may literally be true, but it's unlikely they'll regard themselves as average. If you say a character has medium-length hair, you're essentially saying they have hair. Find something that isn't average about it. Don't overload the story with physical descriptions; one or two salient features will allow a character to resonate, to be 'seen', while alluding to what lies beneath the surface.

So how do you create characters that aren't counterfeits, that manage to convince the reader they are 'real'? Firstly you need to understand *people*. Their motivations. What's *really* making them behave the way they do? Become an amateur psychologist, always observing, seeing past someone's veneer, their public face. Listen in on conversations, looking at the nuance of body language that may betray the words uttered. Study the characters in the best stories; how is their nature revealed, woven into the narrative?

Dialogue is one of the best ways to reveal character, so you need to develop a good ear for it. Reading it aloud, or even recording and playing it back, can be useful. Remember, though, dialogue never mimics the way people actually speak. It is an illusion of speech; it is distilled and cuts out the dull parts of a conversation (such as saying 'hello' at the beginning of a telephone conversation). And always avoid using it as exposition.

Lacunae in the Short Story

Think about the best meal you've ever prepared, where flavour and texture and aroma all coalesced perfectly into a sublime dish, one your taste buds can almost recall as you imagine it. Now, instead of focusing on all the ingredients, the methods used, consider what you didn't put in, what you didn't do to the food. Because this was just as important to the outcome.

Giving the reader space through maintaining narrative silence can create powerful short fiction. By holding back, by resisting flagging every tiny aspect of the story in an expository smörgåsbord, you're letting the reader (more than that: you're inviting them to) do some work, allowing meaning to germinate from them. At first this can feel risky, but once you've learned to trust the reader, respecting their intelligence and instinct, their ability to read between the lines, you can begin to leave out more and more, merely evoking something's (an emotion, an event, a feeling) presence. Being force-fed a story is never satisfying – the food analogy again is a good one, with every facet of exposition and character spooned without pause into someone's mouth. Instead let the reader become active, to be part of the storytelling process, sensing the minutiae of a piece, its allegories, motifs and metaphors often only felt on completion. Of course there is a fine line, which when crossed you've become too arcane so as to frustrate – what is absent must still be implied – but try holding back as much as possible without compromising the story's dramatic tension and narrative progression.

Remember: short fiction is often served well by the reader coming away with more questions than answers.

The short story is perhaps concerned with what Susan Sontag termed of photographs as their 'inexhaustible invitations to deduction, speculation, and fantasy'.

Think of a classic Turner seascape – how the observer is invited to speculate, to look deeper and longer, to return and see things they hadn't before.

The author Graham Mort refers to lacunae's role in his discussion of a reader 'rescuing the text', of them not merely experiencing it but activating it.

> As well as language operating at the level of signification, the setting of a story and its sensory detail also signify in an affective way. The story is formulated as an aspect of the writer's consciousness and activated or catalysed by the reader's consciousness. It follows that the story only really exists when this activation takes place. We can't express the actual dimensions of time and space, because the task of writing could never keep up with the density and pace of actuality, so lacunae are inevitable.

Reminiscent of Kipling's fire that has been poked, its pieces raked out, Mort goes on to liken fiction's structure to the game Jenga.

> It helps us to decide how we can remove elements of the text whilst implying their presence. So narrative structures become lighter but also more resonant and intimate places for the reader because readers are more active in their realisation.[3]

Indirectness

Earlier I mentioned a number of qualities the short story tends to possess – but, it being the vibrant, versatile form that it is, none of these are requisites. Except for two: indirectness and subtext (which is dealt with below). Yes, something needs to happen, a shift in vision, perspective perhaps, for either the character, the reader, or both. But there are some great stories that take delight in nothing occurring, the character as stuck as they were in the opening, no epiphany, no progression. Certainly stories need conflict, but then all fiction requires this, so we can take this as a given, along with compelling, interesting characters.

Often the story relishes a lyrical style, yet as Carver points out, this too is not necessary: 'It's possible, in a poem or a short story, to write about commonplace things and objects using commonplace but precise language, and to endow those things – a chair, a window curtain, a fork, a stone, a woman's earring – with immense, even startling power.'[4]

Why indirectness? If we come straight at the story's theme, placing it on a plinth, adorning it with flashing lights, with song and dance, we deny the reader one of storytelling's most ancient allures: the frisson of working it out for themselves. Less is always more. By holding back, leaving space within the narrative, by never saying how a character feels, by paring down exposition, we create narrative tension and drive. Think of a ghost story, or a horror film. Of the power in what is only glimpsed, of what is suggested. This activates our primal emotions and senses, piques our attention, raises anticipation, encourages speculation. This is the art of storytelling. If you included every detail, every event, every emotion and motivation, the story would read like a textbook. Stories should need unlocking on some level.

If the short story were a painting, it would most likely be impressionistic, its strength coming from what is left out, what is merely hinted at. Or more crudely, think of your story's meaning or theme as being the core of an onion: make your reader peel back all the layers before they can get to it.

Subtext

The author Grace Paley is often quoted as saying, 'Every good story is at least two stories.' This goes to the heart of short fiction's purpose, of its desire to be complex and layered, to amply reflect the minutiae of the human condition. As with real life, the best stories have stories within them, worlds within worlds, kernels of truth that resonate deep below the piece's surface. Within your surface story, there must exist a portal or portals, liminal spaces that access this subtext, allusions or symbols that allow the reader's (often unconscious) mind to experience thematic qualities beyond those foregrounded. This 'other' quality is often intangible, felt but not entirely understood, its currents passing through your story, amplifying it, charging it. Perhaps your protagonist feels a deep sense of shame or guilt or sadness that isn't explicitly connected to the story, in that it's not explored or narrated. It's part of the character, yet exists separately. Perhaps this transforms as the story develops, perhaps not. As a writer, you may not even know this second story until after you've written the surface one, because it's emerged from your own subconscious mind – one of the beautiful processes in composition. And it's this subtext, as it quietly reverberates for your reader, that gives the story a ghostly quality, something all the best pieces have.

The short story, as we have seen, is a complex beast. It likes to punch above its weight, is so often more than the sum of its parts. Writing these compressed narratives is far from easy; the form demands much. But in unpicking its constituent parts, some of the mystery begins to fall away, and, with practice, something wonderful can start to emerge.

Notes

1   Charles E. May, 'Discovering Patterned Text vs. Exploring Amplified Context', *Thresholds*, http://thresholds.chi.ac.uk/reading-the-short-story/ (accessed 19 April 2017).

2   Viorica Patea (ed.), *Short Story Theories: A Twenty-First-Century Perspective*, (Amsterdam: Rodopi, 2012).

3   Graham Mort, interview for *Short Fiction*, www.shortfictionjournal.co.uk/?page_id=515 (accessed 19 April 2017).

4   Raymond Carver, 'A Storyteller's Shoptalk', *New York Times*, 15 February 1981, www.nytimes.com/books/01/01/21/specials/carver-shoptalk.html (accessed 19 April 2017).

9

Point of View

The viewpoint character is your host, the person from whose perspective – perhaps even from within whom – we experience the story, and every work of fiction has one.

Because point of view may be confused with opinion, which it isn't, Janet Burroway in *Writing Fiction: A Guide to Narrative Craft* suggests 'vantage point' as a more precise term. The viewpoint is the vantage point from which we experience the story. Burroway goes on to suggest that 'it might be better to think of viewpoint as being about speaking: Who speaks? To whom? In what form? At what distance from the action? With what limitations? All of these issues go into the determination of the point of view.'[1]

Perhaps, then, in beginning a piece of fiction writing, the first decision to make is: who is speaking?

Who Speaks?

From the earliest literature all the way through to the end of the nineteenth century, the use of an unapologetically omniscient narrator was common practice. The narrator of Guy de Maupassant's 'The Necklace' (1884) is a good example of this kind of authorial omniscience:

> She dressed plainly because she could not dress well, but she was as unhappy as though she had really fallen from her proper station, since

with women there is neither cast nor rank: and beauty, grace and charm act instead of family and birth. Natural fineness, instinct for what is elegant, suppleness of wit, are the sole hierarchy, and make from women of the people the equals of the very greatest ladies.[2]

Such omniscient narrators have somewhat fallen from favour. In recent decades, the idea that there is one truth has been as much disputed as the existence of God. For this and other reasons, an omniscient narrator who sounds genuinely all-knowing is less often used. Omniscient narration where the vantage point is at some distance from characters in their situations – narration that uses an authoritative but not all-knowing voice to set the scene – is more often the norm, as here in Tessa Hadley's story 'One Saturday Morning':

> Carrie was alone in the house. It was a Saturday in the mid-nineteen-sixties, and her parents were out shopping: she was ten years old, and doing her piano practice. She had borrowed her parents' alarm clock and put it on top of the piano to time herself.[3]

This perspective is useful to set the scene or to convey expository material, but in my view it should be used sparingly. It won't take long before readers tire of being told things; they want to experience the story more often than they are willing to be given information relating to it.

Your next narrative choice is deciding from whose point of view the fiction should be written. It may be the protagonist's. In John Updike's 'A & P', for example, the author has chosen the protagonist-narrator viewpoint. This means that for the duration of the narrative the reader is trapped inside one character's consciousness. An alternative is to have a narrator who is not the protagonist but an observer, a reporter. In the novel, one of the best-known examples of this is F. Scott Fitzgerald's *The Great Gatsby*, where the narrator-reporter is the confidant of the protagonist, Jay Gatsby. This viewpoint choice is almost always in the first person, as it is in *Gatsby* and in Conan Doyle's Sherlock Holmes stories, where Holmes' friend Dr Watson is the narrator-reporter, but it's equally possible in the third person. Fitzgerald has used a third-person narrator-reporter himself, in his story 'The Lost Decade', where Orrison, a journalist, reports on the protagonist, Trimble:

> 'The weight of spoons,' said Trimble, 'so light. A little bowl with a stick attached. The cast in that waiter's eye. I knew him once, but he wouldn't remember me' …
>
> … It was all kind of nutsy, Orrison decided.[4]

Writing Burst
- I wish you had told me this before.

To Whom?

Mostly the person being addressed in a piece of fiction is you, the reader – Hi! – and Janet Burroway stresses taking care in the way we go about this: 'The one relationship in which there must not be a distance, however, is between author and reader.'[5] When we write fiction, most of us assume the reader is somebody we can confide in, someone who shares our education and culture and will understand our references. Our narrators usually speak to somebody we assume is somewhat like us. Usually. Sometimes you will come across fiction where the explicit audience is not the reader, though: fiction where the narrator speaks to another character.

In Richard Burns' emotive story 'Perfect Strangers', the narrator is an adult looking back on a childhood holiday with his divorced father. The whole story is addressed to another character, the father, who has since died.

> You took me straight home to Mum, the clumsy caravan still fastened to the back of your Maxi. 'I'll not come inside,' you said. 'Your Mum might have visitors.'
>
> This didn't seem likely but I wasn't going to argue. 'Thanks then,' I said. 'I'm glad you enjoyed it.'
>
> 'Oh Dad, I did. Really. The best holiday ever.'
>
> And you drove off, as you always drove off, alone.[6]

The emotional impact is amplified through the narrator's direct address to his father, and further enhanced by son and father being largely separated by divorce and later death. If you can emulate it, having your narrator address the narrative to another character within it may achieve a wonderfully resonant emotional effect.

In Which Person?

You've decided which of the available characters narrates your story and you have an audience in mind. The next decision facing you is the form or *person* this narrator will take.

First person offers the possibility of an intimate bond between narrator and reader, which is desirable. Fiction is primarily about people and as readers we all decide, as we do in life when making friends, who we get on with and who we don't. First person opens up the inner world of the narrator and if readers empathise with what they experience there, a relationship may be formed. This is what we're all hoping for when we create a fictional world. First person is highly appealing to beginner writers. Perhaps this is because first person appears to be the form in which it is easiest to create a character; becoming your character may seem less of a leap when you are doing it using the 'I' form.

One of the great advantages of first person is that the narrator may address readers directly, which is friendly, and may also confide in them, as Truman Capote does many times in 'My Side of the Matter':

> I know what is being said about me and you can take my side or theirs, that's your own business … The day Marge and I got off the train at the L&N depot it was raining cats and dogs and do you think anyone came to meet us? … Eunice and Olivia-Ann had seen us coming and were waiting in the hall. I swear I wish you could get a look at those two! Honest, you'd die![7]

First-person narration has shortcomings, as Orson Scott Card observes: 'The main limitation on first-person narrative is that your narrator has to be present at the key scenes. A first-person narrator who merely hears about the major events of the story is no good to you at all.'[8]

Also, it's far too easy in first person to go into claustrophobic interior monologue mode; I can't be the only reader in the world to lose the will to live during protracted interior monologues, can I? It's like getting trapped at a party by somebody who loves the sound of their own voice.

More flexible and more potent than first-person narration is what often gets referred to as *third-person limited*. John Gardner here suggests why this particular point of view is preferable:

> First person locks us in one character's mind, locks us to one kind of diction throughout, locks out possibilities of going deeply into various characters' minds, and so forth. Third-person-limited or third person subjective is the same as first person except the 'I' is changed to 'she'.[9]

Note Gardner's reference to 'third-person subjective'. Part of the flexibility, the fluidity, that third person offers is that it may be subjective or objective – in other words the author may inhabit the consciousness of the character or remain on the surface of that character. Thus you (and, of course, the reader) may be privy to his or her thoughts and feelings, or not. One advantage of third-person limited is what Jenny Newman refers to as its 'tight focus'.[10] As we will see in a moment, the use of third person also offers you the facility of adjusting the focus – or, if you like, zooming in and zooming out again – which first person does not.

Here's a summary of the advantages and disadvantages of the various viewpoints just explored, plus a couple of rarities I haven't so far examined.

At What Distance from the Action?

John Gardner talks of 'psychic distance', which he defines as 'the distance the reader feels between himself and the events in the story'. This is something you can control in a couple of ways.

	First Person Singular ('I')	Second Person ('You')	Third Person ('He' or 'She')	First Person Plural ('We')
For	Immerses reader in narrator's heart and mind and may thus create an intimacy between narrator and reader, which is helpful if you want the reader to keep turning. First person would be the obvious choice if you want your narrator to be unreliable – and one of the advantages of unreliable narrators is that they make for active readers: the reader has to form views of the characters and situations different from those of the narrator.	Second person shares most of the virtues of first person singular. Also, it may appear to make the narrator and the reader one – not a bad trick if the reader buys it. Stories in second-person viewpoint are fairly common these days. You can find examples in Jennifer Egan's 'Out of Body' from A Visit from the Goon Squad, Melissa Banks' 'You Could Be Anyone' from The Wonder Spot and Jon McGregor's 'We Wave and Call' in Best British Short Stories 2012.	Whereas first person singular only permits you to adjust the distance between the narration and the story being narrated, third person allows you to adjust the distance between narrator and reader. Stories told in third person can be omniscient and wide focus, or stay on the surface of the point-of-view character's consciousness, or enter it.	First person plural in novels is rare. Jeffrey Eugenides' The Virgin Suicides is narrated by a group of teenage boys, and Joshua Ferris' And Then We Came to the End is narrated by the staff of an advertising agency. A more recent example is a chapter focusing on Dan, one of the characters in Anne Enright's The Green Road. She has described this viewpoint as 'the communal voice'. At least some of the time, Kevin Barry's 'Beer Trip to Llandudno' uses a communal voice. Put me straight if you can, but in my experience first person plural is even rarer in the short story than it is in the novel.
Against	Excludes readers from entering the minds of other characters; can be claustrophobic; your narrator cannot be everywhere, and so will inevitably miss key action.	Readers may find it mannered. They may find it presumptuous that the author is assigning responses and emotions to them.	In my view, there are no major disadvantages to third person. It may be as subjective as first person but also as objective as omniscient. Although most of us start out thinking first person is easier and more comfortable, it probably isn't. Henry James described first-person narration as 'barbaric'.	Lacks one particular character with whom readers may empathise. Shares the disadvantage of second person – may seem mannered.

First of all, you may adjust the position of Burroway's vantage point. You could, for example, shift from third-person omniscient to third-person limited. William Trevor's story 'The Ballroom of Romance' opens in the former:

> On Sundays, or on Mondays if he couldn't make it and he often couldn't, Sunday being his busy day, Canon O'Connell arrived at the farm in order to hold a private service for Bridie's father, who couldn't get about any more, having had a leg amputated after gangrene had set in. They'd had a pony and cart then and Bridie's mother had been alive: it hadn't been difficult for the two of them to help her father on to the cart in order to make the journey to Mass.

Within two paragraphs, the focus has narrowed and the camera has zoomed in, as we enter third-person limited:

> As she cycled back to the hills on a Friday, Bridie often felt that [some of the girls she'd been at school with] truly envied her her life, and she found it surprising that they should do so. If it hadn't been for her father she'd have wanted to work in the town also, in the tinned meat factory maybe, or in a shop.[11]

These two short passages illustrate part of John Gardner's suggestion that 'the beginning of [a] story find[s] the writer using either long or medium shots. He moves in a little for scenes of high intensity, draws back for transitions, moves in still closer for the story's climax.'[12]

Here you can see that the distance between both character and action affects readers' emotional response to the fiction. The first passage from 'The Ballroom of Romance' sets the scene; the second focuses on a character within that scene ('As she cycled back to the hills on a Friday, Bridie …') before moving the vantage point inside the consciousness of the character ('If it hadn't been for her father she'd have wanted to work in the town also …'). To my mind, the move from omniscient to third-person limited represents a much greater change in the reader's perception than any that might result from choosing first rather than third. It's in adjusting the distances between character, story and reader, not in choosing between, say, first-person and third-person narration, that you make decisions about viewpoint that offer you greatest control and flexibility. In the end, such decisions help you control the reader's responses – which is your overriding goal as a fiction writer.

You can control the distance between the reader and the events of the story in a couple of ways. The first, which we have just seen in the Trevor story, is adjusting the position of your vantage point by moving from third-person omniscient to third-person limited. The second way is by adjusting the position of the narrator in relation to the events of the story and to the reader.

At the beginning of Haruki Murakami's 'Yesterday', the viewpoint character addresses readers directly, conducting a one-sided conversation with them:

> As far as I know, the only person ever to put Japanese lyrics to the Beatles song 'Yesterday' (and to do so in the distinctive Kansai dialect, no less) was a guy named Kitaru. He used to belt out his own version when he was taking a bath.
>
> Yesterday
> Is two days before tomorrow,
> The day after two days ago.
>
> This is how it began, as I recall, but I haven't heard it for a long time and I'm not positive that's how it went.[13]

Later in the story, you will find the viewpoint character in a different position in regard to the readers, within the action:

> I recognized Erika Curtain right away. I'd only seen her twice, and sixteen years had passed since then. But there was no mistaking her. She was still lovely, with the same lively, animated expression. She was wearing a black lace dress, with black high heels and two strands of pearls around her slim neck.

The point-of-view character has changed from the role of narrator to that of protagonist, and has moved from addressing the reader directly to being a character within the action.

Writing Exercise: Make Friends with the Reader

Think of a situation where you found it difficult to do what you knew you really ought to do, and write a 250-word piece of fiction. Your brief is to express to the reader the viewpoint character's thoughts and feelings, but without monologuing; he or she should address the reader directly while remaining a character within the action.

Writing Burst

- Put 'Andrew Wyeth, Christina's World' in your search engine and use this painting as your prompt.

Omniscient Narrator

Here the narrator speaks as though he or she were God. John Gardner says of the omniscient narrator:

> He sees into all his characters' hearts and minds, presents all positions with justice and detachment, occasionally dips into the third person subjective to give the reader an immediate sense of why the character feels as he does, but reserves the right to judge (a right he uses sparingly).[14]

If you're going to use an omniscient narrator in the twenty-first century, chances are you will not want to wear your omniscience on your sleeve. Nobody likes a show-off. This may well mean keeping it fairly quiet that there is an omniscient narrator in the house, as Flannery O'Connor does here, in 'Everything That Rises Must Converge': 'Behind the newspaper Julian was withdrawing into the inner compartment of his mind where he spent most of his time.'[15] The narration is omniscient, but O'Connor can pass it off as third-person limited; at a casual reading, the viewpoint may seem to be Julian's. Alternatively, you need to use a tone so arch, so dripping in irony, that the reader is bound to realise you know full well that the omniscient narrator went out of fashion in 1899. See how Joyce Carol Oates does so in 'Is Laughter Contagious?':

> Christine Delahunt. Thirty-nine years old. Wife, mother. Recently returned to work – a 'career.' A woman of moral scruples, but not prim, puritanical, dogmatic. Isn't that how Mrs. D. has defined herself to herself? Isn't Mrs D., in so defining herself, one of us?[16]

Whichever way the whims of fashion may blow, the thing to remember about omniscient narration is to use it as a means of pulling back, of giving the bigger picture, and to do so subtly, sparingly.

First-Person and Third-Person Limited

If you opt for one of these, you are either narrating submerged in the viewpoint character's consciousness, thinking and feeling what she is thinking and feeling, or staying on the surface, following her around like a reality TV crew, recording her every word and deed, but leaving readers to deduce from these what she is thinking and feeling. In first person, the reader is stuck with the consciousness of your narrator, but, as I've already mentioned, if you adopt third-person limited you have the option of pulling back for a spot of omniscient narration. This will allow the reader room to breathe. Imagine a film entirely shot in medium close-up and close-up: that's what first-person narration means for readers. It's pretty intimate, which may or may not be a good thing.

Dual Viewpoint

In a story, dual viewpoint, alternating between the viewpoints of two characters, is appealing because it lends the fiction some variety; it gives the reader a temporary holiday from one viewpoint character when you move to another. Another advantage of dual viewpoint is that the shift from one character's perspective to another's generates movement and change, and any kind of motion, any kind of change, is beneficial in narrative. (As I say elsewhere, a story should be like a shark, constantly moving through the water.) Using dual viewpoint also means that you get two perspectives on the story, which will benefit from offering conflicting views. Having two viewpoints also creates the opportunity to run a separate narrative in each one, which may converge at the end. This is artful and, if handled skilfully, satisfying for the reader. (For examples of dual viewpoint, see Chapter 24: 'Transitions'.)

Writing Exercise: Dual Viewpoint with Jack and Meg

It can be both appealing and dramatic to look at a relationship from the perspectives of the two characters in it. Jack and Meg have been on tour for two months now. Jack is having a terrific time, but is unaware that Meg is tiring of playing second fiddle to him. Only at the end of the story does it emerge that Meg has been rehearsing with Rocky the sound engineer and that the pair of them have secured a recording deal with Huge Records. Imagine Jack's surprise!

Making this a dual-viewpoint story might well work better than single viewpoint. For one thing, narratives are in large part about movement and changing viewpoints is a form of movement, one that keeps readers interested.

Begin a dual viewpoint story based on my tongue-in-cheek Jack and Meg scenario.

The Short Story Cycle

Because of its length, carrying off multiple viewpoint in a single short story is difficult, but that's the most common viewpoint choice within collections of short stories that are in some way related to one another, and I'd like to take a little detour at this point to consider the short story cycle.

In 'Only Connect', his essay in *Salon.com*, Robert Morgan suggests that the short story cycle has 'the advantages of the integration and interconnection of a novel and the intensity and compression of a short story'.[17] Short story cycles may be the most common term for collections of linked short stories, but they have also been dubbed 'novels-in-stories', 'composite novels' and, simply, 'linked story collections'.

Publishers' marketing departments often pass off short story cycles as novels. You may well have read one. From Alice Munro's *The Beggar Maid* through Louise Erdrich's *Love Medicine* to Elizabeth Strout's *Olive Kitteridge,* the short story cycle often comes disguised as a novel.

Generally speaking, short story cycles do not have a single, unifying plot, or a single point of view – though of course, the latter is true of many novels – but are linked by other attributes. In James Joyce's *Dubliners* and Robert Olen Butler's *A Good Scent from a Strange Mountain,* the element that links the stories is place. In Denis Johnson's *Jesus' Son,* Melissa Banks' *The Girls' Guide to Hunting and Fishing* and Pam Houston's *Cowboys Are My Weakness,* it is the focus throughout on one central character (or in the case of Junot Diaz's *This Is How You Lose Her,* on very similar characters) that unifies the collection. In William Faulkner's *Go Down, Moses,* Sherwood Anderson's *Winesburg, Ohio,* Tim O'Brien's *The Things They Carried* and many examples by Amy Tan or Louise Erdrich, what connects the stories is their focus on a set of characters, often a family. However, as the critic Susan Garland Mann argues, 'There is only one essential characteristic of the short story cycle: the stories are both self-sufficient and interrelated.'[18]

The connections between characters and locations that you may devise will link your short story collection and give it some of the fulfilment that a novel may offer the reader – but, to pull that off, there will have to be some sort of drawing together of the threads of the different narratives at the end of your short story cycle. One model is that which Carol Shields uses in *Larry's Party,* where the final chapter suggests a conclusion not only by being about the eponymous party, but also by drawing together at it most of the major characters from Larry's life – from the rest of the book, in other words. Another way of drawing together the threads of a short story cycle is a technique used by Amy Tan in *The Joy Luck Club.* The book has been about the relationship between Chinese mothers and their Chinese-American daughters and specifically about the difficulty the daughters have had in coming to terms with the two halves of their identity. The final story is narrated by one of the daughters, Jing-Mei, and in it she goes to China to meet her half-sisters, the daughters her mother was forced to leave behind when she had to flee to America. When the half-sisters at last meet, Jing-Mei feels she is becoming fully Chinese for the first time; she also finally comes to terms with being both American and Chinese. This bringing together of the two worlds, the two identities of the novel, suggests a cohesion and a completion that perhaps isn't in reality present.

Writing Burst

- Put 'Joni Mitchell, Chelsea Morning' in your search engine and use the song as your prompt. Listen without any visuals; you just want the experience of hearing the lyrics and the music.

Floating Viewpoint

In the same way that you can move the vantage point of a story from third-person omniscient to third-person limited, or shift between point-of-view characters in a dual-viewpoint story, you can, if you're skilful enough and if you establish a clear pattern for the reader, shift your viewpoint from one character to another within the one scene. Hemingway does it in 'A Clean, Well-Lighted Place'. The story is more often than not in third-person omniscient, but it shifts occasionally between two third-person limited viewpoints. The story begins in omniscient ('It was very late and everyone had left the café except an old man who sat in the shadow the leaves of the tree made against the electric light.'). Later on, it's for a while in the viewpoint of the young waiter, who

> took the brandy bottle and another saucer from the counter inside the café and marched out to the old man's table. He put down the saucer and poured the glass full of brandy ... [He] poured on into the glass so that the brandy slopped over and ran down the stem into the top saucer of the pile.

Following that, the young waiter returns to the table where the older waiter sits and the viewpoint returns to third-person omniscient, where it remains until after the young waiter goes home, at which point the viewpoint becomes that of the older waiter, who carries on in his head the conversation he had been having with the younger waiter before he left:

> What did he fear? It was not a fear or dread. It was nothing that he knew too well. It was all a nothing and a man was a nothing, too. It was only that and light was all it needed and certain cleanness and order.

Three kinds of viewpoint – the omniscient narrator's, the young waiter's and the old waiter's – and you wouldn't notice it unless you were studying the story for an exercise like this. This is deft, subtle control of viewpoint. What happens when you fail to control viewpoint, though?

The Viewpoint Lapse

It's possible to destroy in a flash the reader's engagement with your narrative by falling into inadvertent multiple viewpoint. Your first-person viewpoint character is film director Orson Welsh, who is growing increasingly frustrated with his female lead, Rita Hayseed. The story is trucking along nicely, the reader is enjoying being immersed inside the head of this genius of film-making, and then on page 2 line 3 runs into this little landmine: 'On the twenty-second take, Rita thought she might faint.' Bye-bye, reader. In any piece of fiction, point of view is crucial – but only if you maintain control of it.

Control

Breaking fiction-writing craft into separate elements, as this book does, has to have its limitations. One technique always bleeds into another, and in the case of viewpoint there is an unavoidable overlap with character and voice. Perhaps because of that, viewpoint can achieve many things simultaneously, and a story where the author confidently controls it will excite and delight, sweeping the reader away. A great example of controlled use of viewpoint is Muriel Spark's story 'The House of the Famous Poet'. Here's the opening:

> In the summer of 1944, when it was nothing for trains from the provinces to be five or six hours late, I travelled to London on the night train from Edinburgh, which, at York, was already three hours late. There were ten people in the compartment, only two of whom I remember well, and for good reason.
>
> I have the impression, looking back on it, of a row of people opposite me, dozing untidily with heads askew, and, as it often seems when we look at sleeping strangers, their features had assumed extra emphasis and individuality, sometimes disturbing to watch. It was as if they had rendered their daytime talent for obliterating the outward traces of themselves in exchange for mental obliteration. In this way they resembled a twelfth century fresco; there was a look of medieval unselfconsciousness about these people, all except one.[19]

I began with Janet Burroway's interpretation of viewpoint as vantage point and here it is certainly that. I sometimes think of the vantage point as a little figure on a platform who indicates to the reader the focus of the story. In this passage, the vantage point leads readers through the focal points of the narrative and commands their perceptions of the story.

The first sentence communicates the era (the 1940s) and the setting, both general (Britain) and specific (a train from Edinburgh to London), and subtly suggests the tone: the train is hours late and the implication is that the narrator is frustrated, and perhaps also languorous.

The second sentence gives my little figure on a platform a broad view of the compartment before moving in on a couple of particular passengers. In the latter half of that second sentence, the narrator turns from the scene to confide in the reader that something dramatic is about to happen ('only two of whom I remember well, and for good reason').

The swift, confident movement of the vantage point through the era, the country and the compartment to the source of the story has taken control of the reader. The economy (57 words), the suggestion of character (someone educated, intelligent and with a taste for an anecdote) and the voice, which is weary ('it was nothing for trains from the provinces to be five or six hours late'), exasperated ('was already three hours late') and one of experience (she knows all about this train journey). Our little figure on a platform has also moved us from the present, whenever that might be, to the past: 'In the summer of 1944, when it was nothing …'.

Besides the skilfulness I have noted, one other feature of this story plays an important part in exercising control: the author has complete command of language. Just as much as she controls the focal points of the story and the delivery of the necessary information, she also moves through sentences with perfect efficiency. Quite important, that. (See Chapter 16: 'Style'.)

In the second paragraph, the narrator reminds us that this all happened some time ago ('looking back on it') and demonstrates in her description of the row of people opposite a beady eye for detail and a skewed sensibility: she finds sleeping strangers 'disturbing to watch' and thinks in terms of people 'obliterating' aspects of themselves.

Next the figure on the platform takes us momentarily out of the compartment and into a medieval painting, before turning sharply to the passenger who is different from the others. And this difference lets us know that here is the precise focus of the story.

Does this give you an idea of what control of viewpoint looks like and how powerful it can be in controlling the reader? I hope so, because if you can't control the reader you will most likely be wasting your time.

Notes

1   Janet Burroway, *Writing Fiction: A Guide to Narrative Craft*, 6th Edition (New York: Longman, 2003), p 254.

2   Guy de Maupassant, 'The Necklace' in *A Parisian Affair and Other Stories* (London: Penguin Classics, 2004), p 296.

3   Tessa Hadley, 'One Saturday Morning', http://www.newyorker.com/magazine/2014/08/25/one-saturday-morning (accessed 15 April 2016).

4   F. Scott Fitzgerald, 'The Lost Decade', https://ebooks.adelaide.edu.au/f/fitzgerald/f_scott/short/chapter52.html (accessed 15 April 2016).

5   Burroway, *Writing Fiction*, p 289.

6   Richard Burns, 'Perfect Strangers' in Duncan Minshull (ed.), *Telling Stories* (London: Sceptre, 1995), p 30.

7   Truman Capote, *The Complete Stories* (London: Penguin Classics, 2005), p 47.

8   Orson Scott Card, *Characters and Viewpoint* (London: Robinson Publishing, 1990), p 144.

9   Gardner, *The Art of Fiction*, p 76.

10 Jenny Newman, 'Short Story Writing' in Newman et al., *The Writer's Workbook*, 2nd Edition (London: Arnold, 2004), p 57.

11 William Trevor, 'The Ballroom of Romance' from *The Stories of William Trevor* (Harmondsworth: Penguin, 1983), p 185.

12 Gardner, *The Art of Fiction*, p 111.

13 Haruki Murakami, 'Yesterday' in 9 and 16 June 2014 issue of the *New Yorker* (accessed 15 June 2016).

14 Gardner, *The Art of Fiction*, p 158.

15 Flannery O'Connor, 'Everything That Rises Must Converge' in the collection of the same name (Harmondsworth: Penguin, 1975), p 13.

16 Joyce Carol Oates, 'Is Laughter Contagious?' in Robert Stone (ed.), *The Best American Short Stories* (Boston: Houghton Mifflin Company, 1992), pp 218–19.

17 Robert Morgan, 'Only Connect', Salon.com, http://www.salon.com/2000/11/03/morgan_3/ (accessed 22 September 2005).

18 Susan Garland Mann, *The Short Story Cycle: A Genre Companion and Reference Guide* (Westport, Connecticut: Greenwood, 1989).

19 Muriel Spark, 'The House of the Famous Poet' in Malcolm Bradbury (ed.), *The Penguin Book of Modern British Short Stories* (London: Penguin Books, 1988), p 181.

10

Characterisation

Helen Newall

According to Janet Burroway, 'Human character is at the forefront of all fiction,'[1] although writers will do well to note Hemingway's caution that 'a writer should create living people; people not characters. A character is a caricature.'[2]

The important difference between people and characters lies in the nuances of the word 'character' as defined in the Oxford and Cambridge online dictionaries: in both, character is defined firstly as 'the mental and moral qualities distinctive to an individual', but secondly as 'a person in a novel, play, or film'. Characters in long and short fiction are always the second, but they must seem to be the first. They *are* the story, for according to John Gardner in *The Art of Fiction*: 'However odd, however wildly unfamiliar the fictional world … we must be drawn into the characters' world as if we were born to it.'[3]

So, since short stories more often than not involve people, and their interactions, emotions, hopes, dreams, desires and disappointments, how should writers craft effective characterisation and write living, breathing people? The answer, ultimately, is the way that works best for you, but what follows are provocations, ideas and techniques for play and experimentation, which will hopefully help expand your skill.

Telling Details

Telling is a punchy and direct way of offering information: it is stated, or told, rather than shown, and because we tend to believe what is baldly stated by an authorial voice, it is accorded the weight of an indisputable fact. Take for example the statement:

> The banker, spoilt and frivolous, with millions beyond his reckoning, was delighted at the bet.[4]

But sources of such character information are multiple: we might be told about the attributes of a character from:

* the writer (as shown above)
* the narrator
* the character in the spotlight
* another character.

Each of these sources may subtly alter the value of information given to the reader. In her collection of interconnected short stories *Olive Kitteridge*, writer Elizabeth Strout tells us about Henry, the character on whom she focuses in 'Pharmacy':

> Inwardly, he suffered the quiet trepidations of a man who had witnessed twice in childhood the nervous breakdowns of a mother who had otherwise cared for him with stridency.[5]

This offers a lot of information very swiftly and allows the narrative to move on to more revelations, and because it is information given by the authorial voice, we trust it. Contrast this with the following example taken from J.D. Salinger's collection *Nine Stories*, in which we see one character giving us an impression of another who is not present:

> 'That dopey maid,' Eloise said without moving from the couch. 'I dropped two brand new cartons in front of her nose about an hour ago. She'll be in, any minute, to ask me what to do with them ...'[6]

Eloise might be a reliable source of information and the maid might be dopey, but such a statement might also tell us much more about Eloise than about the maid.

Sometimes it is the characters themselves who claim self-knowledge and reveal information about themselves, but bear in mind that they might be deluded, or naïve. Sometimes it is first-person narrators (who are different, after all, from writers) who give us that information. These are two forms of telling found in this sentence from Sandra Cisneros's story 'Linoleum Roses':

> She says she is in love, but I think she did it to escape.[7]

The power of this sentence lies in the context in which it is given: 'Linoleum Roses' is a vignette in which each sentence reflects onto the others like a jagged piece of mirror. The sentence given above is powerfully shifted by all the others around it. Take this for example, which causes the reader to reassess previous given information:

> She sits at home because she is afraid to go outside without his permission.

So the information given about this character, about any character, is cumulative, and dependent upon the reliability of the narrator, the context, the information given elsewhere in the work. A canny writer can exploit this, as Harper Lee does in her long-form work *To Kill a Mockingbird,* where what we are told about Boo Radley, and what Boo Radley does, are very much at odds, which leads us onto a discussion of how characters reveal themselves through behaviour.

Showing Details

While telling is a shorthand way of offering detail to the reader, showing is also a powerful option, for characters are revealed in what they do and how they do it, and by what they say and how they say it. Ian Rankin's collection of John Rebus stories, for example, offers some very finely drawn characters exposed in actions and conversations. In one such example, Rebus and a colleague, Gilmour, have found a watch on a body they have legally exhumed. The following exchange happens afterwards in the pub:

> When Rebus returned from the bar with their whiskies, he saw that Gilmour was playing with the pocket watch, trying to prise it open.
>   'I thought you handed it over,' Rebus commented.
>   'You think he'll miss it?'
>   'All the same …'
>   'Hell's teeth, John, it's not like it's worth anything.'[8]

The scene is small, but the detail is huge and characterises the men. We learn that they like a drink, but that they are never quite off duty; we learn that Gilmour has taken the watch rather than handing it in as he should; we learn of their dark humour in Gilmour's comments that the dead man won't miss it; and in the final explosive outburst, that he considers the object's theft to be justified by its worthlessness. Both men then try to open the watch, from which we surmise that Gilmour's lack of adherence to correct police procedure is matched by Rebus's, albeit after a certain hesitancy denoting perhaps a slightly less shaky moral compass. Rankin thus expertly shows us character in the actions, and in the conversational tone of five or six lines of tight prose and dialogue.

The differences between telling and showing might be summarised in this table.

She is an impatient woman.	A statement of fact; an undemonstrated attribute that tells the reader nothing of how impatience manifests itself in the action of the narrative. The reader is passive in understanding the character.
She waits impatiently in the queue to buy a train ticket.	The character's attribute is now given a narrative context, but the reader is still left to imagine how the characteristic of impatience might manifest.

She checks the time, taps her fingernails against the screen of her phone, then cranes her neck to see over the shoulder of the man in front as he slowly counts change and unzips and re-zips a wallet, and she shuffles as if the stone beneath her shoes is burning hot.	The reader is shown the character behaving in the scene without the characteristic being named as impatience: the behaviour speaks for itself. The reader must now actively infer the qualities of the character.

None of these examples is better than the rest: the best one is actually the one which is best for the context in which the writer is using it – but you have to be aware, and in control, of how you're using it.

Knowing and Understanding

Such masterly writing as Rankin's or Chekhov's comes from knowing *and* understanding your characters, and how they will behave, and what they will say in situations. It's worth considering, therefore, John Gardner's distinction between knowing and understanding:

> The writer's characters must stand before us with … such continuous clarity that nothing they do strikes us as improbable behaviour for just that character, even when the character's action is, as sometimes happens, something that came as a surprise to the writer himself. We must understand, and the writer before us must understand, more than we *know* about the character.[9]

There is much work to do to get to this stage of understanding. Janet Burroway is one of many writers on writing who suggests one way to do this is by keeping what she calls a *character journal*: 'A journal', she writes, 'lets you coax and explore without committing yourself to anything or anyone. It allows you to know everything about your character whether you use it or not.'[10]

A character journal might be a scrapbook of useful names; your scribbled observations of the peculiar or idiosyncratic things people do and say; habits or mannerisms that you notice in your friends and enemies that might be useful. Describe them in written sketches; observe their natural histories. Artists practise life drawing; you should practise life writing.

Writing Exercise: Writing from Life

Sit quietly watching people you know or people you don't know in the house, in a café, in a train station. Discreetly write short paragraphs on the people you see, catching appearance and actions, getting down as much detail as you can. If you hear any, now is also the time to jot down those weird little bits of conversation you might catch to tune your ear in to how people speak. Such observation exercises train your eye and offer you raw material and telling detail that can tighten up your characterisation and thus your writing.

The companion exercise to this is for the brave and the emotionally stable.

Sit quietly and watch yourself: what are you like, what do you do when you're angry or sad or happy, curious, excited, jealous ...? And what does your astrological birth sign – whether you believe it or not – say about you? Which birth sign should you be? You might think of this as a critical self-examination – a sort of reality-check horoscope of the self captured in words. And of course this material need never be shown to anyone, merely plundered for material in future writing projects.

A Method

Both the life-writing and self-appraisal approaches might be compared with Lee Strasberg's famous Method, whereby actors achieve effective characterisation through the psychological techniques of emotional recall and sense memory of previous experience. But bear in mind Lawrence Olivier's comment to Dustin Hoffman on the set of *Marathon Man*: after Hoffman, an advocate of the Method, played hard to portray a tired and hung-over character by being tired and hung-over, Olivier retorted: 'Why don't you just try acting?' For writers this might translate as 'why don't you just try writing?', because sometimes knowing everything about a character in advance might make a writer feel as if things are progressing, but can become a sort of displacement activity: in other words, you might never get round to writing, because you're so busy researching your characters ... I have always been an advocate of the happy medium in which I find out what I need and no more: I don't know what my characters would order in restaurants if they don't appear in restaurant scenes. This is understanding them, but not exhaustively knowing them. But on days when the writing is stuck, a playful exploration can move the writer through an impasse.

Writing Exercise: The Questionnaire

Think of a character from an ongoing project, or take someone you sketched in the previous observation exercise, or invent someone completely new.

What's your character's name? What shoes are they wearing? Any jewellery?

What's in their pocket? What's their favourite song? Favourite book? Star sign? If they own one, what is the inside of their car like? How would they react to a surprise birthday party? And so on …

It's likely you're answering as the writer, and thus from an exterior point of view. Now answer them 'in character' from an interior point of view. This is the equivalent of what actors call 'hot seating': the actor 'in role' answers a series of unexpected questions posed by others. If you're feeling fearless, and you're in a writing class, try hot seating. Don't take anything personally. Get someone to scribe the answers. Have fun.

You can also answer questions about a character from the point of view of another character: this might reveal what character A feels about character B, which is also invaluable information.

Useful sources of ready-made questions include the Q&A celebrity features in magazines, or, if you're in a writing class, invent weird, wildcard questions by writing them on slips of paper and passing them to the question reader – it might be your lucky writing tutor. Whatever your technique, respond as quickly as you can: don't question the question; write down or speak the first response. You never know: you might find a diamond.

The information such an exercise yields might not always get used in your writing projects, but it's likely it will help you understand your characters better.

Attributes that you assign to a character should obviously be much more complex than fixed characteristics tagged arbitrarily onto a name. Consider Jonathan Culpeper's concept of character attributes involving a triad of possibilities: a character might laugh at a film, for example, because:

- He or she is a jovial person – which Culpeper thus defines as a 'person attribute'.
- It is a funny film – which he defines as a 'stimulus attribute'.
- He or she is drunk while watching – which is deemed a 'circumstance attribute'.[11]

These qualities are, according to Culpeper, moderated by three further dimensions: their distinctiveness (the extent to which a character reacts distinctively to different things); consistency (the extent to which he or she reacts in the same way to similar stimuli); and consensus (the extent to which such a reaction would be expected across a larger number of respondents). It may tell you a lot about a character who is, for example, laughing uproariously at a film no one else is finding funny. So, in considering your characters and their attributes and behavioural responses, analyse how Culpeper's dimensions, rather than the attributes themselves, illuminate character, as shown in this table.

Behaviour	Distinctiveness	Consistency	Consensus
Laughing at her dead pet kitten	Yes – in contrast, she weeps at sad films	Yes – she laughs about it on several occasions	No – most people mourn dead pet kittens
Stridently and publicly condemning those who drink	No – he has strong beliefs about other things he calls immoral	No – he secretly drinks to excess himself	No – most people are not as extreme and do not condemn drinking
Spending too much money	No – she is profligate in other areas too	No – she has periodic guilty economy drives	Yes and no – some budget; others do not

It's not always necessary to analyse the dimensions of your characters' attributes in such detail, especially if it becomes another displacement activity, but it can be valuable to understand that attributes are not fixed; for what people do and say can shift radically in different circumstances.

Writing with Photography

Writing that is visual is powerful and allows the writer to use the devices of showing rather than telling. Visual cues for writing are thus a good source of inspiration. Street photography in particular is a great source of inspiration: unlike life observation, it affords the writer time to look deeply at people, to stare at them, without getting arrested or thumped. The effect of a good photograph is that the viewer perceives a narrative, and a 'what-happened-next?' reaction.

Writing Exercise: Reading People

Try online image searches for the work of Heather Buckley, Joel Meyerowitz, Vivian Maier or Daido Moriyama. The war photography of Don McCullin is also effective for this exercise. You will find depicted a wealth of characters in a variety of settings, all of them currently anonymous, and inviting the viewer to supply narratives. So supply those narratives. Select an image and use or abuse the following checklist: don't think too hard; swift, playful first impressions are useful. You can always edit later.

What name does this person use?
What is happening?
What is this person's greatest fear?
What is this person's greatest love?
What happens next?

Now craft mini-narratives using material you've generated. Such short exercises are comparable with practising scales on a piano: they flex your writing muscles before you start work on something longer.

Keep the scenes short: nothing much need happen, and nothing need finish; concentrate instead on capturing characters' behaviour, and how thoughts, feelings, hopes and fears are either revealed or concealed.

Now look again at the section on showing and telling. Redraft your scenes and concentrate on how character information is revealed by the writer, by what the character does or says, and how much is shown, and how much inferred or implied.

Conflict

The main character in your narrative is sometimes termed the *protagonist*. I prefer this term to *hero* or *heroine*, because main characters in stories aren't necessarily heroes or heroines. The etymology dictionaries will tell you that *protos* means first; *agonizesthai* means to struggle for a prize; and *anti* means against. The protagonist is, therefore, not necessarily a conventional hero or heroine, but the first or main character struggling to gain something, and the *antagonist* is the character or obstacle standing in the way of the protagonist's success. And therein lies a great source of conflict, for we are frequently told that characters must want something, but that if they achieve their goals too easily, then stories are less satisfying.

Narratives need conflict, and characters show what they are really made of when things don't go to plan. Well-drawn protagonists must therefore be matched by well-drawn antagonists, so don't research one and neglect the other. And remember: most people have both strengths and weaknesses; anti-heroes, as much as heroes, can win the day. Remember too that it's easy for writers, and readers, to fall for the evil charms of antagonists: make sure that the characterisation of the protagonist is robust enough to be in the same narrative as the antagonist: you don't want your readers cheering for the wrong character …

Other chapters in this book deal with external conflict. They will be useful to read in conjunction with your studies on character. But consider internal conflict, for the protagonist might be his or her own antagonist: perhaps he or she self-sabotages. Ray Bradbury's story 'The Fruit at the Bottom of the Bowl' is a case in point: the antagonist here is not another character, although Huxley plays a part, but the obsessive-compulsive disorder growing within Acton, the protagonist. It's also a great story to study how a character shifts from nervous visitor to crazed criminal through the course of the short form, and how tension ramps up in a narrative of very few players. Acton is cleaning fingerprints away from a crime scene:

> 'Look at it, you idiot! See how the whorls go? See?'
> 'That proves nothing!'
> 'Oh, alright!' Raging, he swept the wall up and down, back and forth, with gloved hands, sweating, grunting, swearing, bending, rising, and getting redder of face.[12]

It's all the more sinister because the argument he is having is with himself. Conflicted characters – those with strong and deep internal struggles – are often thus extremely valuable to a writer.

Writing Exercise: Action Sketches

Take a character from a previous exercise. Write them into a scene. Don't worry too much about how the scene starts; write excerpts and get straight into the immediate action. The following are situations you could use:

- Your character is late for a train when an old man asks for help carrying a large case in the opposite direction …

- At dusk, your character sees a gang of children about to throw kittens off a bridge into the water ...
- Your character, short of cash, finds a large diamond ring in the street ...

You might now see that your characters really start breathing when they want something, badly, madly, deeply. And when they are conflicted, things get interesting: what do your characters want? And what do they do when confronted with a problem?

Final Remarks

There is much, much more to say, and you might seek out texts dealing exclusively with characters in fiction: Orson Scott Card[13] and Nancy Kress[14] are good places to start. Those studying characterisation should also now read chapters about dialogue, conflict, point of view, because as we've seen, they are strongly related. But I'll finish with a recommendation for you to consider also your bit part players: the waiters, hairdressers, taxi drivers, the extras who populate stories and assist the protagonist and the other main characters. They too, although they might appear but briefly, can be inflected with telling detail – Ian Rankin's stories are worth studying for this – because characters, large or small, significant or insignificant, can be the making or breaking of your work.

Notes

1 Burroway, *Writing Fiction*, p 118.
2 Ernest Hemingway, *Death in the Afternoon* (London: Vintage, 2000), p 168.
3 Gardner, *The Art of Fiction*, p 43.
4 Anton Chekhov, 'The Bet' (1889), available at www.copan.edu.mx/docs/Dessec15-16/TheBetAntonChekhov.pdf (accessed 19 April 2017).
5 Elizabeth Strout, *Olive Kitteridge* (London: Simon & Schuster, 2008), p 4.
6 J.D. Salinger, 'Uncle Wiggily in Connecticut' from *Nine Stories* (New York: Little, Brown and Company, 1970).

7   Sandra Cisneros, 'Linoleum Roses' in *The House on Mango Street* (London: Bloomsbury, 2004), p 101.

8   Ian Rankin, 'Dead and Buried' in *The Beat Goes On* (London: Orion, 2014), p 5.

9   Gardner, *The Art of Fiction*, p 45.

10 Burroway, *Writing Fiction*, p 119.

11 Jonathan Culpeper, *Language and Characterisation* (Abingdon: Routledge, 2014), p 127.

12 Ray Bradbury, 'The Fruit at the Bottom of the Bowl' in *The Golden Apples of the Sun* (London: William Morrow, 1997).

13 Orson Scott Card, *Characters and Viewpoint* (London: Robinson Publishing, 1990).

14 Nancy Kress, *Write Great Fiction – Characters, Emotion & Viewpoint: Techniques and Exercises for Crafting Dynamic Characters and Effective Viewpoints* (Cincinnati: Readers Digest Books, 2005).

11

Plot

Maybe there are some writers around who give birth to plots the way salmon spawn, but I haven't met one of them. Most of us struggle with the whole business of constructing a storyline that will ensnare, retain and move – not to say change the whole life of – the reader. Plotting is hard, but let's see if we can't make it a little easier.

As you know, all genuinely creative art originates in the unconscious and you will be best able to tap that most fertile part of your mind when you are closest to a state of unconsciousness. (See Chapter 1: 'How a Writer Works'.) A corollary of this is that too much planning will not benefit your fiction. Here's the author Henry Green on the subject:

> As to plotting or thinking ahead, I don't ... I let it come page by page, one a day ... try and write out a scheme or a plan and you will only depart from it. My way you have a chance of something living.[1]

What's wrong with too much planning? Well, you will almost certainly plan with your conscious mind; it is after all partly for ordering and structuring. Rather than putting a lot of energy into planning, you might be better to concentrate on maximising your access to the unconscious. Your unconscious knows what it is doing. You might find it helpful to think of your story as something which already exists somewhere on the far shore of consciousness. Your job is to tap in to the appropriate part of your mind so that you can go and live there. Then, over as much time as the length of your story dictates, slowly collect all the pieces of it on a computer file. Like Raymond Carver: 'I made the story just as I'd make a poem; one line and then the next, and the next. Pretty soon I could see a story, and I knew it was my story, the one I'd been wanting to write.'[2]

When you have your fiction safely home from the other side, all assembled there on your computer, your conscious mind comes into its own, analysing, judging, editing, ordering and reordering. But that's much later. Your initial task is to go and live where your story, mysteriously, already exists. 'Plot', says Ashley Stokes, 'is part of the process of writing. It is something we find in the activity itself. More importantly, it comes to us in the amorphous work of notebooks, long walks, versions, false turns, hard decisions, insomnia and staring out the window.'[3]

For fiction writers, living where the story already exists means that your social circle consists of their characters. If you read Colm Tóibín's *The Master*, a biographical novel about Henry James, you will gain some idea of the kind of monastic servitude to literature to which those who go all the way are called. In order to make your fiction live and take readers on an enthralling journey, to some extent you will have to emulate Henry James; instead of rubbing shoulders with colleagues, engaging in the challenges of the workplace, you will be living your life elsewhere, in your imagination, and living your life vicariously through your characters. In a recent interview in the *Daily Telegraph*, the writer Rupert Thomson enthused about just this, saying that he found the experience of living day after day in his mind so exhilarating that he couldn't imagine not doing it. Anne Tyler, the *doyenne* of American women's fiction, concurs:

> For many years, my writing had to work itself in around the rest of my life – first because I had a 9 to 5 job, then later because I had small children. I don't think I gave my fiction proper attention, which may be why my first four novels are so much weaker than the later ones. But along about the time I started *Celestial Navigation*, I began to see how deeply absorbing and fulfilling it could be to sink completely into an imaginary character's world.[4]

Finding this other world has to do with tuning in to the part of your mind where it exists, as Michèle Roberts explains: 'The unconscious is part of yourself: it's like this big country which sends you messages if you tune in and do your work.'[5]

Now unless you're somebody who thrives on solitude, this may not appeal; it will involve sacrifice. But the more time you can spend living elsewhere, the better you will be able to bring your fiction back and send it out into the world to be enjoyed.

So relax. In one sense, you don't really have to think up a plot. It's more a case of positioning yourself where you are most likely to discover and then bring it home with you.

What Is Plot?

Here's a useful definition of plot, from Ansen Dibell's book on the subject:

> Plot is built of significant events in a given story – significant because they have important consequences … Plot is the things characters do, feel, think, or say, that make a difference to what comes afterward.[6]

Two things worth noting here, right away. First of all, the events aren't any old events; they are *significant*. The King has indigestion. The Queen has a corn on the little toe of her left foot. Insignificant. You'll have heard Oscar Wilde's dictum that drama is life with the dull parts left out. Keep it in mind. Like every other writer on the planet you will all too often produce fiction that fails to omit the dull parts. That's okay. Just remember to take them out afterwards. The second thing to note is that these significant events have consequences – they alter what ensues. In this regard, analyses of an author's craft often speak of *causality*. The King dies and then the Queen dies could be regarded as two random events, but stories are never random. In stories, one thing leads to another. The King died and the Queen died of a broken heart. Causality. Because *this* happened (the King died) *that* resulted (the Queen died of a broken heart).

Conflict

It's a given that a story almost always needs conflict. (I would say always, but that's a subjective view.) However, not all kinds of conflict are beneficial. James N. Frey[7] says there are three kinds of conflict – static, jumping and steadily rising – and suggests that only one of them will work.

> Scene One: Molly tells Harry that he is lazy and useless; he won't ever help with the dishwashing.
> Scene Two: Molly tells Harry that he is lazy and useless; he never does any cleaning round the house.

Static conflict. Readers want news, not history. They already know she thinks he's no help to her.

> Scene One: Molly tells Harry that he is lazy and useless; he won't ever help with the dishwashing.
> Scene Two: Molly arrives home with her solicitor friend Rose, who declares Molly's intention to divorce Harry.

Jumping conflict. This has gone from a skirmish to the Battle of Trafalgar.

> Scene One: Molly tells Harry that he is lazy and useless; he won't ever help with the dishwashing.
> Scene Two: While Harry is sitting in a deckchair in the front garden picking fluff from his belly button, their hunky new neighbour Bill offers to relieve Molly of the four bursting bags of shopping she is straining to carry in from the car. Molly gives Harry a significant look.

Steadily rising conflict.

Writing Burst

- Put 'Sam Walsh, The Dinner Party' in your search engine and use this painting as your prompt.

What's at Stake?

So. It's a good idea to place your characters in a situation which involves some conflict. 'What's at stake?' is one of my most common comments on student work. If you want your reader to read on, there has to be something at stake – right from the start. This means that you will need to raise a question in readers' minds in the first paragraph of your story, maybe even in the first line. Then, having hooked readers with some initial intrigue, you will have to either develop that reader question or introduce further ones. Both, probably.

Your first sentence establishes that Amy, your protagonist, has awoken in a strange bed with a thundering headache. She doesn't know where she is. Your reader is hooked and wants to read on – to find out, with Amy, where she is and what she got up to last night. In the second sentence, Amy hears the sound of water running in the bathroom down the corridor and realises she is not alone in this strange flat. She looks at the walls, where the framed art prints indicate nothing much about the owner of this room. Her head still hurts and she is having trouble waking up. She realises she is naked. You are now reeling your reader in very nicely. Amy hears the shower go off and, presently, footsteps coming down the corridor towards her. A young woman wrapped in a towel comes into the room, drying her hair with another towel. She seems not to notice Amy. As she moves to the dresser, the woman in the towel's glance falls on Amy, and she nods a silent greeting. At the dresser, she turns on a radio and the presenters are bantering about something as they move towards the news headlines.

'I must have put some drink away last night,' Amy says.

The woman in the towel hums 'Uptown Girl' and fidgets with her hair. Your reader, like Amy, is deeply intrigued about what's going on here. You have been thickening the plot quite effectively. More footsteps coming down the corridor. What now? Amy wonders. A naked man carrying a towel walks into the bedroom and chucks the towel he is carrying at the woman by the dresser, who goes '*James*!' and indicates Amy under the duvet. 'Whoops,' says James.

Reader questions abound. What did Amy do last night? Who are these strangers? What is their relationship to Amy? To each other? What will happen next?

I don't know the answer to any of these questions, but I do know that creating those questions in readers' minds is essential to fiction writing. If you don't generate similar questions on page one of your story, you will be, in F. Scott Fitzgerald's phrase, *chewing with no gum*. You can write the most exquisite prose in the world, but unless you create and sustain narrative tension, readers will desert you in droves. Picture them stampeding away from your beautifully crafted sentences, a vast herd of buffaloes, careering across the prairies.

Writing Exercise: 1. Intrigue 2. Thicken the Plot

Write the first two or three paragraphs of a story in which you

1. Keep your protagonist and your reader in the dark about what's going on and
2. Keep building on the initial intrigue by quickly creating new reader questions.

I'm trying to make plotting your work feel easier to you, but every writer knows it's a struggle. It may help to think of plot in the following, terribly basic way. Order exists before the story begins. (It's safe to swim at a particular New England beach.) The start of the story is a disruption of that order, which is often known as the inciting incident. (A shark attacks and kills an attractive woman in a bikini.) No matter how much the protagonists fight against the forces of disorder (the shark, in this instance), things go from bad to worse. Eventually when everything has got about as bad as it can possibly be, the protagonists snatch victory from the jaws – sorry – of defeat. (The shark is killed.) Order is restored. (Okay to go swimming on that beach again – although personally I wouldn't.)

The American writer Anne Lamott came up with my favourite description of the way fiction writers wrestle with plots; she speaks of 'flail[ing] around, *kvetching* and growing despondent, on the way to finding a plot and structure that work.'[8] That's pretty much the way I've felt about making stories for as long as I've been trying to do it. For me, one of the most helpful explanations of plot is Michael Baldwin's breakdown (in *The Way to Write Short Stories*[9]) of what he calls the simple linear plot. As he claims, this plot structure covers most of the stories in the world.

The Simple Linear Plot

A character has a goal. It could be that he wants to win the Tour de France. Maybe he's been smitten by this beautiful woman who has started to work at the desk opposite him and he has to win her heart. Or he and his two companions have crashed their light aircraft into a snowdrift in the Himalayas and they have to find their way back to safety. The goal could be anything. Now ask yourself this: if this character pursues his goal and gets it just like that, is it a story? You're right: it isn't. Character pursues goal and achieves it right away is okay as an anti-narrative joke in those ads they used to run for the new Mini – you know, Martians invade the earth … new Minis thwart invasion … The End … It's a Mini adventure. But as a story you want to engage and retain readers with, this won't stand up. If the conflict is too easily overcome, there's no narrative engagement.

The simple linear plot is an easy way of understanding the necessity of conflict that isn't easily or quickly overcome. Here, the protagonist's goal meets one obstacle after another, right from the start. The *Roadrunner* cartoons illustrate this. What is Wile E. Coyote's goal? To kill Roadrunner. What are the obstacles he encounters in pursuit of this goal? You name it, really. Roadrunner is faster, smarter and luckier than Wile E., the other side of which is that Wile E. is probably the stupidest, slowest, unluckiest creature on the planet. Added to which he gets all his supplies from the Acme Corporation, the shoddiest manufacturer in the field of munitions. That's your simple linear.

How does it end? In Wile E's case, always badly. He never achieves his goal, but the effect of that is always humorous. It's in not achieving his goal that the laughs are raised. In most examples of the simple linear, the protagonist is likely to achieve his goal. Rocky, against all the odds, becomes heavyweight champion of the world. In *Finding Nemo*, Marlin overcomes every obstacle the story throws at him and rescues his son. Catastrophe, in the simple linear, is almost always averted, usually many times. Check the number of obstacles overcome in *Finding Nemo*. In the normal run of things, each of these obstacles may be a little greater than its predecessors, with the final obstacle being the greatest of all. But don't forget Ansen Dibell and causality:

> Each set piece (after the first) should be set in motion, at least in part, by what happened in the previous one. This present scene should dramatize and arise from the effects created by what's gone before, and in turn have effects played out in the story thereafter. Cause sparks effect, which in turn becomes cause, right up to your story's end.[10]

In all of the above, the kind of story implied has the three-stage structure that goes all the way back to Aristotle in ancient Greece. However, in the kind of short story which has dominated the form in world literature in English ever since Chekhov, plot has become secondary to character.

Writing Burst
- Everything begins with a question, and not all questions have answers.

Chekhov

Vladimir Nabokov pointed out that in Chekhov's best-known story, 'The Lady with the Dog', 'All the traditional rules of storytelling have been broken in this wonderful short story ... There is no problem, no regular climax, no point at the end. And it is one of the greatest stories ever written.'

Not all fiction, especially short fiction, is plot-driven. In Chekhov, there isn't always a sense of conflict and resolution, or rising action. There is usually no nineteenth-century sting in the tail. Instead, he focuses on character, which is slowly revealed, distilled to its essence.

Perhaps the key to Chekhov's approach to characters is his compassion for them, his empathy. Eudora Welty observed that 'The depth of Chekhov's feeling for man is the very element out of which his stories spring.'

What I admire most about Chekhov is this compassion, his graciousness towards his characters, the way in which he regards them more kindly than they deserve. Chekhov looks at characters with a fresh eye and with considerable generosity of spirit. We see this demonstrated in his story 'Lady with Lapdog'. Gurov is a tawdry character, a seasoned, cynical philanderer, who in middle age has grown jaded. He might be unsympathetic in many respects, but Chekhov treats him better than he deserves. And the result for the reader is that we sympathise, possibly even empathise, with somebody we might normally look down on or not look twice at. It's the Tony Soprano effect. Tony is a murderous womaniser, but he's also fragile and warm-hearted. Chekhov's instructive approach to characterisation is illustrated in his 1891 letter[11] to another writer, which proposes the importance for the fiction writer of seeing the value in everyone:

> Noah had three sons, Shem, Ham and Japhet. Ham noticed only that his father was a drunkard, and completely lost sight of the fact that he was a genius, that he had built an ark and saved the world. Writers must not imitate Ham, bear that in mind.

We are all flawed human beings, and if you can show the good side of a character who isn't obviously virtuous, readers will be affected and it will chime with their experience; people are complicated. 'Chekhov's wish', says Richard Ford, 'is to complicate and compromise our view of characters we might mistakenly suppose we could understand with only a glance.'

To return to my earlier metaphor, living elsewhere may just mean living inside your chosen character, walking a mile in his shoes, and showing us what he's like. Sometimes your short story may be an exploration of two or three characters and their particular situation, by the end of which they or the reader or all of them have realised something. Characters and situations have been revealed. (See also Chapter 13: 'Scenes'.)

Writing Exercise: The Tony Soprano Effect

Think of the most difficult person you know. Not only somebody who annoys you and makes your life hard, but ideally someone who you also suspect is plain nasty.

Write a piece of fiction for fifteen minutes in which you show both the unsympathetic and the sympathetic side of this person. Before you start, take another look at Chekhov's Noah letter above.

Notes

1   Quoted in Plimpton (ed.), *The Writer's Chapbook*, p 191.
2   Raymond Carver, 'On Writing' in Ann Charters, *The Story and Its Writer*, 5th Edition (Bedford Books of St Martin's Press, 1997), p 1529.
3   Ashley Stokes, 'Plotting a Novel' in Julia Bell & Paul Magrs (eds), *The Creative Writing Coursebook* (Basingstoke: Macmillan, 2001), p 207.
4   Online interview with Anne Tyler in Readers' Club, www.eastoftheweb.com/short-stories/UBooks/Bet.shtml accessed 23 May 2017.
5   Michèle Roberts, interviewed by Jenny Newman in Monteith, Newman & Wheeler (eds), *Contemporary British and Irish Fiction*, p 128.
6   Ansen Dibell, *Plot* (London: Robinson Publishing, 1990), pp 5–6.
7   James N. Frey, *How to Write a Damned Good Novel* (Basingstoke: Macmillan, 1988).
8   Anne Lamott, *Bird by Bird: Some Instructions on Writing and Life* (New York, Anchor Books, 1995), p 55.
9   Michael Baldwin, *The Way to Write Short Stories* (London: Elm Tree Books, 1996).
10 Dibell, *Plot*, p 74.
11 In *A Life in Letters* (London: Penguin, 2004), p 68.

12

Dialogue

First, the easy part: practicalities. If readers are to connect with your story without being confused, it makes sense to present your dialogue in one of the established ways. Here are the ones I know about. I don't know of any others but if you do, drop me a line.

Presentation

The most common convention for laying out dialogue, the one that has been used more than any other, is to put the speech inside speech marks, like this, from V.S. Pritchett's story 'The Lady from Guatemala':

> 'Guatemala! Of course I must see her!' he exclaimed. 'What *are* you thinking about? We ran three articles on Guatemala. Show her in.'
> 'It's your funeral,' said the girl and gave a vulgar click of her tongue.

That's the way most of us present dialogue. There are variations, of course, as here, in 'The Dead', where, instead of speech marks, James Joyce opts for preceding speeches with dashes:

> – I don't mind in the least, Miss Morkan.
> – But I've a nice partner for you, Mr Bartell D'Arcy, the tenor.[1]

In 'The Things They Carried', Tim O'Brien goes further, omitting any kind of punctuation that would indicate what's said and leaving the reader to distinguish between what's been said and narration:

> Like cement, Kiowa whispered in the dark. I swear to God – boom, down. Not a word.
> I've heard this, said Norman Bowker.
> A pisser, you know? Still zipping himself up. Zapped while zipping.

Speech marks: easy for the reader; dashes instead of speech marks: slightly harder; no punctuation to distinguish what is said from the narration: harder still. I wouldn't recommend one any more than the other. Readers are smart, always smarter than you think they are. You could say Tim O'Brien's method will keep you on your toes, though. Your aim should be to make all dialogue entirely characteristic of the character speaking, which is a challenge. Making sure that all your dialogue is unmistakably dialogue is surely a corollary of that challenge.

Writers almost always take a new paragraph for each new speaker, which you know from your fiction reading, of course, and see in all the examples quoted above. You will find exceptions, though, and Malcolm Bradbury's method, in 'Composition', is one:

> 'I'm not a woman, pal. I'm a person.' 'Of course, right', says William. 'I really believe in all that. I wasn't trying to role-type you, honestly. I'd have asked anybody.' 'Oh, sure. Anybody who's historically supposed to be seen around with a needle', says the girl. 'Like a woman. Come on, how come you picked on me?'[2]

Layout like this makes it more difficult than it should be to work out who is saying what, whereas taking a new paragraph each time there's a new speaker makes it easier for the reader to follow where the focus of the story is at any given moment. You can also help the reader out in this respect by keeping the action and dialogue of a character in the same paragraph:

> She paced the wings, getting more anxious by the minute. Finally she strode onto the little stage. 'I've got something you should all hear.'

Imagine this with the action and dialogue in separate paragraphs; the reader might be left wondering if the speech and action were those of one character and not two.

Because you want the reader to focus on what is said rather than the attribution of the dialogue, avoid using speech tags (*he said*) if you can possibly manage without them. For the same reason, don't let your speech tags draw attention to themselves – *he expostulated*. Rather you should make them as plain as possible – *he said, she asked*.

If you use adverbs on speech tags – *she cried distressingly* – you risk drawing attention to the tag and distracting the reader from what is said. More importantly, using an adverb with a speech tag will always be an attempt on our part to explain the tone of what's been said. If you get the speech right, though, the tone will be self-evident.

When you can't avoid using a speech tag – and remember you should – you have more options than you might think about where you place it. The tag may be positioned before, during or after what is said. Note that sometimes the rhythm of the dialogue will require it to go in the middle. *'There is no question in my mind,'* Henry said. *'She is dead.'*

A canny way of attributing speech is to use an action instead of a tag. *Jenny caught his eye. 'Hello.'* Not only does this minimise the use of speech tags, it's also a variation, and readers like variety. Hopefully we've now looked at enough variety to be going on with.

Writing Burst
- Put 'Hail, Caesar! Would that it were so simple' in your search engine and use the film clip as your prompt. (If it doesn't inspire you, it will at least make you laugh.)

The Craft of Dialogue Writing

Much of what you need to learn about dialogue can be found in this edited passage from Elizabeth McCracken's story 'It's Bad Luck to Die'.

In the scene we're looking at, the viewpoint character, Lois, is visiting her mother. Lois is married to Tiny, a tattoo artist, who has covered most of her body with tattoos. (Later in the story, Tiny is referred to as a great artist and Lois his gallery.)

> My mother poured me a cup of coffee and said, 'Sweethearts carve their names on trees, not each other. Does it ever occur to you that you are not leading a normal life?'
> 'Yes,' I said. 'Thank you.'
> ...
> 'I just feel that you're painting yourself into a corner,' Mom said to me. 'How's Tiny?'
> 'Doing very well,' I said. 'Business is up.' My mother winced.
> ...
> [She] took me to her bedroom closet to give me some of her old clothing. She was almost as tall as I was and very fashionable, her hand-me-downs nicer than my new things.
> 'Here,' she said, handing me a pile of skirts and dresses. 'Try them on. Don't take what you can't use.'
> I started for the bedroom to change.
> She sighed. 'I'm your mother,' she said. 'I used to fit girdles on women with stranger bodies than yours. You don't have to be modest.'
> So I undressed there and tried on the clothes, and my mother looked at me and frowned. Afterwards, I sat down on her bed in my underwear and lit a cigarette.
> ...
> My mother, who only smoked in airports and hospital waiting rooms ('All that cleanliness and worry gets to me,' she'd say), slid a cigarette from the pack, took mine from my hand, and lit the end of hers. She looked at all of me stretched along the bed, started to touch my skin, but took her finger away.
> 'Well,' she said, blowing out smoke, 'you've finally made yourself into the freak you always thought you were.'
> I looked at her sideways, not knowing what to say.[3]

We can see some of the attributes of dialogue in this passage.

1. Dialogue creates and builds narrative tension, which, you will notice, rises steadily

Lois's mother's opening remark is sarcastic and confrontational ('Sweethearts carve their names on trees, not each other') and expresses naked disapproval of Lois's tattoos – and by implication of her husband and chosen lifestyle – ('Does it ever occur to you that you are not leading a normal life?')

The tension is developed when Lois's mother in one breath says 'I just feel that you're painting yourself into a corner,' and 'How's Tiny?' The statement expands our understanding of her disapproval while the question, by implication, lays the blame at Tiny's feet. This very short speech generates the initial tension, and engages the reader with the scene.

Lois's response ('Doing very well ... Business is up') rejects her mother's point of view. She isn't in fact trapped with Tiny; they are flourishing together. This conflict of opinion increases the narrative tension.

When Lois baulks at undressing in front of her mother, the response she gets shows once more that her mother disapproves of the fact that Lois has allowed herself to become a canvas for her tattooist husband: 'I used to fit girdles on women with stranger bodies than yours.'

The tension reaches its peak when Mom takes in the full extent of Lois's tattoos and says 'Well ... you've finally made yourself into the freak you always thought you were.'

In only five short speeches (75 words!), McCracken has generated steadily increasing conflict, which climaxes in a vitriolic insult.

2. Dialogue reveals character

Everything the mother says is consistent, and in it we see that she is judgmental and exasperated with her daughter ('Does it ever occur to you that you are not leading a normal life?') and venomous ('You've finally made yourself into the freak you always thought you were'). She is also, as we've already seen, sarcastic ('Sweethearts carve ...') and disapproving (the remark about girdles and about what constitutes a normal life).

Lois's dialogue shows us that she is polite and gracious ('Yes ... Thank you'), although the alternative interpretation, that she too is being sarcastic here, makes us active readers – we are intrigued to know which interpretation is correct. When she ignores the subtext in her mother's by implication unenthusiastic enquiry about

Tiny's welfare and replies 'Doing very well … Business is up,' we can deduce that she is positive, possibly long-suffering and clearly unwilling to engage in the argument her mother's remarks could easily provoke.

3. In dialogue, what remains unsaid may be as significant as what is said

Readers will understand that there is much that Lois could say, but declines to, and may understand the argument that might have been happening, had Lois reacted to her mother's barely veiled criticism of her. It's perhaps in this, Lois's refusal to fight back, that we learn most about her. That may be nothing beyond what I've just suggested, but what she doesn't say reinforces what we can tell about her from what she does.

4. Dialogue is characteristic of the person speaking it

Because of what has been established about the mother so far – principally that she disapproves of Lois's tattoos – her saying 'I used to fit girdles on women with *stranger bodies than yours*' (my italics) is entirely characteristic. Similarly, even with the little knowledge of her character which this short passage affords, it would seem uncharacteristic for Lois to say anything as judgmental, disapproving and confrontational. Thus it's always a good idea when redrafting dialogue to check that you've got the right character saying the particular line. If it sounds exactly in character, readers' understanding of the character is confirmed. They are not in doubt about the nature of the character. This is important. If readers are going to be able to engage with them, and so with the story itself, they need to reach an understanding of your characters. Clarity is essential. If characters say something uncharacteristic, the focus may become blurred and readers' view of them muddied, which may diminish their commitment to finishing the story.

5. Dialogue is often at its most effective when it comes in short speeches

The longest speech in this extract is twenty-one words, and it's often the case in short stories that a speech is no more than one or two lines long. Why? Short means snappy, so your pace is enhanced, but it may mean, too, that you've a better chance of keeping things clear. You want your readers to grasp straight away what you intend to say (or not say); you want to avoid the possibility that they won't be able to tell the difference between the important and the unimportant. Also the longer the speech, the greater your chances of writing flaccid dialogue, the greater the danger of producing a monologue from which readers begin to fear they will never escape. There are exceptions, of course, but try flipping through an anthology and see how often you find a short speech.

6. Dialogue is multi-purpose

You may have noticed that I have used the same speeches to make different points here. In well-crafted dialogue, an individual speech may be short, characterising, characteristic and indirect; it may generate narrative tension, and signify something by what is unsaid. 'How's Tiny?' for instance.

7. People don't listen

Here's the artist James McNeill Whistler on what he and his friend Oscar Wilde spoke about when they got together: 'Oh, we always talk about me.' To which Wilde responded, 'We always talk about you, but I'm always thinking about me.' People don't listen to each other, and for this reason characters shouldn't always respond to what has been said to them. Non-sequiturs make for good dialogue, as here, earlier in 'It's Bad Luck to Die', when Lois confronts Tiny about cutting reproduction paintings out of an art book of hers:

> 'What do you think you're doing?' I asked, hand on my hips, the way my mother stood when she started a fight.
> 'Take off your pants,' he said.

Non-sequiturs make the reader work, and active readers are happy readers. They also create tension: the character responding has dismissed what the speaker wanted to discuss.

8. Less is more

There are those who fly in the face of this – Hemingway and Murakami, for instance – but too much dialogue has a tendency to make your fiction feel loose and diluted. A balance between dialogue and narrative passage is the norm, and many great short stories have prioritised narration over dialogue. Arbitrary examples are Cheever's 'The Swimmer', which has approximately three times as much narration as dialogue, and Kafka's 'The Metamorphosis', which is about 90 per cent narration. Most of us will write stories that have more dialogue than either of these. At the same time, most writers will produce early drafts that contain superfluous speeches. When redrafting, all of us will have to excise unnecessary dialogue. What needs cutting? What should stay in? Although I'm generalising all over the place in this book, it's hard to do so about that. You'll know best yourself. In our heart of hearts we always know what needs fixing in our drafts. If you don't know where to start with cutting dialogue, though, you could do worse than to look back at the seven sub-sections above and think about your draft with them in mind.

As in almost everything, less really is more, and this applies especially to the use of dialect. Because you don't want your story to grind to a halt while readers work out syllable by syllable just exactly what has been said, phonetically rendered dialect – *There's yin or twa lambs on thonder hillside yet* – is very hard to get away with in dialogue. Use dialect words very sparingly, as Clare Wigfall does in 'The Numbers', situating her story in the Scottish islands with only a few words: 'ken' for know, 'awfy' for awfully, 'lassie' for girl. Very spare use of dialect, but we're never in doubt that we're in a remote part of Scotland.

9. Good dialogue is often indirect

Characters say one thing and mean another. This is authentic – we spend our lives saying one thing and meaning another – but, authenticity apart, indirect dialogue is desirable because it will involve readers in some thinking: they will have to deduce what it is the character really means.

My mother poured me a cup of coffee and said, 'Sweethearts carve their names on trees, not each other. Does it ever occur to you that you are not leading a normal life?'

'Yes,' I said. 'Thank you.'

...

'I just feel that you're painting yourself into a corner,' Mom said to me. 'How's Tiny?'

'Doing very well,' I said. 'Business is up.' My mother winced.

Her mother asks if it has ever occurred to Lois that it isn't normal for a person to express their love by tattooing the one they love. She replies, 'Yes ... Thank you' and the subtext here is that she refuses to argue. The reply also indicates that she is happy for this to be an abnormal expression of love and, by implication, happy with the life she has chosen. With the understanding we have (quickly) developed of this mother–daughter relationship, we know right away that when the mother says 'How's Tiny?' she isn't genuinely interested. Just the reverse: she would be happy to hear that Tiny wasn't doing well.

10. Bad dialogue is often direct

The opposite of indirect dialogue is that which tries to convey information. For the same reason that you would try to avoid telling the reader things (because Flannery O'Connor told you not to, right?), avoid using dialogue as a vehicle for exposition: *'Is that your medal?'* / *'The one I won for running two marathons in the same day? Yes, it is.'* More common, but just as much to be avoided, is literal dialogue, known amongst screenwriters as *on the nose*. Dialogue that's on the nose has no subtext; what you see is what you get and nothing is going on between the lines. It might look something like this:

'So that was your dialogue chapter?'

'Yep.'

'Think it'll be helpful?'

'Hope so.'

'What's next?'

'A project.'

Writing Exercise: Dialogue

See how much of this chapter has stuck: write a short scene in which an unfortunate passenger in a non-smoking train carriage confronts the only other passenger on board – who is smoking.

1,000-Word Story Project

Family Project

As your stimulus this time, I want you to think of one of those occasions when your family has got together. The obvious ones are the key holidays: Christmas, New Year, Easter, Eid, Passover, Diwali. This story doesn't have to be set in the here and now. It may be inspired by experiences you had when you were a child or a teenager. Maybe you are more drawn to another kind of family gathering – a wedding, a birthday party, a funeral or an anniversary of some kind.

Once you have the setting – Christmas Day 2012 or your cousin's *bar mitzvah* – settle on a relationship. You and your father. You and your big brother. Your father and his mother-in-law. You and your younger sister, the usurper who simply by being born bumped you out of pole position in the universe. Within the relationship you have opted for, choose your viewpoint character. A fictional version of yourself at the age of ten. Your mother. Your precocious only-child cousin.

Next, focus on an habitual perspective your point-of-view character has on the other person in this relationship. The view that has hardened in you over the years that your big brother is only concerned with himself and, worse, that your existence barely matters to him – in fact, it's an irritation. Here's a mocked-up illustration:

Family Gathering Your grandparents' golden wedding anniversary.
Family Relationship You, aged fourteen, and the cousin who has always bullied and tormented you. (When you were both seven he would always greet you by wrestling you to the ground. When you

were eleven, he would taunt you with how useless you were at soccer, or how uncool your tastes in TV programmes were.)

Viewpoint Character Your fourteen-year-old self.

Habitual Perspective That this cousin is ridiculously competitive, a sadist whose role in life is to make people feel worse about themselves.

Your challenge is to come up with a story in which, during the course of the family gathering, at least one of your characters arrives at a new understanding of the other.

Remember, this is a very short story. All you should aspire to do is reveal the situation between these two characters and show how the understanding of one of them is altered by something that happens to them. Finally, a further challenge: you may only include what the characters say (dialogue) and what they do (action).

Write a 500-word reflection, too, and include a bibliography of any texts that have informed the creative work.

Notes

1   V.S. Pritchett, *Collected Stories* (London: Penguin Books, 1984), p 415.
2   In Malcolm Bradbury (ed.), *Modern British Short Stories* (London: Penguin Books, 1988).
3   From Elizabeth McCracken, *Here's Your Hat, What's Your Hurry?* (London: Vintage, 1996), pp 12–15.

13

Scenes

The screenwriter William Goldman on beginnings: 'We must enter all scenes as late as possible. We must enter our story as late as possible.'[1] While it's true that cinema is a more impatient medium than the short story, fiction readers are impatient enough. I regularly receive student work in which the story doesn't actually begin until late on page 1, or 2, or 3. Sometimes this is because the authors don't discover what the story is about until they have warmed up their engines. Sometimes it's because they aren't fully aware of the reader's need to commit to the story. How often have you set aside a story or a novel because you have not been able to do that? Isn't it nearly always because you haven't been hooked? The bottom line is that your reader will not commit until you have established the story, until you have shown that something is at stake.

Writing Burst
- 'You can't do that.'

A couple of thousand years ago, the Roman lyric poet Horace suggested that epics ought to begin in the middle of the action and coined the phrase *in medias res*, which literally means in the middle of things. Nothing has changed. Your story begins with the clock on the terrorist bomb counting out the final ten seconds before Big Ben blows up – not with the terrorist's trip to Bombs R Us to buy supplies, not with his difficulty attaching the timer to the explosives, not with the five-mile tailback on the M25 on the way into London. As Goldman says, enter your scene as late as possible. Why? Because it dramatises, raises the narrative tension and ups the stakes. These are good steps to take if you want to grab a hold of your readers. Here's a little checklist for your story, scene, chapter, novel beginning:

* Have you started *in medias res*, in the middle of the action?
* Ask yourself what the hook is. How soon does the hook appear?
* Have you spent half a page, a page, or even two pages warming up your engines? If your reader hasn't been snared by the end of page 1, it's unlikely that they will remain with you for much of page 2. When you revise, and discover that the hook comes in the fifth paragraph of the story, it's easily fixed: cut the first four paragraphs. Some of what's in there may seem to you like essential information about, say, character and setting. Okay. Chop it up and distribute it through the first few pages of your story. If you give it to the reader in dainty morsels, if you offer it on the hoof, while action and dialogue are moving the story on, you will get away with it. If your story opens with a page of scene-setting or character description, you can forget readers and go back to the day job.
* Remember the lessons of page design. The notion that shorter paragraphs are more desirable than longer ones is never truer than at the beginning of your fiction, and an excellent place to locate a very short paragraph is right slam at the start of the first page.

Writing Exercise: Beginnings

Here are five films you may know: *Dr Zhivago, Annie Hall, The English Patient, The Incredibles* and *Whiplash.* (You'll be able to find plot summaries online.) Imagine you've been given the job of transposing one of them into prose fiction. Write an intriguing and compelling first paragraph.

Dramatisation

Which would you prefer: seeing, say, *Interstellar* in a state-of-the-art cinema, widescreen, in the highest-definition digital quality, or sitting there as I recount the story of the film to you? Nobody wants to be told about a movie; we want to *experience* it. The same is true of fiction. Readers will barely register what you tell them, but they will take what you dramatise to heart and, if you're doing your job well enough, they will join your characters on the emotional journey you send them on. Rather than summarising, explaining, recounting, telling the readers about what your characters are going through, the idea is to let them see for themselves. Flannery O'Connor got it right when she said, 'No reader who doesn't actually experience, who isn't made to feel, the story is going to believe anything the fiction writer merely tells them.'[2]

Showing

A good starting point in learning how to show is to think of your story as a piece of theatre. Picture a hologram theatre in front of you right now. Imagine yourself, the author, sitting in your office chair in the wings. It's a comfortable chair with its own wheels, so you can slide around. The most potent elements of your story, though, are those that happen onstage. In fiction, you are creating an imitation of life, and if you can imagine this hologram theatre now, it's what goes on between your characters onstage, on the set, that will impact the reader. Should you wheel yourself in your office chair onto the stage to address the audience, to explain something, you will disrupt their suspension of disbelief. If you're doing it right, your audience has been emotionally involved by your characters, swept along with the quest of your protagonist, Stanley, to track down the dealers who dealt the drugs that killed his son. In other words, at least some of the time and arguably most of it, you will not be telling readers anything; rather, you will be using your skill with words to create a drama in their heads.

Often, showing a reader something means what it says: the way your characters behave will show us how they feel. When the blood rises to

Kath's face, it shows us that she is embarrassed. Your telling us so would not have nearly as much effect. Why? Because when you show, the reader has to do the detective work; you have made your reader active and readers like being active. Readers who are forced by bad writing to become passive soon weary of the fiction they are reading, so when you want to convey a character's feelings, resist the urge to explain them. 'The writer should especially avoid comment on what his characters are feeling,'[3] is John Gardner's advice. Become a student of human behaviour and show us how your characters' actions, gestures and facial expressions demonstrate what they are feeling.

It's commonly said that immersive fiction is all about what characters do and say. Action, what they do, will always be showing. Dialogue, what they say, will also always be showing. Why? Because both constitute the story's reality unfolding. 'In a scene,' James N. Frey says, 'the narrator describes actions as they happened.'[4] It's more than the actions, though: it's what the viewpoint character experiences, and since we experience the world through the senses, sensory writing creates immediate, immersive fiction. The American writer Robert Olen Butler's theory is that fiction engages readers when the author focuses on the viewpoint character's 'moment-by-moment sense-based events and impressions'.[5] Remaining on the surface, sticking to what characters say and do, is the most basic way to ensure that you are showing, but if you want to bring your story to life, Butler's advice is worth learning by heart. Fiction comes alive when you focus on the viewpoint character's moment-by-moment sensory perceptions. That's the best advice on showing that I know of.

Telling

Telling is when the narrator addresses the reader. Maybe instead of presenting characters in dramatic situations the narrator delivers notes on character. If you find yourself describing a character, you are telling.

> Sue had always been sharp as a pencil and thin as a rake; until now, she had never had a problem with her weight.

If, however, you use action and dialogue to show a character in a dramatic situation, you will be *showing*.

> Sue held her old summer dress against herself and studied her reflection in the mirror. Her body extended beyond the edges of the dress by a good six centimetres on either side. She sighed and threw the dress onto her bed.

Telling crops up in fictional discourse when authors try to give the reader information they think important. The irony is, readers only regard as important information they deduce for themselves. (See Flannery O'Connor above.) Which brings us to exposition: background information. Jo, your protagonist, is now a respected primary school head, but you want readers to know that, to pay her way through teacher training, she worked for an escort agency. The last thing you should do with significant data like that is deliver it on a plate as a piece of exposition. Readers don't want much on a plate, but they definitely won't thank you for conveying dramatic back-story in this way. As John Gardner says, 'A good writer can get anything at all across through action and dialogue ... he should probably leave explanation to his reviewers and critics.'[6]

Exposition is easy to spot: it's usually in the pluperfect tense.

> Boris had always been a buffoon. On his first day at Oxford, he had nearly caused a riot by cycling into a party of Korean tourists.

The pluperfect is the 'had been' tense and, because it's so far removed from the immediate, it's lethal. The pluperfect feels as if it didn't happen today, or even yesterday. It feels as though it took place weeks, months or years ago. Avoid the pluperfect like the plague.

Telling, then, is when you try to give your readers information on a plate. It's when you explain, lecture, summarise, recount. It's second- or third-, not first-hand information. No good for you, Fictionist. The kind of writing you are aspiring to produce is, in Ansen Dibell's words, 'dramatised, *shown*, rather than summarised or talked about'.[7] Clearly there aren't many short stories that don't feature telling, so as a narrative mode it does have a place. Many arresting short story openings are told. The narrator may address the reader as here in Sean O'Faolain's 'Persecution Mania':[8]

> There are two types of Irishman I cannot stand. The first is always trying to behave the way he thinks the English behave. The second is always trying to behave the way he thinks the Irish behave.

Or the telling may take the form of exposition, as it does in Bernard Malamud's 'In Retirement':

> He had lately taken to studying his old Greek grammar of fifty years ago. He read in Bulfinch and wanted to re-read the Odyssey in Greek. His life had changed.[9]

If telling is a valid option, even at the beginning of a story, how do you judge when to use it? A good rule of thumb might be to avoid telling the reader any part of your story that has dramatic substance. 'Many unimportant parts of a story may be *told* rather than shown,' Barnaby Conrad advises, 'but the reader will feel cheated if not "present" at the important ones.'[10]

Learning writers are often blind to the difference between telling and ordinary description of action. They can think that this is telling: *Rosie tuned her mandolin.* Yes, it does tell you something, but it isn't *telling*. It's action.

Another problem is that sometimes the difference between showing and telling is too fine to spot. That's okay. There are grey areas in anything. And sometimes what you write may be interpreted as both showing and telling – simultaneously. That's fine, too. But learning the difference between telling and showing in their purest forms is one of the most important steps a fiction writer can take.

Your job is to make the reader forget that she is reading, and give her the illusion of being in the story, seeing and hearing and smelling and feeling what's happening to your characters. Your job is to create scenes.

Writing Burst

- A situation: any relevant app notwithstanding, a young couple can't find their destination and walk round and round for a long time, getting increasingly frustrated.

The Scene

Scenes are where the reader sees your characters live in person, speaking and acting. The word 'scene' makes you think of films or plays, which is only right, as a scene should be *dramatic*. Something is dramatic when it has been dramatised. You dramatise when you use conflict to reveal character. If the author tells the reader about it, it has not been dramatised. Dramatising is *showing*.

Apart from revealing characters in conflict, what is the function of a scene? Simple: it moves the action forward. 'A *scene* is one connected and sequential action,' according to Dibell. 'It's built on talk and action. It arises for a reason, and it's going somewhere. It has meaning. It has a point: at least one thing that needs to be shown or established at that spot in a story.'[11]

At the end of a scene, things are no longer as they were at the beginning. The way a scene moves the action forward is by having characters *act* and *speak*. It explores and reveals character and motivation. By the end of each scene the reader should know more about the characters. Also, the scene makes clear where and when the action is taking place. And, because it has a mood or atmosphere – funny or tragic, hopeful or desperate – a scene will affect the reader's emotions.

How to Make a Scene

A scene will always be immediate. 'It seems to happen', Ansen Dibell says, 'just as if a reader were watching and listening to it happen.'[12] The point of writing immediate fiction is to put the reader right inside the action, experiencing it vicariously. How do you do this? Well, an approach that seems to work for me is a writer's bread and butter: imagining that you, the author, are this character in this situation and trying to convey the experience in words so direct that the reader will share the experience with you. Writing fiction is not so different from method acting. You need to immerse yourself in character and situation, *become* the character, as De Niro does in *Raging Bull*.

A scene, especially if it is an opening scene, may well have a hook to snare the reader. Sometimes this will be terribly dramatic: 'As he neared the top, Ben wondered how much weight this old drainpipe could hold.' But sometimes the hook will simply be a matter of intrigue: 'I swore I was never going to do this again.'

A scene will often have a reversal. Lester, who wanted to send Callum to the gallows, ends up being hung himself. Nina, who had seemed so sympathetic to begin with, turns out to be an obnoxious character.

A scene often builds up to some kind of climax that will conclude it. Maybe this will be a nail-biting moment where readers will wonder whether or not Ann is going to get the sack. It may be the moment where Poppy announces that she has to go to Rio de Janeiro, and we will want to move swiftly to the next scene so that we can find out why.

You ought to be able to learn a few things about writing scenes by looking at the following extract from Denis Johnson's story 'Emergency'. First of all, the opening maximises reader engagement. It may be obvious, but if you can write down why this opening is engaging, it may help you to emulate it in the exercise that follows. (And you will have noticed that it could not be more *in medias res*.) Next, see how much is told (very little), how much shown and what, in this case, showing involves. You might say that in this scene, rather than tension rising – it's pretty high from the start – the plot thickens. Note down how this is done.

Around 3.30 a.m. a guy with a knife in his eye came in, led by Georgie.

'I hope you didn't do that to him,' Nurse said.

'Me?' Georgie said. 'No. He was like this.'

'My wife did it,' the man said. The blade was buried to the hilt in the outside corner of his left eye. It was a hunting knife kind of thing.

'Who brought you in?' Nurse said.

'Nobody. I just walked. It's only three blocks,' the man said.

Nurse peered at him. 'We'd better get you lying down.'

'O.K., I'm certainly ready for something like that,' the man said.

She peered a bit longer into his face. 'Is your other eye,' she said, 'a glass eye?'

'It's plastic, or something artificial like that,' he said.

'And you can see out of *this* eye?' she asked, meaning the wounded one.

'I can see. But I can't make a fist out of my left hand because this knife is doing something to my brain.'

'My God,' Nurse said.

'I guess I'd better get the doctor,' I said.

'There you go,' Nurse agreed.

They got him lying down, and Georgie says to the patient, 'Name?'

'Terrence Weber.'

'Your face is dark. I can't see what you're saying.'

'Georgie,' I said.

'What are you saying, man? I can't see.'

Nurse came over, and Georgie said to her, 'His face is dark.'

She leaned over the patient. 'How long ago did this happen, Terry?' she shouted down into his face.

'Just a while ago. My wife did it. I was asleep,' the patient said.

'Do you want the police?'

He thought about it and finally said, 'Not unless I die.'

Nurse went to the wall intercom and buzzed the doctor on duty, the Family Service person. 'Got a surprise for you,' she said over the intercom ...

... [The doctor takes his time getting there] ...

He peeked into the trauma room and saw the situation: the clerk – that is, me – standing next to the orderly, Georgie, both of us on drugs, looking down at a patient with a knife sticking up out of his face.

'What seems to be the trouble?' he said.[13]

Writing Exercise: Making a Scene

Divide a page in two. On the left side, list five different kinds of journey. On the right, make a list of five things a person might take on a journey. Now write a scene structured around one of the journeys on the left of your page, and use in it two of the items on the right side of your page.

You need a minimum of two major characters. Don't forget to use dialogue.

Follow this chapter's advice on scenes as well as you can.

Spend twenty-five minutes on this.

Endings

Stories don't just stop. They have to end, and this is true no matter what kind of an ending you write. (For some of the possibilities, see below.) Finding your way to the appropriate ending is, as William Goldman admits, 'just a bitch. (Tattoo that behind your eyelids.)'[14] Because pulling off a story that works all the way through is a challenge that not many people succeed in the world is littered with flawed endings. Here are a few things to ponder as you struggle to perfect the ending of your story:

* More is riding on your ending than on any other part of your story. You do not want to screw it up.
* Have you written past the ending? This is common. When you reach the end, stop. If your story begins with the blue touchpaper burning, it ends with the largest rocket exploding in the sky, not with the dish-washing after the firework party guests have gone home. If you've resolved the major conflict, answered the major questions, your story is over and you should exit stage left *prontissimo*.
* Has your ending gone on forever, or have you failed to end the story in one decisive action? Bad endings can be like a stuck record. You think it's over, but no, that wasn't the ending; here comes another. And another.
* Is your ending an explanation of something, possibly of the whole story? (*Fred was never going to like Phyllada; he had been educated in a sink school and didn't even know what an unpaid internship was.*)
* Is your ending too told? (*Once he had finished his course of therapy, Billy gave up being an IT consultant and became a gardener.*)
* Had it all been a dream? (*When she woke up, Florence was in the bunker again, sitting on the same deckchair, fiddling with the same Rubik's cube. Had she never escaped?*)
* Is your ending clear? A deliberately ambiguous ending is one thing, but watch out for one that is accidentally ambiguous. Readers won't be happy.
* Is there a sting in the tail? (*While he is away on a business trip to China, Jen leaves her boss's solid gold Shearker fountain pen lying around and somebody steals it. Her boss, Michael Underhand, is a harsh man who she knows will sack her when he finds out, and she can't afford that; she has to keep paying off her student loan. Desperate, Jen sells her body night after night for the whole fortnight Underhand is away, and manages to buy an identical gold Shearker just before her boss's return. When he comes in the next morning, Underhand has a present for her: a Shearker gold fountain pen. 'But that's too much,' she says. 'These pens cost a fortune.' 'Don't*

worry about it,' Underhand says. *'It's a counterfeit I picked up in Hong Kong. So's mine. I buy a few every time I'm out there.'*) Cue groaning readers. In every aspect of fiction writing, you can make anything work, of course, but my view is that it's difficult to pull off the sting in the tail and that this kind of ending is really a bit nineteenth century.

* Is your ending appropriate? Have your characters got what they deserved? Have your readers been given what they were fervently hoping for? They thought the antagonist would get his just deserts but she didn't. Everything indicated that the story was upbeat, but the ending had all the joy of Munch's 'The Scream'.

There are all kinds of short stories, of course, and all kinds of endings, but here are three that you might consider using.

The Let Readers Decide Ending

Alice Munro's 'Five Points' has an open and ambiguous ending, the kind that hands over to the reader the decision about what happens in it and what will happen after it. The relationship between Neil and Brenda has been stretched, possibly (but we don't know) to breaking point.

> He has lost some of his sheen for her; he may not get it back. Probably the same goes for her, with him. She feels his heaviness and anger and surprise. She feels that also in herself. She thinks that up till now it was easy.[15]

What is it that will no longer be easy? Going on without Neil or staying with him and working on their relationship? Munro isn't telling us; it's up to us to decide, based on the evidence of what has happened prior to the ending. She hands the decision over to the jury, the readers.

The Allegorical Ending

Edna O'Brien's story 'In the Hours of Darkness' has a similarly open ending. Lena, the viewpoint character, has brought her son to Cambridge, to begin his degree, and she knows that the permanent separation of mother from child that is about to begin is going to be difficult:

> She was facing the predicament she had read about in novels – that of a divorced woman, bereft of her children, having to grow old without these beloved props, having in some indescribable way to take the first steps into loneliness.[16]

After she has parted from her son, she returns to her hotel and can't sleep. 'Then she sank into the gaping armchair and waited stoutly for morning.' Like the one above, this is an open ending, but it's also allegorical. On one level, it's about what it says: she isn't able to sleep and decides to accept it and give up trying. However, readers don't need to be taking a degree in Literature to see that the action and the resolve is really about her getting to grips with her future as a mother in an empty nest.

The Let's Leave It There Ending

Elsewhere, I've mentioned the new approach to short stories that Chekhov is credited with introducing at the end of the nineteenth century. Here we don't really get a beginning or an ending. We arrive in the middle of something, after the beginning, and leave before the end. A situation or a character has been revealed, and readers have been given an understanding of either or both; we've walked in on something and once we've got the gist of it, we walk out again. The Let's Leave It There ending. Any number of examples of this kind of ending are available, but let's go with Lorrie Moore's 'Debarking'. As the US gets ready to invade Iraq, Ira is a recently divorced man trying to come to terms with his new situation. In the final scene, he is getting very drunk in a bar and making inflammatory, sarcastic remarks about Easter and the resurrection.

> 'The dead are risen! The damages are mitigated! The Messiah is back among us squeezing the flesh – that nap went by quickly, eh? May all the dead arise! No one has really been killed at all – OK, God looked away for a second to watch some "I Love Lucy" re-runs, but he's back now.

Nothing has been lost. All is restored. He watching over Israel slumbers not nor sleeps!'

'Somebody slap that guy,' said the man in the blue shirt down at the end.[17]

Let's leave it there.

Notes

1   William Goldman, *Which Lie Did I Tell?* (London: Bloomsbury, 2000), p 198.
2   Flannery O'Connor, *Mystery & Manners* (London: Faber and Faber, 1972), p 91.
3   Gardner, *The Art of Fiction*, p 111.
4   Frey, *How to Write a Damned Good Novel*, p 127.
5   Robert Olen Butler, *From Where You Dream: The Process of Writing Fiction* (New York: Grove Press, 2005), pp 14–15.
6   Gardner, *The Art of Fiction*, pp 110–11.
7   Dibell, *Plot*, p 8.
8   In *The Stories of Sean O'Faolain* (Harmondsworth: Penguin Books, 1970).
9   In Bernard Malamud, *Rembrandt's Hat* (Harmondsworth: Penguin Books, 1970).
10 Barnaby Conrad, *The Complete Guide to Writing Fiction* (Cincinnati: Writer's Digest Books, 1990), p 118.
11 Dibell, *Plot*, p 8.
12 Dibell, *Plot*, p 8.
13 Denis Johnson, 'Emergency' in Robert Stone (ed.), *Best American Short Stories 1992* (New York: Houghton-Mifflin, 1992), pp 111–12.
14 Goldman, *Which Lie Did I Tell?*, p 104.
15 In Alice Munro, *Friend of My Youth* (London: Vintage, 1991), p 49.
16 In Edna O'Brien, *Mrs Reinhardt and Other Stories* (Harmondsworth: Penguin Books, 1980).
17 In Lorrie Moore, *Bark* (London: Faber & Faber, 2014), p 14.

14

Setting

SEAGOON: What are you doing down here?
ECCLES: Everybody's got to be somewhere.

The Goon Show

As in Spike Milligan's script, everybody has to be somewhere, and this is true of your characters and their situations. Interior monologue, authorial summary and exposition might be included in a list of exceptions, but as far as scenes in fiction go, you will have to set them somewhere, because according to Elizabeth Bowen, 'Nothing happens nowhere'; and, for Jerome Stern, 'A scene that seems to happen nowhere often seems not to happen at all.'

Setting in fiction serves several purposes. It contributes to the solidarity of your fictional world and so makes it more convincing. It is a means by which you can make the world your readers imagine when they read your fiction more vivid, more real. It can play a major part in creating both character and emotional tone. You can use setting to dramatise, to generate and enhance the conflict. The setting may help build narrative tension, advance the plot and amplify the theme. The setting, in fact, is nearly as important as character and plot and will sometimes function almost like a character. This is the case in, for example, John Cheever's 'The Swimmer',[1] where the suburban swimming pools are almost as significant as the protagonist, and in Wells Tower's 'On the Show',[2] where the fairground underpins every character and all of the plot developments.

For these reasons, it's worth spending as much time developing the setting of a story as you would your characters and your plot. This will require you to thoroughly familiarise yourself with the place where your story happens, whether it is based on a real place (the Midlands tram system in D.H. Lawrence's 'Tickets, Please'[3]) or entirely invented (the futuristic, dystopian world of Michel Faber's 'Fish',[4] which is distinguished by fish swimming through the air). It will require research on your part, often research that takes place on location. 'I needed to describe a hotel room,' Stanley Elkin wrote. 'I've been in lots of hotel rooms, but I didn't want to depend on my memory. And so I went to the Royal Garden Hotel in Kensington and rented a room, simply to study the furniture there … Somebody watching me would have thought I was a madman.' You will note remarkable characters or images or capture stray thoughts about any aspect of your story in your journal, but you should also use it to collect the details of real places with which to build your setting.

You should devote time to studying how other writers use setting and make notes on their techniques and the effects. In Jhumpa Lahiri's 'Interpreter of Maladies',[5] the setting is the approach to the Sun Temple at Konarak, in India. The viewpoint character is Mr Kapasi, a taxi driver who has brought the Das family to visit the temple: Mr and Mrs Das, a young Indian couple born and raised in America, and their three sons, Ronnie, Bobby and Tina. Setting is used for all the purposes listed above.

The Solidarity of the Fictional World

The world created here is brought to life and made real through the use of specific detail and sensory writing. The details specified build a particular setting and come from researched information, from books and online sources or visits to relevant locations. There are too many examples to list in 'Interpreter of Maladies', but here are some.

A goat is tied to a stake in the ground; locals sing a Hindi love song; Mrs Das fans herself with a Bombay film magazine; an emaciated man in a dirty turban is seated on top of a cart of grain sacks; and the temple, which dates from the thirteenth century and was built by a ruler of the Ganga dynasty, is decorated by friezes of the entwined naked bodies of the Nagamithunas, half-human, half-serpentine couples.

One of Robert McKee's ten commandments for writers is 'Thou shalt know your world as God knows this one'. The pro-research commandment. Jhumpa Lahiri clearly knows her chosen setting, and the effect of her many specific details is to make the world of the story real to the reader, and thus believable.

Sensory writing makes 'Interpreter of Maladies' more felt. It's dry and bright at the temple; an ocean breeze tempers the July heat; Mr Das's thumbnail makes a scraping sound as he drags it across the pages of his guide book; Mrs Das speaks dreamily, her gaze is drowsy, she wobbles on her heels as she climbs to the temple; monkeys emit soft swooping sounds; Mr Kapasi's skin prickles in the heat; and a breeze blows a slip of paper away. These details bring the setting alive and make it vivid.

Creating Character

Signifiers of India create Kapasi's character for us. He is Indian and is confirmed as being so by the details listed above and by other signifiers of the sub-continent: the popcorn dipped in mustard oil; the desert setting of the temple and the dry riverbed close by; the procession of elephants carved on it; the life-size statues of Surya, the Sun God; the tribe of dangerous monkeys. His car is outdated (Austin Ambassadors were built in the early 1980s); the handles on the back doors are crank-like; it has no air-conditioning. His other job – interpreting patients' descriptions of their ailments for a doctor – has no equivalent in the West. In these and other specifics, we understand the context in which Kapasi lives and his character is filled out.

The characterisation of Mr and Mrs Vas is achieved in the main through the ways in which they contrast with the country they are visiting. India, with wildlife, ancient buildings and friezes, poverty and livestock, is presented as real, genuine; but Mr Vas, with his tour guide and his camera, is presented as a tourist: shallow, inauthentic, alien. Despite their Indian roots, the Das family are continually shown to be at odds with the story's setting. Mr Kapasi observes that Ronnie and Bobby, in their brightly coloured clothes and caps with translucent visors, are dressed as foreigners. Even when the family aren't at odds with the setting, the contrasts between India and the West are used to characterise them. Mr Kapasi's other job, interpreting for a doctor what patients say, is novel to the Dases. Unlike the Indian women Kapasi is familiar with, Mrs Das's legs are uncovered. When they drive to Udaghiri, the setting turns against the Westerners; monkeys surround them and eventually one of the tribe attacks Bobby and beats him with a stick. In one way or another, the Das family are almost always at odds with the setting, and that conflict helps us understand their characters.

Creating Emotional Tone

The setting often contributes to a story's emotional tone, and this is an effect you can achieve through small details, and not many of them. A good example is the way Lahiri creates a melancholy tone in the passage that is set in Lahiri's principal workplace, the doctor's office where Kapasi interprets maladies. That tone, that mood, is suggested by the specific details and the vocabulary the author chooses to communicate them, and the tone is made real for the reader because Lahiri never once tells us what the office and the infirmary it is in is like, doesn't tell us it's a bleak, melancholy, miserable place. Instead, she suggests the place's tone by the details she includes, and they are few enough for me to list all of them. Swollen bowels, 'spots on people's palms' that changed color, shape or size', the doctor's (by implication) ridiculous bell-bottom trousers, his humourless jokes, the stale infirmary in which Mr Kapasi's clothes 'clung to him in the heat, in spite of the blackened blades of a ceiling fan churning over their heads'; and the fact that Kapasi's job involves changing bedpans. (The underlining is mine.) The way Lahiri creates the emotional tone of Mr Kapasi's workplace amounts to less than ten details and a few key vocabulary choices.

Conflict, Narrative Tension, Plot Development, Theme

The setting in 'Interpreter of Maladies' helps dramatise the conflicts between Mr and Mrs Das and between Kapasi and Mrs Das. It is almost always referred to in a negative way, usually involving discomfort of some kind, which often has to do with the heat in Konarak. Characters, especially the Das family, but to a certain extent Kapasi, too, are at odds with the setting, which helps to generate conflict. One part of the setting – the hill that's populated by monkeys – is the most potent source of conflict here. Throughout the story, the monkeys are a threatening presence, prompting us to be anxious about what will happen to this family. The first time they appear, the monkeys are ominous:

> Their long gray tails dangled like a series of ropes among the leaves. A few scratched themselves with black leathery hands, or swung their feet, staring as the car passed. (p 47)

Later they line up on either side of the characters ('All along the path, dozens of monkeys were seated on stones, as well as on the branches of the trees') and soon surround Mr Das and the children, and the threat begins to approach actual danger. The tension rises a few pages later when the adults find Bobby

> surrounded by a group of monkeys, over a dozen of them, pulling at his T-shirt with their long black fingers [and] his bare legs were dusty and red with welts from where one of the monkeys had struck him repeatedly with [a] stick ... bleeding slightly where the stick had broken the skin. (p 67)

Lahiri has used the monkeys, a key aspect of the setting, to generate conflict and steadily increasing narrative tension, which leads to ever-greater suspense. The setting is throughout inimical to the visiting Westerners, and Lahiri advances the plot by demonstrating how at odds they are with this setting and then using the setting – in the form of the belligerent monkeys – to dramatise this conflict and develop the plot to a tense climax. One of the themes of the story is the relationship of the East

(India, Kapasi) with the West (Das, an American family), and this theme has been communicated to the reader through the way the characters interact with the landscape, through the conflict between the culture of the setting and that which the Dases are used to – the West.

Writing Burst

• Put 'Henri Fantin-Latour white cup and saucer' in your search engine and use this painting as your prompt.

Setting and Viewpoint

Jhumpa Lahiri's story is a useful model of how setting may be used to create character, advance the plot, dramatise, enhance narrative tension and amplify theme, but also an example of good practice in other, subtler, but no less instructive ways, some of which you can find in this passage:

> It was no longer possible to enter the temple, for it had filled with rubble years ago, but they admired the exterior, as did all the tourists Mr Kapasi brought there, slowly strolling along each of its sides. Mr Das trailed behind, taking pictures. The children ran ahead, pointing to figures of naked people, intrigued in particular by the Nagamithunas, the half-human, half-serpentine couples who were said, Mr Kapasi told them, to live in the deepest waters of the sea. Mr Kapasi was pleased that they liked the temple, pleased especially that it appealed to Mrs Das. She stopped every three or four paces, staring silently at the carved lovers, and the processions of elephants, and the topless female musicians beating on two sided drums.
>
> Though Mr Kapasi had been to the temple countless times, it occurred to him, as he, too, gazed at the topless women, that he had never seen his wife fully naked. Even when they made love she kept the panels of her blouse hooked together, the string of her petticoat knotted around her waist. (p 57)

First lesson from this passage: you will reveal the setting more effectively through the use of concrete, specific detail. But use telling detail, not every detail; leave the reader space to complete the picture you begin. The temple is made solid to us through only a few specific details – 'figures of naked people ... the half-human, half-serpentine ... the carved lovers ... the processions of elephants ... the topless female musicians beating on two sided drums' – but these details combine with the little we already know about Indian art and enable us to imagine the actuality of the temple.

Second lesson. An unglossed, expositional descriptor of the setting makes the reader passive; you will be telling them about it rather than showing it. If however, you write with immediacy and show the setting, you give them a vicarious experience of it. Bringing the setting alive for the reader is a matter of experiencing it through the point-of-view character's perceptions and what they are doing within it at any given time. Perceiving the setting from the viewpoint character's perspective will involve incorporating description into action and dialogue, which will keep your story moving and help you avoid static description. Writing with the senses creates the protagonist's perceptions of the setting. Remember Robert Olen Butler's crucial advice, quoted in the last chapter: 'Writing fiction is about rendering the world primarily through the viewpoint character's moment-to-moment, sensual and emotional perceptions.' The carvings on the temple and Mrs Kapasi's inhibiting clothing are brought to life through sensory description.

Perceiving the setting from the viewpoint character's perspective rather than your own brings it to life. 'Mr Kapasi was pleased that they liked the temple, pleased especially that it appealed to Mrs Das.' Lahiri hasn't described it in the factual manner of a guidebook. Kapasi isn't objective about the place; he feels more positively than he might have on any other day because he is attracted to Mrs Das, and she is enjoying the visit. The author inhabits the protagonist's viewpoint and a protagonist will of necessity have thoughts and feelings about the setting, will have a relationship with it. As a result, the reader will, too. And don't forget that this relationship between viewpoint character and setting is also a characterising device. The setting is brought to life through the character having a relationship with it, and that relationship tells us more than we had known about the character.

And, to some extent, readers will have to deduce the character's feelings about their context, which fosters active readers. Kapasi 'gazed at the topless women' and it occurred to him 'that he had never seen his wife fully naked'. The significance of the fact that he had never seen his wife fully naked isn't made explicit, but from the very fact that he makes the comparison and that he is clearly attracted to Mrs Das readers can deduce that Kapasi isn't sexually fulfilled. And we surmise this through the character's relationship with the setting.

It may be easy to neglect setting in your writing. The most obvious elements of craft – character, plot, dialogue – tend to be what writers focus on, but I would argue that setting is almost as important. Don't forget to give it your attention.

Writing Exercise: Setting

Pick a workplace you are familiar with: a supermarket, a college, a restaurant, a newsagent's. Think of somebody you know well who would both fit in and be at odds with the place.

Now write for twenty minutes using this character in this setting.

Your task is to see if you can manage to deploy four of the setting-related skills that we have just observed in Jhumpa Lahiri's story:

creating character
advancing plot
dramatising
enhancing narrative tension.

Notes

1   In John Cheever, *Collected Stories* (London, Vintage Classics, 2010), p 776.

2   In Wells Tower, *Everything Ravaged, Everything Burned* (London: Granta, 2009), p 185.

3   In D.H. Lawrence, *England My England* (London, Penguin Twentieth Century Classics, 1996), p 58.

4   In Michel Faber, *Some Rain Must Fall and Other Stories* (Edinburgh: Canongate, 2000), p 19.

5   In Jhumpa Lahiri, *Interpreter of Maladies* (London: Flamingo, 1999), p 43.

15

Description

Ursula Hurley

Writers have been creating virtual realities since before computers were even dreamed of. Good fiction conjures an alternative world, gives you a window into someone else's life, takes you somewhere other. Above all, it's convincing. Effective description is fundamental to this process. The aim is to entrance your reader by the cunningly set stage to the extent that they don't notice the ropes and pulleys supporting it all. The craft is in judging what is salient and what is boring, when to zoom in and when to draw back, when to show and when to leave intriguing gaps, when to elongate and when to contract.

While these considerations apply to all prose narratives, they are particularly, urgently important in short fiction, where we don't have time to elaborate. A larger text, like a novel, may be able to carry a little extra weight. But a short story offers no hiding place – it must be lean and built for speed. As Alice Munro puts it, 'You're much more thinly clothed. You're like somebody out in a little shirt.'[1] So if we have to travel light, we must choose very carefully what to pack in the case marked 'Description'.

Less Is More

Narrative drive is paramount, a lesson I learned the hard way after wasting a lot of time and effort on pages and pages of beautiful (to me) but pointless (to everyone else) description. As Stephen King says,

In many cases when a reader puts a story aside because it "got boring," the boredom arose because the writer grew enchanted with his powers of description and lost sight of his priority, which is to keep the ball rolling.[2]

Just because you can doesn't mean that you should. When it comes to setting the scene, the bare minimum can be more than enough. To illustrate this, I'm going to use a very short piece of flash fiction by David Gaffney, called 'The Kids Are Alright'. The piece is so short that we can read it in full to understand how specific description contributes to the functioning of the narrative:

The Kids Are Alright

When I heard about the boy whose parents dressed him as a girl until the age of twelve I thought, lucky kid. My parents dressed me until I was thirteen as popular crooner Perry Como. They even encouraged me to carry, but not smoke, a beautiful briarwood pipe and I would stab the air with its stem to emphasise a point and suck on it when deep in thought. Yet I wasn't unhappy; it was normal. My cousin had it much worse as Max Bygraves. One day I was house-training the dog. The sleeve to *Swing Out Perry* was on the floor and before I could stop him Engelbert squatted and squeezed a neat little turd right on the middle of Perry's polished inane features. The next day my mother let me have my fringe cut like Dave Hill out of Slade. Kids have to be allowed to express themselves.[3]

This is a strong example of a 'tip of the iceberg' story, in which an apparently 'off the cuff' anecdote suggests an alternative reality beneath the surface of the narrative, where families condition their children to perform bizarre and inappropriate identities. The focus on a single concrete detail, the 'beautiful briarwood pipe', brings the narrator's reality to life. The gestures that the child is encouraged to make with it, as he mimics the behaviour of a much older man, evoke the situation vividly and with great economy. This single object and its active description ('carry', 'stab', 'suck') show us the effects on a person who grew up experiencing this strange environment. Crucially, however, we are not told why a family would impose such rules on its children ('my cousin had it worse'). Like all effective short fictions, this narrative prompts the reader to do their own imaginative work, conjuring the parents and their motivations beyond the frame of the story. It is the subtle and carefully selected concrete detail that helps the story to live beyond the written text, resonating in the reader's imagination.

The humour and oddity of this narrative are generated by the deadpan first-person voice ('it was normal'). Gaffney's skill here is in maintaining the simplicity and brevity of the voice, using cultural markers to do the work for him. So Perry Como, Max Bygraves and Engelbert Humperdinck are invoked to represent the easy-listening, blazer-and-slacks ethos in which the narrator's childhood was steeped. In case the reader is completely nonplussed by the cultural reference, Perry Como is introduced as a 'popular crooner'. Those two precisely chosen words sound like the blurb from a record sleeve – they not only describe Perry for those in need of guidance, but they also enact his identity as a cultural icon for safe, family-friendly entertainment. The narrator's own attitude to Como is expressed unambiguously through the two-word description: 'polished inane'.

By the time we get to the dog, Engelbert, the reader is left to pick up the logic that, given the context of this family, he must be named after Engelbert Humperdinck, another icon of the 'easy listening' culture. Implication is key here and the reader is expected to make the imaginative leap. This is a risk, because it relies on pre-existing cultural knowledge that the reader brings to the story. Not all readers will 'get it', but those who do will enjoy the in-joke. And with most readers now having an internet search capability at their fingertips, this technique is perhaps less risky than it used to be.

Despite the quirkiness of Gaffney's story, we might read it as encapsulating the near-universal experience of teenagers finding their own cultural reference points and rejecting those of their parents. Much of this work is carried by the use of records and song titles. Readers with relevant cultural knowledge will associate the story's title with The Who's 1965 song, 'The Kids Are Alright', and the rebellious youthful attitudes with which it is associated. We read the dog's defecating on Perry Como's

LP as a symbolic rejection of the parents' culture. The parents' acceptance of this cultural shift is coded in the narrator's mother allowing him a fashionable haircut. Again, it is a particular entertainer who carries this symbolism, 'Dave Hill out of Slade' representing rock music and its attendant unconventional, self-expressive culture that would be anathema to Como and his ilk. Again, a reader unsure of Dave Hill's appearance is left to work it out for themselves, but they are given a pointer as to which band he was with.

It is such precisely chosen cultural markers and concrete details that achieve big contributions to the depth and power of even the shortest stories. As Rust Hills tells us, when writing short fiction, 'Everything must work with everything else.' And description, when used skilfully, can be a vital component in a form where 'Everything enhances everything else, interrelates with everything else, is inseparable from everything else.' The key to succeeding in this aim is, as demonstrated so ably by Gaffney, to incorporate description with 'a necessary and perfect economy'.[4]

Writing Exercise: Using Description to Achieve Depth and Resonance

Take a draft story (even a first paragraph will do). Look for a moment when a character performs an action. Immediately following that action, introduce a sensory detail. What is the first and most important thing that they notice? If you can, locate a detail in their environment that comes from touch, taste, sound or smell. Sight is fine, but it's sometimes more obvious and therefore less interesting. Have your narrator or point-of-view character note or perceive this detail in a way which resonates with the theme or plot of your story. If you aren't yet sure of plot or theme, great! Consider this detail and think about what it might contain. The character's own perceptions of the world around them could tell you what the theme really is. Rewrite or tweak in light of these insights.

Then ask someone to read your work. Ask them to explain the effect that your description has on them. What does it look like in their imagination? What themes are present? What have they surmised/understood/anticipated from your writing? How do their impressions differ from your intentions? What would you change in the light of their comments?

Try asking someone else to read your paragraphs and compare their responses with those of your first reader. Are they similar or different? Why might this be?

Multi-Tasking and Multi-Layering

As we have seen, description is the consummate multi-tasker. Amongst other things, it can:

* create atmosphere/suspense
* introduce something the reader needs to know
* help the drama
* show character/build voice
* contribute to the plot
* work on symbolic, allegoric and prosaic levels.

One of the most memorable and unsettling short fictions that I have ever read is 'Four Institutional Monologues' by George Saunders. This unconventional narrative uses four different forms, narrated by four different voices, to achieve a sinister implication that is never stated outright, but which builds in and across the voices so that what is unsaid is sometimes more powerful than what is voiced. In each case, the voice of the narrator and the unsettling implications are created by effective use of description.

The first section is a memo from a middle manager. The voice and status of this character are established via a deliberate imprecision in his ability to describe feelings: 'we got sort of excited'. We deduce from his enthusiastic but incompetent expression that his team has been criticised for attitude and performance by those more senior in the organisation. What the organisation is, its purpose, and the work that it does, are all carefully withheld. We get references to 'the tasks that we must sometimes do around here that maybe aren't on the surface all that pleasant'. One employee is praised for his productivity in terms that suggest violence: 'God he was really pounding down and you could see the energetic joy on his face each time he rushed by us to get additional clean-up towels.' Disturbing possibilities lurk under the surface of what is being described, and these intensify as the story progresses. What it is that he's pounding, why the work may be morally suspect, and what goes on in Room 6 ('no-one is walking out of Room 6 feeling perfectly okay') is never actually revealed.[5]

The second monologue is a 'Design Proposal', which makes deliberate use of impenetrable jargon, including a chilling reference to the

'Forward-Anticipating Temporary Community'.[6] Just who this community contains and the reason for its temporary nature (which is emphasised repeatedly) is never revealed. Following this is a third monologue, written in mistake-ridden English by a worker who is clearly considered to be of the lowest status. This section is a pitiable plea for other departments to cease their mockery of the narrator and his co-workers:

> And also you don't have to say Ouch whenever one of our throwed Knuckles goes too far and hits the wall, it is not like the Knuckle could feel that and say Ow, because it is dead dumbass, it cannot feel its leg part hitting the wall, so we know you are being sarcasmic.[7]

Again, it is inarticulacy, and a withholding of what is actually going on, that give this description its power.

The final, and most disturbing, section is titled '(93990)' and is written in the language of a scientific experiment. Through the jargon and technical terminology, an affecting narrative about a 'diminutive male' monkey emerges. The monkey survives all of the toxic substances which kill the other subjects of the experiment. The horrific deaths of the other monkeys are recorded in cold, objective language, while the sentience and humanity of the 'diminutive male' are there for us to see, if we read attentively:

> Also at times it seemed to implore. This imploring was judged to be, possibly, a mild hallucinogenic effect. This imploring resulted in involuntary laughter on the part of the handlers, which resulted in the animal discontinuing the imploring behaviour and retreating to the NW corner where it sat for quite some time with its back to the handlers. It was decided that, in future, handlers would refrain from laughing at the imploring, so as to be able to obtain a more objective idea of the duration of the (unimpeded) imploring.

Through the sparse and 'objective' description, the reader understands that the narrator has completely missed the point. This 'diminutive male' monkey (his small stature described repeatedly in order to establish him as deserving of our sympathy) is pleading for his life while the handlers dismiss entirely the possibility that the monkey understands what is happening and is trying to communicate with them. The narrator's description of their decision to stop laughing relies on the basis of scientific observation and excludes any sympathy with another living creature. The reader sees through the narrator's description, to the real point of the narrative, which remains unspoken. The unflinchingly scientific voice is sustained to the end, where they mindlessly 'sacrifice' the monkey, having failed to recognise or investigate the far more interesting finding, which is the great intelligence of the creature they have killed. The intended outcome of the experiment is not explained. While the four narratives are never linked explicitly, we are left with a sense that they are all connected via descriptions of institutional blindness and immorality.

The most useful lesson that we can draw from Saunders' story is that description works best when it reflects the voice and world-view of the character who is perceiving or narrating the events. What's important to them? What would they notice first? How do they understand and respond to the world around them? In some cases it may be more effective to create inarticulate or even misguided descriptions of feelings, events and settings because that is more accurately the experience of the characters involved.

Maintaining the integrity of the fictional world that you are creating means never describing things just for the reader's benefit. All the characters in the sinister world of the 'Institutional Monologues' know exactly what is going on and what they are all involved with. For the narrator to state, 'As you know, we are all working on X in order to achieve Y,' would be clunky in the extreme. Avoiding this requires self-confidence – the temptation when we are drafting work is to make clear what is happening because we are so keen for our readers to understand our message, and anxious that they may not 'get it'. However, as Saunders demonstrates, the unspoken is often a more powerful tool of communication. Using description to hint, suggest or even mislead can be very effective, offering the reader the space to read between the lines. As Sara Maitland reassures us, 'A powerful piece of writing is always teamwork: respect your readers, and you will find there is nothing to be self-conscious about.'[8]

Writing Exercise: Description Is Character

Write about an everyday process, such as making a cup of tea, getting dressed or switching on a computer, using the techniques and strategies that we have covered in this chapter. Make sure that you describe the events from within the world-view of your character. If they are bored, angry, or inarticulate, make sure that your description supports and intensifies this feature of their personality. Think about what could be left implied or unsaid. Consider gaps that could build intrigue and suspense. Try to make space for your reader's imagination to work. Above all, make it a gripping read.

Notes

1   'Go Ask Alice', Alice Munro interviewed by Alice Quinn in the *New Yorker*, 19 February 2001, http://www.newyorker.com/magazine/2001/02/19/go-ask-alice (accessed 19 April 2017).

2   King, *On Writing*, p 207.

3   David Gaffney, 'The Kids Are Alright', in *Transmission*, Issue 2, 2005, p 12.

4   Rust Hills, *Writing in General and the Short Story in Particular* (Boston: Houghton Mifflin, 2000), p 4.

5   George Saunders, 'Four Institutional Monologues', pp 13–33 in Dave Eggers (ed.), *The Best of McSweeney's* Vol. 1 (London: Penguin, 2005), pp 14–16.

6   Saunders, 'Four Institutional Monologues', p 19.

7   Saunders, 'Four Institutional Monologues', p 24.

8   Sara Maitland, *The Writer's Way* (London: Capella, 2005), p 119.

16

Style

Style has to do with accuracy of expression, sentences, syntax, vocabulary choice, imagery and voice. (More on this in the next chapter.) Put simply, style is proper words in their proper place, as Jonathan Swift suggests. Rust Hills, in *Writing in General and the Short Story in Particular*, lists all of the above, plus the use of tenses, italics and punctuation (specifically exclamation points and semi-colons), plus paragraphing, plus choices in dialogue writing. In only a short chapter, I can't cover every facet of style; what follows is a little advice on a few of them.

Influences

Your influences will have shaped your style. These may be the fiction you've read over many years (and last week); the way people around you speak, both wherever you are now and in the place where you grew up; the poetry and songs you listen to; and *you*. Your style comes out of who you are, out of your evolving personality and out of who you are this moment when your coffee doesn't taste right and you're looking out of your window at the house behind.

Meaning, Sense and Clarity

The University of Iowa's Writers' Workshop is the most prestigious graduate writing programme in the USA, and it's also the oldest in the world. Graduates of the Iowa Writers' Workshop include Flannery O'Connor, Raymond Carver, John Irving and Jane Smiley. Philip Roth and Kurt Vonnegut both taught there, and for many years Marilynne Robinson was on the staff. Creative Writing was first introduced into British higher education when the University of East Anglia began its MA in 1971 – with a cohort that included Ian McEwan – but it was as long ago as 1922 that the University of Iowa set the ball rolling by announcing that creative work would be acceptable as theses for advanced degrees.

The novelist Madison Smartt Bell, in his teaching handbook *Narrative Design, A Writer's Guide to Structure*, claims that 'It was [at Iowa] that the workshop method, now common to about 95 per cent of all writing programs across the academic landscape, first evolved. The Iowa workshop, in short, is the Ur-creative writing program.'[1]

Some years ago, I paid a visit to Iowa. I went to learn. I surmised that this university, with a fifty-year head start on universities in the UK, must have learned a thing or two. On one of the days, I was a guest in one of the late Frank Conroy's classes. At the time, Frank was the Director of Iowa's Writers' Workshop. During the class I witnessed, Conroy was at pains to convey to his students the difficulty of achieving 'meaning, sense and clarity'. In the following, from his essay 'The Writer's Workshop',[2] Conroy expands on his beliefs about accurate expression.

In my opinion the struggle to maintain meaning, sense and clarity is the primary activity of any writer. It turns out to be quite difficult, demanding constant concentration at high levels, constant self-editing, and a continuous pre-conscious awareness of the ghostly presence of mind on the other side of the zone [the reader] …

1. Meaning. At the literal level, the writer's words must mean what they say … *He sat down with a sigh* means that the sitting and the sighing are happening at the same time, which precludes a construction such as *'I'm too tired to think,' he said as he sat down with a sigh.* The reader will undoubtedly get the drift and will separate the sighing from the saying, but the writing is sloppy from the point of view of meaning. It doesn't, at the literal level, mean what it says. Errors of meaning are quite common in lax prose, and there are more ways of making them than I can list here.

2. Sense. The text must make sense, lest the reader be excluded. *The boy ate the watermelon* makes sense. *The watermelon ate the boy* does not, unless the author has created a special world in which it does. Unmotivated behaviour in characters doesn't make sense to the reader, who is also confused by randomness, arbitrariness, or aimlessness in the text. The writer must recognise the continuous unrelenting pressure from the reader for the text to make sense. It can be a strange kind of sense, to be sure, but the reader must be able to understand the text to enter it.

3. Clarity. Strunk and White[3] tell us not to use ten words where five will do. This is because the most compact language statement is almost always clearer than an expansive one. The goal is not brevity for its own sake, but clarity. The reader expects the writer to have removed all excess language, to have distilled things to their essences, whether the style is simple or complex … As well, clarity has aesthetic value by itself.

In using language, accuracy and direct communication are essential. They are also important considerations if you want to keep language properly arranged with everything in its place. Language is, if you like, a medium, and your fiction the message it delivers. Your use of language is a tool.

Years ago, I went on a lighting course at the Royal Exchange Theatre in Manchester. The most helpful advice during that week was made by Vince Herbert, then in charge of lighting at the theatre. 'Lighting is there to allow the show to be seen and to create effects,' he said. 'If the audience notice your lighting, you've failed.' Joyce Carol Oates says virtually the same thing about the way writers use language: 'I think that's one of the problems with the really elegant writers; you stop reading and start admiring the words. So you lose the narrative flow. I don't want that to happen.'[4]

I'm as fond of beautifully crafted prose styles as the next person, but I think the point being made here deserves your attention. All of us want to use words beautifully, but the beauty of the style should never distract from the function of language in fiction, which is not primarily to be attractive. 'Mannered writing', John Gardner argues, 'is writing that continually distracts us from the fictional dream by stylistic tics that we cannot help associating, as we read, with the author's wish to intrude himself, prove himself to be different from all the other authors.'5 The words are there to deliver the story, not the other way round. Words are the material from which you create your story.

Writing Exercise: Meaning, Sense and Clarity

If you're at university or college, it shouldn't be too hard to find a play to see, or a gig. Whatever kind of performing rings your bell, go and see a live show of some kind.

Your brief is to write a record of what you saw and experienced, but not to express the kind of opinions that a reviewer might. Instead, stay at the level of what happened, both onstage and in the audience. You have 500 words in which to produce a record of your chosen event, one which complies with Frank Conroy's observations about meaning, sense and clarity. Do it properly: word-processed and double-spaced.

Concision

Economy is a given in the short story, and one aspect to it is concision. In a letter of 1899, Chekhov gave a rationale for concision.

> You understand it at once when I say, 'The man sat on the grass'; you understand it because it is clear and makes no demands on the attention.
>
> On the other hand, it is not easily understood, and it is difficult for the mind, if I write, 'A tall, narrow-chested, middle-sized man, with a red beard, sat on the green grass, already trampled by pedestrians, sat silently, shyly, and timidly looked about him.'
>
> That is not immediately grasped by the mind, whereas good writing should be grasped at once – in a second.

The long-winded version here has too much detail for readers to take in. You need to leave them space to work. For one thing, readers require that so that they can engage with your text. They engage by being given work to do, work such as supplementing your outline of something with more detail from their own minds. An additional reason to keep it brief is that since the last century, the century of the image, of photography, billboard advertising, cinema and television, people have become visually oriented, and impatient of lengthy descriptions of what they will already be familiar with from these media. Less is almost always more.

If you want to make your prose concise, you might think about writing with verbs and nouns. This means as far as possible avoiding adjectives and, especially, adverbs. It has to do with hitting the nail on the head first time, so that the reader accesses the information immediately. Compare:

* Buffy walked angrily out of the room.
* Buffy stormed out of the room.

Which is more direct? An adverb ('angrily') and the verb it qualifies can usually be replaced with a single verb that means the same thing. This is concision. This is choosing to leave out words you can manage without. But Hemingway (see below) talks about something else: the omission of information. What his theorising of omission says to me is that we will often have far more material for a piece of fiction than we actually use. Yes, you should know the world you have imagined inside out, but you don't have to exhibit all of that knowledge in the final draft.

Chekhov's story 'The Kiss' includes the following: 'He raised his stick and hit his son on the head; the son raised his stick and struck his father just on his bald patch such a blow that the stick bounced back. The father did not even flinch, but hit his son again and again on the head. And so they stood and kept hitting one another on the head, and it looked not so much like a fight as some sort of game. And peasants, men and women, stood in a crowd at the gate and looked into the garden, and the faces of all were grave.'[6] How clean is that? Moment by moment as you read this, you can picture the scene he describes as easily as reading it. (Note that Chekhov uses only one adjective and no adverbs.)

Using adjectives sparingly is effective. This sentence, from Katherine Dunn's story 'The Allies', is instructive: 'Her eyes went soft, turning to the grey sky outside the window.' Two adjectives, both of which tell you something significant that the reader can easily absorb.

Concision may also be a matter of removing the superfluous and the redundant, two slightly different things. You might say the superfluous is what you can manage without. The redundant is that phrase or word which amounts to stupid repetition of one kind or another: 'Sunrise at this time of the year comes at 6.30 a.m.' (It's never going to be p.m., is it?) Or: 'This CD was electronically recorded in LA.' (How else but electronically?)

Following on from Chekhov's aesthetic of simplicity and economy, two twentieth-century writers have particularly influenced fiction writers with their succinct prose. The first was Ernest Hemingway, a great theorist of style. One of Hemingway's ideas about fiction is that it is strengthened by omission. We've already looked at omitting adjectives and adverbs, but Hemingway is talking of a different kind of omission.

Omission

Hemingway speaks of omitting at a deeper level, which he illustrates by suggesting that leaving out the fact that his protagonist commits suicide at the end of one story makes it stronger: 'This was omitted on my new theory that you could omit anything if you knew that you omitted it and the omitted part would strengthen the story and make people feel something more than they understood.'[7]

He elaborates by using the analogy of an iceberg: 'There is seven-eighths of it underwater for every part that shows. Anything you know you can eliminate only strengthens your iceberg. It is the part that doesn't show. If a writer omits something because he does not know it then there is a hole in the story.'[8]

Omission is perhaps a first cousin of concision, and Hemingway majored in it. He seems to have taken to heart Ezra Pound's advice about what makes for good writing:

* direct treatment of the 'thing', without evasion or cliché

* the use of absolutely no word that does not contribute to the general design, and
* fidelity to the rhythms of natural speech.[9]

In Hemingway's story 'Hills Like White Elephants', a couple sit at a bar in Spain waiting for a train. Reading between the lines of their conversation – information is conveyed indirectly (see 'Dialogue') – it is clear that they are going to a city where she will possibly have an abortion. As we approach the end of this very short story, we know the train is close. Here are the last two lines of the story:

'Do you feel better?' he asked.
'I feel fine,' she said, 'There's nothing wrong with me. I feel fine.'[10]

Do the man and woman get on the train? Does the woman have an abortion? If so, do they remain together afterwards? It's possible that Hemingway had some or all of the answers to these questions, but it's certain that the story is made stronger because he has decided to omit all of this apparently vital information. As with words, with less can be more.

From the second half of the twentieth century onwards, any short story writers who write tight, mean and lean owe a debt to Hemingway. He may be the most influential prose fiction writer of the twentieth century. (Which is not to say that he is the best.)

Writing Burst
* A lot of people leave this town, and sooner or later most of them come back.

Precision

The heir of Chekhov and Hemingway is Raymond Carver, and what Carver brings to the table is precision ('the language must be accurate and precisely given'). His work has been perceived as minimalist, though he himself preferred to see it as 'precisionism'. Jay McInerney finds in Carver's work 'the naïve clarity ... of Hemingway's early stories'.[11] Carver may not have done anything much that Hemingway hadn't half a century earlier. He gives a rationale for his precisionism here, and it should sound familiar:

> What creates tension in a piece of fiction is partly the way the concrete words are linked together to make up the visible action of the story. But it's also the things that are left out, that are implied, the landscape just under the smooth (but sometimes broken and unsettled) surface of things.[12]

In promoting precision, Raymond Carver said that 'the words can be so precise they may even sound flat; but they can still carry; if used right, they can hit all the notes.' This excerpt, from Carver's story 'One More Thing', may include flat words, but they carry, and, I would say, hit all the notes:

> [Maxine] unbuttoned her coat and put her purse down on the counter. She looked at L.D. and said, 'L.D., I've had it. So has Rae. So has everyone who knows you. I've been thinking it over. I want you out of here. Tonight. This minute. Now. Get the hell out of here right now.'
>
> L.D. had no intention of going anywhere. He looked from Maxine to the jar of pickles that had been on the table since lunch. He picked up the jar and pitched it through the kitchen window.[13]

All of the above notwithstanding, economy is not the only game in town.

Writing Exercise: Concision, Omission, Precision

Write a scene 500 words long and composed of concisely, precisely expressed prose in which you omit what you might yesterday have considered key information. In the manner of Hemingway in 'Hills Like White Elephants', try to avoid your characters communicating directly or expressing emotion. Here's a sentence to start you off:

Tammy arrived back earlier than Jon expected.

Some Other Kinds of Sentences

This sentence, by Henry James, a master of fiction writing, may make the case for erring on the side of economy and favouring the concise and precise:

> The money was far too much even for a fee in a fairy-tale, and in the absence of Mrs Beale who, though the hour was now late, had not yet returned to the Regent's Park, Susan Ash, in the hall, as loud as Maisie was low and as bold as she was bland, produced, on the exhibition offered under the dim vigil of the lamp that made the place a contrast to the child's recent scene of light, the half-crown that an unsophisticated cabman could pronounce to be the least he would take.[14]

The meaning doesn't fly off the page and into the reader's mind, does it? What this sprawling, sagging sentence means, I think, is: *The sum the cabby asked for was ridiculously high, but Susan Ash produced a half-crown and he accepted it.* Does Henry James communicate this directly and effectively? No. Is this scenic route sentence in some way stylish? Not to me. However, not all longer sentences are bad.

Long Sentences

It may be true, as I say elsewhere, that long sentences make long paragraphs and long paragraphs make dense pages; and, in our visual era, none of us is very good at reading monolithic chunks of black ink. We prefer some white space on our pages. But, but, but. Longer sentences offer more opportunities to vary the rhythm and to build musicality. There's something beautiful about a sentence that extends for line after line without losing your attention.

> She herself had already had her own troubles, losing her kids and keeping her ex-husband, Danny, from breaking in her house and stealing her things while she was at work, which was really why I had moved in in the first place, that and needing to give my little daughter, Cheryl, a better shake in things.[15]

Here, Richard Ford puts one phrase on top of another, like someone building a house of cards, and each new card that he sets in place builds the rhythm of the sentence and, I would argue, makes the reading pleasurable. (And let's not forget that Henry James has written many elegant and beautiful long sentences.)

Lush Sentences

Hemingway and Carver are famous for cutting their prose to the bone, so it's not just the longer sentence that's a viable alternative to the models of economy we've just examined, it's also the texture of the writing.

> The fringed lampshade glowed with a warm light that exposed the lovers on the bed. Her mother was transformed into a round, rosy, moaning, opulent siren, an undulating sea anemone, all tentacles and suckers, all mouth and hands and legs and orifices, rolling and turning and cleaving to the large body of Bernal, who by contrast seemed rigid and clumsy, moving spasmodically like a piece of wood tossed by inexplicable high winds.[16]

This passage from Isabel Allende's story 'The Wicked Girl' shares Ford's house of cards layering of phrase upon phrase, but the prose is also more sensual, lush, and lavish. It is ornate if not baroque. After Carver's American cold cuts and salad, Allende's prose is Chilean *empanadas*; the meat and vegetables have been stewed in an exotic blend of spices and herbs. If you're having difficulty coming to terms with the contrasting models in this chapter, it might help to think of my friend who, when he's on his bike, thinks motorists are a pain in the ass, but when he's in his car, thinks cyclists are. Flowery and elaborate has its uses just as much as lean and wiry.

Lyrical Sentences

One of Hemingway's major concerns was to eschew emotionalism and sentimentality in his work. In 'Hills Like White Elephants', powerful emotions are at work between the man and the woman, but none of these emotions is directly alluded to or expressed. Lyrical writing is just the opposite. Rather than being ducked, characters' emotions are poured out in an effusive manner, as Bertha's are here, in Katherine Mansfield's 'Bliss':

> And the two women stood side by side looking at the slender, flowering tree. Although it was so still it seemed, like the flame of a candle, to stretch up, to point, to quiver in the bright air, to grow taller and taller as they gazed – almost to touch the rim of the round, silver moon ... Both, as it were, caught in that circle of unearthly light, understanding each other perfectly, creatures of another world, and wondering what they were to do in this one with all this blissful treasure that burned in their bosoms and dropped, in silver flowers, from their hair and hands?[17]

Effusive characters with deep emotions may engage readers just as much as stories where sentiment is avoided. Up to a point. In an interview on French television, the American film director Frank Capra, whose emotive, populist work includes *It's a Wonderful Life,* once said, 'I made mistakes in drama. I thought drama was when actors cried. But drama is when the audience cries.'[18]

As we've already seen, 'Hills Like White Elephants' concludes like this:

> 'Do you feel better?' he asked.
> 'I feel fine,' she said, 'There's nothing wrong with me. I feel fine.'

All of the dialogue prior to this point suggests – in an impressively indirect way – that tensions between this couple are riding high and that the woman is feeling far from 'fine'. The question is, which is likely to give the reader the emotional experience – being effusive like Mansfield or restrained like Hemingway? You'll have to decide for yourself. If you want to have the best of both worlds, you could do worse than emulate a model that bridges these two extremes: Philip Roth's long story *Goodbye, Columbus.*

> We had to take about two too many steps to keep the approach from being awkward, but we pursued the impulse and kissed. I felt her hand on the back of my neck and so I tugged her towards me, too violently

perhaps, and slid my own hands across the side of her body and around to her back. I felt the wet spots on her shoulder blades, and beneath them, I'm sure of it, a faint fluttering, as though something stirred so deep in her breasts, so far back it could make itself felt through her shirt. It was like the fluttering of wings, tiny wings no bigger than her breasts. The smallness of the wings did not bother me – it would take an eagle to carry me up those lousy hundred and eighty feet that make summer nights so much cooler in Short Hills than they are in Newark.[19]

Deep feelings are involved here, but they remain implicit, rather than explicit. There is no pouring out of emotion, but neither is there the repressed restraint of the Hemingway. Is it a case of the character or the reader having an emotional experience? Again, you decide.

Writing Burst
- 'I feel so pathetic crying,' he said.

Musical Sentences

The rhythms of good prose may suggest music. Creating musical prose is often about descriptive writing, but there are other ingredients beyond descriptive prose. This kind of writing has to do with sculpting and shaping your words and clauses so that they are more beautiful than their function demands. It's also about having a love for words, for their sounds as much as their meaning. We are approaching the realm of poetry here, and it's no coincidence that Jackie Kay, the author of this next passage, is as much acclaimed for her poetry as for her short fiction.

Today the morning had started with Vadnie saying to herself, Time to get up, Vadnie Marlene Sevlon. Preston was up and out and had not brought her the usual cup of hot tea. The girls had already grown up and left home. Grace was the first of the family at university. Sometimes she'd find herself doing a big shop and telling people the family was coming home, that's why her trolley was loaded. Today nobody was there and nobody was coming home and she felt suddenly tired.[20]

This paragraph features sibilance throughout, alliteration ('Preston was up and out and had not brought her the usual cup of hot tea), assonance ('doing a big shop and telling people the family was coming home') and consonance ('telling people the family was coming home, that's why her trolley …'). In addition, hard and soft sounds have been artfully knitted together ('Grace was the first of the family at university'). You're a writer, you love words. You could do this. But bear in mind the wisdom of Elmore Leonard: 'If it sounds like writing, I rewrite it.'[21]

Writing Exercise: Long, Lush, Lyrical and Musical

In the previous exercise, you wrote a concisely, precisely expressed prose scene, starting with this sentence. See if you can learn from Ford, Mansfield et al., and rewrite that exercise so that it becomes almost the opposite of itself. Aim for some or all of the attributes listed in the title of this exercise.

Writing all you can all of the time will necessarily develop your style for you. Robert Olen Butler, whom I've mentioned once or twice, suggests that none of us knows what we are doing until we have written a million words of fiction. Equally, reading all you can all of the time will shape your style, too. When discussing the Oscar Wilde scandal, one of the minor characters in *Author, Author*, David Lodge's fictionalisation of Henry James' middle years, suggests that a writer has a duty to be a moral person. This was a perhaps unfortunate judgement on Wilde, but the implication of the remark was that who a writer is shapes his or her writing. A corollary of this is that what a writer reads shapes his work. The higher the quality of the prose you consume, the more likely it is that the prose you produce will be worth reading.

Write all you can, read all you can, but also challenge yourself to read work of lasting worth. A diet of, for instance, F. Scott Fitzgerald and – since I've just mentioned her – Marilynne Robinson will increase your chances of developing an elegant, attractive style.

Notes

1   From the chapter 'Unconscious Mind' in Bell, *Narrative Design*, p 4.
2   Frank Conroy, 'The Writer's Workshop' in Tom Bailey (ed.), *On Writing Short Stories* (Oxford University Press, 2000).

3 William I. Strunk & E.B. White (eds), *The Elements of Style* (Allyn and Bacon, 1999) and online at: www.bartleby.com/141/ (accessed 27 March 2017).

4 Joyce Carol Oates, quoted by William F. Buckley in his essay 'Style and Language' in Conrad (ed.), *The Complete Guide to Writing Fiction*, p 94.

5 Gardner, *The Art of Fiction*, p 119.

6 Anton Chekhov, 'The Kiss' in Richard Ford (ed.), *The Essential Tales of Chekhov* (New York: HarperCollins, 1998), p 51.

7 Hemingway, *A Movable Feast* (London: Arrow, 1994), p 75.

8 Quoted by Charters in *The Story and Its Writer*, p 614.

9 Quoted by Charters in *The Story and Its Writer*, p 614.

10 Ernest Hemingway, 'Hills Like White Elephants' in *The Essential Hemingway* (Harmondsworth: Penguin, 1964), p 378.

11 In his introduction to Jay McInerney (ed.), *The Penguin Book of New American Voices* (London: Penguin, 1995).

12 From Raymond Carver, 'On Writing' in Charters, *The Story and Its Writer*, pp 1524–7.

13 Raymond Carver, *Where I'm Calling From: New and Selected Stories* (New York: Vintage, 1989), p 148.

14 Henry James, *What Maisie Knew* (London: Everyman, 1997), p 135.

15 Richard Ford, 'Rock Springs' in *Rock Springs* (London: Bloomsbury, 2006), p 11.

16 Isabel Allende, 'The Wicked Girl' in Janet Berliner & Joyce Carol Oates (eds), *Snapshots: 20th Century Mother-Daughter Fiction* (London: Vintage Books, 2001).

17 Katherine Mansfield, 'Bliss' in Charters, *The Story and Its Writer*, p 923.

18 Quoted in J.M. & M.J. Cohen (eds), *The Penguin Dictionary of Twentieth Century Quotations* (London: Penguin Books, 1995), p 67.

19 Philip Roth, *Goodbye, Columbus* in Richard Ford (ed.), *The Granta Book of the American Long Story* (London: Granta Books, 1998), p 139.

20 Jackie Kay, 'Mrs Vadnie Marlene Sevlon' in Nicholas Royle (ed.), *Best British Short Stories 2013* (Cromer: Salt Publishing, 2013), p 23.

21 J.M. & M.J. Cohen (eds), *The Penguin Dictionary of Twentieth Century Quotations*, p 230.

17

Voice

Jenny Newman

According to the writer Josip Novakovich, that puzzling thing called 'voice' is simply 'a metaphor for a writer's vigour',[1] or that unique timbre or note that makes you the writer you are.

So at what point in your writing life do you find it?

At a recent festival of writing,[2] the noted dub poet Linton Kwesi Johnson divides his career into three parts. First, he says, comes 'urgency of expression'. In other words, deciding what you want to say can initially be more important than pondering how to say it. Too early a concern with voice may lead to a mannered, self-conscious style which rebuffs or estranges the reader instead of luring her in.

Secondly, says Johnson, comes learning your craft – which could include reading fellow writers, creative writing courses, keeping a writer's journal or reading books such as this one.

Finding your voice, says Johnson, comes last of all: a product of artistic maturity rather than inexperience.

Our speaking voices grow strong when gripped by a powerful emotion. This is true of our writing voices, too. Any distinctive voice is born out of the speaker's confidence that she knows how to engross or entertain. Novakovich quotes Evelyn Waugh, author of *Brideshead Revisited*: 'An artist [...] has to stand out against the tenor of the age and not go flopping along; he must offer some little opposition. Even the great Victorian artists were all anti-Victorian, despite the pressure to conform.'[3]

So why not diverge from the crowd, at least in your fiction? For this you need to know what sort of person you are, or might become, and how to chart your periods of change, regression, development, whim, good and bad moods, shifting opinions and wildest flights of fancy.

Writing Exercise: What You Love, What You Hate

Make a list of ten things you love. They may change each time you do the exercise. *That is part of the point.* While you write, remember that:

- Precision engenders confidence in your readers. Rather than writing 'music', write 'scratchy old recordings of Skull and Roses'. Rather than 'beach', write 'a strip of sand off the KwaZulu coast with sharks cruising offshore'.
- Sense memories enliven prose. Instead of listing simply 'Kashmir rugs', describe how they feel under your bare feet; or instead of 'I climbed the mountain', imagine bare knees scraping against the granite.
- Follow poet Gerard Manley Hopkins by treasuring 'All things counter, original, spare, strange.' He mentions, for example, finches' (not birds') wings and 'rose moles' on trout (not fish).[4]
- Now make a list of ten things you hate – but not straight after watching the news. Avoid abstractions (e.g. intolerance, xenophobia) and think instead of people who have frightened or disgusted you; or how you feel when seasick, panicky or hung-over; or how you dislike double-glazing or finding a hair in your pasta.

The most distinctive voices often come from those who know how, in the words of American poet Emily Dickinson, to 'Tell all the Truth but tell it slant'.[5] Such people have, perhaps, like Dickinson herself, explored the edges of their consciousness, or developed an independent take on life or lived on society's margins, amongst those who are not allowed or who would not want to communicate through official bulletins, newspaper leaders, the legal system or the electoral roll.

This does not mean that to write you need to sleep rough, join an underground organisation, take heroin or run away from home. Nor does it mean that you have to speak dialect or belong to a gang. You may, however, wish to listen to people whose views differ from yours or with whom you would not usually mix, or what the Irish short story writer Frank O'Connor called 'submerged population groups'[6] (a good short story can comment not only on the self but on society, directly or obliquely).

Likewise, teenagers and children often have their own cultures, so you can always mine your childhood for suitably wayward voices, as did Twain himself, who at forty-eight created his teenage narrator in *The Adventures of Huckleberry Finn*, for whom he drew on the black and white voices he'd heard in his Missouri boyhood. Or you could draw on household members, as did, for instance, E.M. Forster and D.H. Lawrence, and as do the British writer Jeanette Winterson and the Irish short story writer Bernard MacLaverty.

But a convincing writer's voice is more than mimicry. No matter how close your source, your characters' voices should not – and could not – merely echo those of people you know: pegging yourself to the factual stifles imagination. So you may also wish to draw on your wider environment. For instance, many jobs have their own lexicons and patterns of speech. Twain himself spent part of his early manhood as a riverboat pilot – and put his knowledge to good use in the above-mentioned *Huckleberry Finn* – and he also worked as a printer's apprentice, miner, prospector and reporter. Even if you have not pursued such a vivid range of careers, you may still watch and listen to auctioneers, butchers, estate agents, hairdressers, dog-walkers, mechanics – or even, as Twain did, undertakers, as you will see below.

Writing Exercise: Use a Spy Notebook

Take your writer's notebook to a place where you do not normally go, but to which you feel drawn: a horse fair, for instance, or a wrestling match, street market, bowling alley or fashionable nightclub. Transcribe all the conversations that you can, as exactly as you can, using phonetic spelling wherever possible.

The short story is a refined and developed form that, to be successful, demands maximum expertise (for a fuller examination of its history and potential, read Chapter 8, Tom Vowler's 'What Is a Short Story?'). It is also an excellent place for you to begin: long enough for you to build your characters, try out different plots, and uncover that slant on experience and way of describing it that will distinguish your work from everyone else's: in other words, to experiment with voice.

Point of view is a literary term for the lens through which your reader looks at the world you create and is fully covered in Chapter 9, 'Point of View'. When considering how best to develop your voice, you will need to decide on who is telling your story. Basically, your choice is between a *character-narrator* and writing in the third person.

First-Person Character-Narrator

If one of your characters is telling the story, you are committed to writing in either the first person or, very unusually, the second person.

Frank O'Connor speaks of the narrowness and 'hysterical clarity'[7] of a child's view of the world. If you want to hone your narrative skills, you might experiment by adopting a child's voice: a popular choice amongst postmodern writers because of the child's fragmented view of the world: its half-comprehending vision can easily be pushed to an extreme of subjectivity. Also, it can reflect our sense of ourselves in a complex, global society in which we are privy to only a fraction of the story.

Here is the opening of Donna Tartt's 'The Ambush',[8] which deals with a child's trauma over his father's violent death, the narrator's estrangement from her family, and adult inability to cope with prejudice and grief. The story is narrated by eight-year-old Evie:

> Before I met Tim – who, in spite of everything I'm going to tell you, would be my best friend for the next four or five years – my mother warned me on the way over to his grandmother's house that I had to be nice to him. 'I mean it, Evie. And don't mention his father.'
>
> 'Why?' I said. I was expecting to hear: *Because his parents are divorced.* (This was why I had to be nice to John Kendrick, who I couldn't stand.)
>
> 'Because,' my mother said, 'Tim's father was killed in Vietnam.'
>
> 'Did he get shot?'
>
> 'I don't know,' said my mother. 'And don't you ask him.'

Evie is in the process of learning – and failing to learn – adult codes. Note that her use of the second person ('you') signals an ingenuous directness and emphasises her storytelling role. As she is looking back over at least four or five years, it seems unlikely that she would remember the dialogue. No matter. The opening plants a powerful hook. Will she upset Tim by asking about his father? If so, how will he respond? (The story proceeds to turn the question on its head.) Note the slight but predictable flaw in the grammar ('*whom* I couldn't stand' would make Evie sound pretentious) and also the mention, albeit bracketed, of the barely relevant John Kendrick – Evie is naïvely confident of our interest.

In the narrative that follows, Tartt excludes crucial information, asking her reader to stay alert to clues. It is we and not the child-narrator who anticipate the crisis. But don't be deceived by an 'I' narrator's apparent openness and naïvety. Every effective teller of tales is unreliable to an extent, with a strongly angled vision and only a partial grip on their world, elements pushed to an extreme in, for instance, Mark Haddon's *The Curious Incident of the Dog in the Night-Time* and Nathan Filer's *The Shock of the Fall*.

Writing Exercise: The Unreliable Narrator

Write a story, or a section of a story, in which the teller, though not lying, misses some of the implications of what is said and done around her, while hearing and seeing those words and events in vivid detail.

As in Donna Tartt's story, the first-person narrator is usually the protagonist. But you might also consider writing what is known as *skaz* (from the Russian 'skazat', which means 'to tell'). Here the narrator is not always the central character and indeed can interrupt the action to comment on the protagonist's behaviour. As its name suggests, *skaz* draws on some of the qualities of an oral performance – for instance, using the vernacular, addressing the reader directly or meandering off at a tangent – and can therefore *seem* improvised or unedited. Famous examples include

Toni Morrison's *Jazz*, Patrick McCabe's *The Butcher Boy* and DBC Pierre's *Vernon God Little*, all of which, despite their spontaneous air, are, of course, artfully written novels.

When you step back and let your character 'speak' for herself, you may find the voice that will make your story distinctive and set it apart from the rest. Here is an extract from the American writer Mark Twain's short story, 'The Undertaker's Chat',[9] narrated not by the central character but by the eponymous undertaker, in which a potential client rehearses his own funeral.

> He had me measure him and take a whole raft of directions; then he had a minister stand up behind a long box with a tablecloth over it and read his funeral sermon, saying 'Angcore, angcore!' at the good places, and making him scratch out every bit of brag about him, and all the hifa-lutin; and then he made them trot out the choir so's he could help them pick out the tunes for the occasion, and he got them to sing 'Pop Goes the Weasel,' because he'd always liked that tune when he was downhearted, and solemn music made him sad; and when they sung that with tears in their eyes (because they all loved him), and his relations grieving around, he just laid there as happy as a bug, and trying to beat time and showing all over how much he enjoyed it; and presently he got worked up and excited; and tried to join in, for mind you he was pretty proud of his abilities in the singing line; but the first time he opened his mouth and was just going to spread himself, his breath took a walk. I never see a man snuffed out so sudden.

Note the word 'chat' in the title, prefiguring orality and also the story's confiding, intimate tone. The lexicon, as often in *skaz,* is colloquial ('a whole raft'; 'all the highfalutin'; 'happy as a bug') and contains dialogue such as 'Angcore, angcore', which by its phonetic transcription draws the reader's attention to the mispronounced French. But for all its relaxed, down-home tone and seemingly naïve air, this artful story strongly promotes traditional southern rural values: a modest approach to oneself and one's achievements; the importance of community; a dislike of pretension and sceptical take on churchy solemnity.

Writing Exercise: An Experiment with Style

Reread your transcript from the spy notebook exercise above, then write it out again. This time, experiment with spelling. How does it look, for example, if you miss the last letter of present participles (for example, *missin'* or even *missin*); or use *me* instead of *my*, or a grammatically incorrect verb form (such as *ain't* or *innit*)? Or spell some words phonetically? Or incorporate dialect words (such as *jigger*); or slang (like *chav*)? Or words from an invented argot, as does Anthony Burgess in *Clockwork Orange*? Do short sentences suit your purpose? Or ones without a main verb? Does it weaken or strengthen your style if you use the above sparingly or even inconsistently?

Angels and Demons

'Man is least himself when he talks in his own person,' says Gilbert in Oscar Wilde's *The Critic as Artist*.[10] 'Give him a mask and he will tell you the truth.' In other words, we all have angels and demons under our skin, alter egos waiting to be tapped, and the farther they are from your everyday persona, the likelier they are to free our imaginations and lessen our inhibitions. Why not copy the above-mentioned authors and use a first-person narrative to help yourself find a voice dramatically different from your own everyday speaking voice?

You may, if you wish, portray the person you feel you might have been in a different situation, of another gender, epoch, religion or nationality; or else your past, outgrown or fantasy self; or one you suppress, or hide from family and friends. For instance, in his famous short story, 'The Dead',[11] the Irish writer James Joyce created, in Gabriel, one of his most convincing characters: a powerful version of the man that he, Joyce, might have become had he remained in Dublin. And Hilary Mantel says that Alison, the central character of her novel *Beyond Black*,[12] was what she could have been if education hadn't intervened.

Second-Person Character-Narrator

You shrugged off your dress without stopping to close the curtains, and let it slither silkily to the floor. Wearing only your leopard skin thong, you flopped on to my futon and took a last swig from my bottle of

Thunderbird. Then you passed out with your smouldering spliff still clamped between your fingers.

Although its rarity lends freshness, and is arresting, this is a difficult voice to sustain while telling a story of any length, especially one involving a lot of action and dialogue. But you could always read Jamaica Kincaid's 'Girl'[13] (which is also a fine example of *skaz*), in which the story's introduction, climax and resolution are all created through the mother-speaker's rhetoric, as is the character of the daughter whom she is haranguing.

Third-Person Narrator

Technically, if you choose this point of view, you will be writing as an author-narrator, not as a character-narrator – but this need not lessen the distinctiveness of your voice. The following extract from James Kelman's original and inventive *How Late It Was, How Late* can be seen as an extreme example of the third-person limited:

> He was fucking dying when he woke up the first time. He didnay know where the fuck he was. He looked about, he was on a floor and it smelled of pish, it was in his nostrils, and his chin was soaking wet and all round the sides of his mouth and like snotters from his nose, fucking blood maybe, fucking hell man, fucking sore.[14]

Here the authorial voice remains almost undetectable. But you can, if you wish, allow yourself more latitude, moving outside your character when you wish to describe her appearance and responses. Note how the italicised sentence in the passage below helps modulate between the inner and outer:

> The cloud was lowering itself for a downpour. *Boris felt his forehead tighten, as though an inner machine was winching up the skin.* He raised a grubby hand and rubbed his brow. With his gaunt face framed by a hacked-off haircut, he looked like a missing person in *The Big Issue,* not a prosperous barrister of twenty years' standing with a flat in Southampton Row and a farmhouse in the Dordogne.[15]

Writing Exercise: Swapping Voices

Write a first-person account of a commonplace scene in your life – at work or a family gathering – keeping as close as possible to your character's everyday speaking voice. Include an implicit conflict, a detail that she alone would notice, and at least one feeling that she would usually hide.

Now rewrite the scene in the third person, from the viewpoint(s) of one or more imagined persons of a different class, gender, age or nationality to yours. Next, analyse the results sentence by sentence, deciding on each one's degree of 'psychic distance' between your characters and your authorial voice. Are you equally intimate with both/all? How do you draw back – or go closer? How does this alter your novel's 'temperature'?

If you wish to pull back even further, and maintain an even greater distance between you and your characters, you may always deploy the third-person omniscient, less popular now than in Victorian times, but possibly making a comeback. This point of view does not mean lapsing into a variant of your everyday speaking voice. Your omniscient narrator's voice may diverge sharply from yours and be every bit as distinctive as a first-person voice – as you will see from the examples in Chapter 9 from stories by Guy de Maupassant, Flannery O'Connor and Joyce Carol Oates. Like many wonderful texts written from all points of view, these stories help bring out the writers' angels and demons. Read them, and bring out your own.

1,500-Word Story Project

People with Problems

The more you study the craft of fiction, the more you feel burdened when you sit down to write. (See Chapter 2: 'Writers' Habits'.) As you face the blank screen, you may well be wondering how on earth you are going to remember everything you now in theory know. You may be flapping about whether you will be able to balance consistent use of limited third-person viewpoint with steadily rising plot and indirect dialogue – and what was that important tip Helen Newall had for creating convincing characters?

Don't fret about any of what you've been studying. Just trust yourself to remember what you need to remember, even if you can't consciously bring it to mind. Don't forget your unconscious mind is at work all the time and it's in the nature of the unconscious that you aren't aware of what it's up to. You will absorb all you need to absorb from studying the craft of fiction.

For this story, here are three sites you can use to inspire a story.

Every week, the Saturday magazine of *The Guardian* has a feature called 'Experience': www.theguardian.com/lifeandstyle/series/experience. Here, members of the public who have distinguished themselves in some way or other describe a typical day, from waking up to going to sleep. Go online and look at some examples in the archive. Choose one and write a short story inspired by it. Instead of stealing the author of the piece and making them your viewpoint, use the most colourful of the teachers you had at school.

The *New York Times Magazine* runs a feature called 'The Ethicist': www.nytimes.com/column/the-ethicist. This does what it says on the proverbial: a reader writes in with an ethical problem and a writer from the *Magazine* suggests a solution. Take a look at the archive and see if you can find one that intrigues you. Make it the basis of your 1,500-word story.

The *Huffington Post* has a section called 'What's Working', which runs features about people who come up with solutions to contemporary challenges: www.huffingtonpost.co.uk/news/whats-working/. Just now, I can see one about the 50 per cent rise in recorded hate crimes after the referendum that decided to take the UK out of the European Union. You could use one of these features as inspiration for your story, perhaps focusing on the problem rather than the site's recorded solution to it.

For this story project, focus on rewriting and see how much you've learned from the chapter on redrafting. Redraft it *a lot*. Don't forget to write a 500-word reflection, with a bibliography of texts that have informed the creative work.

Notes

1   Josip Novakovich, *Fiction Writer's Workshop* (Cincinnati: Story Press, 1995), p 201.
2   Liverpool WowFest, 7 May 2017.
3   Novakovich, *Fiction Writer's Workshop*, p 202.

4   Gerard Manley Hopkins, 'Pied Beauty' in *Poetry and Prose* (London: Everyman, 1998), p 48.
5   Thomas H. Johnson (ed.), *The Complete Poems of Emily Dickinson* (London: Faber and Faber, 1975), p 506.
6   Frank O'Connor, *The Lonely Voice: A Study of the Short Story* (London: Macmillan, 1993), p 72.
7   O'Connor, *The Lonely Voice*, p 57.
8   *The Guardian Weekend*, 25 June 2005, pp 17–21.
9   Mark Twain, *Sketches New and Old* (Kindle edition).
10 Oscar Wilde, *The Critic as Artist: With Some Remarks on the Importance of Doing Nothing and Discussing Everything* (Los Angeles: Sun & Moon Books, 1997), p 41.
11 Harry Levin (ed.), *The Essential James Joyce* (London: Triad Grafton, 1988), pp 138–73.
12 Hilary Mantel, *Beyond Black* (London: Fourth Estate, 2010).
13 Tobias Wolff (ed.), *The Vintage Book of Contemporary American Short Stories* (London: Vintage, 1995), pp 312–13.
14 James Kelman, *How Late It Was, How Late* (London: Vintage, 1998).
15 Kelman, *How Late It Was*.

Part III

How to Redraft

18

Redrafting

Redrafting is where you get down to the nitty-gritty. Your first draft is the raw material, and from it you are going to sculpt a thing of beauty and truth. In a sense, with a first draft you have assembled the resources from which you are going to build the finished item. You probably won't need all these resources, and many of them won't initially be up to the task they need to perform. As Tom Wolfe says, 'You go to bed every night thinking that you've written the most brilliant passage ever done which somehow the next day you realise is sheer drivel.'[1] But that's okay. You can make the resources you've assembled better. If you can't, you can get rid of them and generate some new material.

Flaubert, who redrafted his writing obsessively, said, 'It's never finished; there is always something to do over',[2] and Tolstoy, Joyce and Fitzgerald kept reworking right through until the printing presses were rolling. (And sometimes beyond.) More recently, Raymond Carver claimed to go up as far as thirty drafts and never to do fewer than ten. The probability is you're going to spend an awful lot more time redrafting than composing.

When you redraft, you look at what you've written with a view to improving and developing it. That involves revising and remaking the most significant aspects of the story: plot, character, narrative tension, structure, the way you handle time, tone. Here you improve the larger elements of the story; you work above line level or, more accurately, below the surface. Macro-editing. The other side, micro-editing, involves line-level tasks: vocabulary choices, accuracy, concision, syntax, sentences, rhythm, paragraphs. Macro-editing may be about the protagonist you originally thought would return home ending up in Australia, while micro-editing may be moving a conjunction, wondering how the removal of a present participle might improve a sentence's effectiveness, altering the syntax. Whether you're macro- or micro-editing, the process involves looking at the work and seeing what it says to you.

In redrafting, you're aiming to finish off what you've started: complete the work. In this sense, you are trying to perfect something. Before we get down to considering how best to pursue that aim, let's note at the start that it isn't possible. You will spend your life trying to perfect what you've created, but you never will. Bob Dylan has a couplet about how everything will be different when he paints his masterpiece. You can forget that. Each finished work will always in the end fall far short of the form you imagined it taking when you first conceived it. So bear in mind that there's only so much you ought to do in the way of perfecting a story, and recognise that each new work you begin offers you a further opportunity to develop your craft, to try again to produce your masterpiece. There comes a point in the redrafting of everything you write when you will benefit from stopping and moving on to your next story.

Before you set in to redraft, you need something to work on: a first draft. To get as far as that, follow the spirit of Natalie Goldberg's 'Rules of Writing Practice' and worry about what you write later – much later. If you start to criticise what you are writing while you are writing it, you are unlikely to get far. Cut yourself some slack and ignore your inner critic until you have something finished. Writer first, editor second.

Redrafting will be made a little easier if you remember what we looked at in Chapter 1: 'How a Writer Works' – that when you're creating something, you want to prioritise the workings of your unconscious mind. It's when you have a first draft that you want to prioritise those of the conscious mind. If you put the cart before the horse in this respect, you will severely undermine your efforts and reduce your chances of producing the short story that is there waiting to come out of you. Trust yourself. You're a talented writer and can produce a first draft with the potential to be excellent. You're also a skilled rewriter and can make your first draft fulfil its potential – once it's on the page. You need distance and perspective to redraft, and you cannot have that while you are producing a first draft, so leave it alone until that hard-won first draft is complete. Otherwise you may never get as far as completing a first draft.

When you have a holiday, you take a break from your life and move both physically and metaphorically some distance from it. 'The greater the distance, the clearer the view.' W.G. Sebald wrote. 'One sees the tiniest details with the utmost clarity.'³ Distance lends perspective. When you're in the forest you can't see the wood for the trees, but if you leave the woods and stand on a hill, you may be able to see the full picture. This is the essence of redrafting. You need distance to gain perspective, and distance will always involve time. Many writers suggest putting your work away and leaving it alone for weeks or months.

Partly this requires you to distance yourself from your project, but you also need to leave the unconscious mind to go to work on what you have produced. Writing fiction involves composing and redrafting, which leads in turn to more composing and more redrafting. It's a cyclical activity. You leave your draft alone for some time and, even if you scarcely ever think of it, your unconscious mulls it over. You tap the unconscious's thoughts about the draft and then apply your conscious mind to them, weighing them up, judging their efficacy to see what you can use to develop the story – and you redraft it. And after that, you repeat this cycle.

In short, the time to redraft is not when you are producing the first draft, nor when you have finished the first draft, but rather some time weeks or months afterwards.

Redrafting, when you get to it, involves giving all of your attention to an existing draft and reflecting on how you may improve and develop it. The essence of redrafting is studying what you have written and thinking about it and deciding what needs to be done. All redrafting activity can be reduced to these three words: attention, reflection and revision. Pay attention to the story draft, reflect on what you see there and revise it. Everything you do in the process has the aim of making your story what it should be.

Writing Burst

- Put 'Three Reasons: Three Colours: Blue' in your search engine and use this film clip as your prompt.

Methods

To redraft effectively, you will need to print off the story, read it and annotate it. Paper and pen. For whatever reason – and maybe it's just because we live in a physical reality and a document on a computer screen isn't quite physical – it's vastly more effective if you redraft from a print-off. I'll say it again: annotate a print-off. Being careful not to do a line-level rewrite just yet, write your thoughts in the margin. And get a notebook and use it for reflecting about your drafts. Yes, reflect in writing. Remember that E.M. Forster quotation earlier in this book? 'How do I know what I think until I see what I say?' Thoughts are vague and unformed until they are expressed, and your thoughts as you redraft are best expressed in writing. Reflect in writing.

Printing off is also a practical way of looking at structure or chronology. You can take the printed story, cut it up into its constituent sections and lay them out on the floor, which will give you an overview of the whole thing, an aerial shot. On-screen, this isn't possible. On the screen, all you can see is a few hundred words at a time. To see the big picture, you need the parts of the story spread out in front of you. It helps you think about how all the elements are working together, and it shows you what happens when you take a passage, a scene or a section and move it. (Which you may need to do.) You can then see the part you've moved in its new context and contemplate the effect that has on the rest of the story.

Completing a piece of writing takes much longer than you think. In a swift Facebook survey of my writer friends yesterday, one said he commonly goes through three or four drafts; a couple said eight; one said ten or more; one at least twelve; and one 'tons'. John Gardner – frequently referenced in this book – taught Raymond Carver, who describes Gardner's passion, and the reasons for it, here:

> For short story writers in his class, the requirement was one story, ten to fifteen pages in length … The kicker was that this one short story might have to be revised ten times in the course of the semester for Gardner to be satisfied with it. It was a basic tenet of his that a writer found what he wanted to say in the on-going process of seeing what he'd said. And

this seeing, or seeing more clearly, came about through revision. He *believed* in revision, endless revision; it was something very close to his heart and something he felt was vital for writers, at whatever stage of their development.[4]

You don't want to see your work published and read it and cringe, or give a reading and discover mid-sentence that you haven't expressed yourself as well as you might have and be forced to revise it while you're in mid-flow. (Reader, I have.) For these and more reasons, write, step back, reread, redraft, step back, reread, redraft, step back, reread, redraft and so on.

Jenn Ashworth is perhaps best known for her novels – as I write, one of them, *Fell*, has just been published to considerable acclaim – but she is a gifted short story writer too, as you'll see if you go to her website and check out the *Curious Tales* series. When Jenn came in to speak to a group of my students, she recommended a memorable redrafting technique: be your own triage nurse. Prioritise when you're editing. Consider the larger matters first. The plot, the characters, the setting, the load-bearing structure. Don't get sidetracked by undertaking the micro-editing chores too soon. Why? Because if you've got something wrong at the macro level, the likelihood is that many of the sentences you redraft will end up in the bin. Get the big stuff right first and leave the fine details until you have done that.

On that same visit, Jenn also suggested to my students that when redrafting they should project-manage. She recommended having a purpose in each redrafting session: identifying what you want to achieve, but also looking at how much time you have available and cutting your cloth accordingly. If you've only got half an hour, set yourself a goal that can be achieved in that short time-frame – improving dialogue in one scene, perhaps, or adding sensory detail in another. If a whole morning is available, you might identify your goal as studying your story to see if it's coherent and consistent in tone, continuity (does the protagonist's lover have brown hair at the beginning and black at another time?) and control of viewpoint. If you decide on a task that fits the time available to you, you'll have more chance of achieving what you set out to do and less chance of feeling frustrated at not completing all the things you needed to.

In order to look carefully enough at a piece you've written, you will need to read slowly. Everything in life – everything! – is about the amount of attention you can give, and this is certainly the case when you are trying to look at your work with a view to improving it. Read slowly.

Redraft in short bursts. Different writers will be able to concentrate objectively for different lengths of time, but I'd say redraft for forty-five minutes and then, if you can, don't come back to do more until the next day. It doesn't take much redrafting before you begin to lose your perspective. When you're no longer detached enough from the draft, leave it alone and come back to it when you may be.

First, last and always, take your draft out for a walk. Make that a daily walk and always keep a phone or a notebook to record your every thought. In just the same way as ideas for a new piece of writing come from the unconscious mind (see Chapter 1: 'How a Writer Works'), so too do ideas about how to develop and complete it. Don't let a single thought escape you. Whenever one comes – walking, mopping the floor, driving a distance, staring out of the window – make sure you record it. Not every thought will be pure gold and you won't use all of them, but if you collect them all you will have a storehouse of ideas about your drafts and you can select those that count.

Redrafting Beneath the Surface

Writing fiction, according to James N. Frey, is a hundred times more difficult than you think it is 'because a writer has a damn hard time evaluating what he has written, and unless he knows the strengths and weaknesses of a manuscript it will not be possible to turn a draft into a finished piece of work'.[5] This is a large part of the challenge you face.

Cutting Out, Putting In and Leaving In

Cutting out and putting in covers most of what you do when redrafting. How do you judge what to take out? George V. Higgins has this advice: 'It is necessary to remember at all times, especially when most frustrated and cranky, that the writer is always at the mercy of his story.'[6] I've said elsewhere in this book that it often feels as if the story already exists, on the far side of consciousness, in another world, an ideal version of the story you are writing. It is in this way that you are at the mercy of your story. You are straining with all your might to try to get down on paper the story you can hear from the other side, and that listening process will help you decide what to cut.

When you're revising your story, one of the important things to consider is what to include in it. To do this, you need a clear understanding of what it's actually about, what it concerns. If you know what your story is about, you know what to leave in, what to take out and what to add. 'The writer', John Gardner says, 'sharpens and clarifies his ideas, or finds out exactly what it is that he must say, testing his beliefs against reality as the story represents it, by examining every element in the story for its possible implications with regard to his theme.'[7] So if you're Alice Munro revising 'The Jack Randa Hotel', a story about a Canadian woman pursuing her estranged husband to Australia, and you find in your first draft twelve pages about eighteenth-century French garden design, you will know what to do.

Chronology

Some of what you do in revising your work is reordering. 'I wrote and rewrote sections and moved them around until I had what I wanted,' is the way Roddy Doyle describes the process.[8]

When I'm revising, I spend a good deal of time moving around bits of text of various sizes. Low-level reordering might consist of breaking up bits of information that appear all at once at the start of a story. In the first draft, I might have included a fair bit of detail about, say, the petrol station where the story was set. Second time through, I would hopefully spot that the level of description involved stops the story advancing. An easy way round this is to break this block of description down into little details and drop them in later in the story, sprinkled here and there as it progresses.

Higher-level reordering might arise because, when I get some distance and perspective on my first draft, I see that the scene where the narrator realises that his lover has been lying to him should come at a completely different point in the story. Similarly, I might cut a whole scene at some stage in the writing. A couple of weeks later, it might become apparent that this scene, with a nip and a tuck, will fit perfectly ten pages away from its original position. (See also Chapter 23: 'Crossing Timelines and Breaking Rules'.)

Developing Your Characters

An important redrafting task is ensuring that your characters and situations are fully realised. As you read your writing and rewriting, you will learn more about your characters, and you should: 'You can never know enough about your characters,'[9] Somerset Maugham says. You might begin this process by looking at a character you've sketched out in a first draft and ask yourself a few simple questions.

* Have you got the most effective viewpoint character? Sometimes a story will fall into place when you make the decision to change to a different viewpoint character.
* What is the function of a particular character?
* What are their characteristics?
* What would they do? What wouldn't they do?
* What would they have in their homes? How would they dress? What would they eat?
* What would they say that one of the other characters never would?

Struggling to imagine himself in the shoes of a young woman who robs a bank, Andre Dubus had a moment of illumination:

> I could not get inside of her, become her. Then one day or night I decided to try a different approach. I told myself that next day at the desk I would not leave a sentence until I knew precisely what Anna was feeling. I told myself that even if I wrote only fifty words, I would stay with this …
>
> At my desk next morning I held my pen and hunched my shoulders and leaned my head down, physically trying to look more deeply into the page of the notebook. I did this for only a moment before writing, as a batter takes a practice swing while he waits in the on-deck circle. In that moment I began what I call vertical writing, rather than horizontal. I had

never before thought in these terms. But for years I had been writing horizontally, trying to move forward (those five pages); now I would try to move down, as deeply as I could.[10]

Deepening your understanding of your characters may be achieved in part through research. (What does she like eating? Doing? Watching? Wearing?) You also learn much of what you need to know about a character through the first composition phase; a character grows as you write a story and again as you reread and redraft. Partly, this growth comes about through the greater understanding you derive from spending time with them, living with them, but the process will often involve adapting them. The story, as it grows, may require a character to do something, and that in turn may necessitate a rethink. In a story of mine, a plot hole could be solved if Caitlin, who liked a drink, liked a drink even more. I needed her to let slip a secret and one way of doing this was to accentuate her drinking, so that when she spilled the beans it could be explained by her being drunk. Going back and playing up that aspect of her character solved my plot hole. Rethinking a character had solved my problem.

The process of creating characters snowballs, because what you have down in each successive draft will lead you to new conclusions about them. As you get to know your characters better, you will sometimes be struck by inconsistencies in your draft. You come to that section where Tori tries to unwind with a glass of wine and it occurs to you that unwinding with a peppermint tea would really be more consistent with her personality. You get to know characters better the longer they have been living in your mind, but also through the evidence of their characteristics recorded in each successive draft of the fiction. Your characters develop not only in your mind and in your first draft; they will continue to evolve as you contemplate each draft and develop it. They arrive not in one draft, but through many.

Character and Plot

It is from your characters that your plot will grow. You have probably read many times the old saw that character is plot. Fortunately, when it comes to plot, none of us is doomed to settle for our first attempt. When we revise, and come to understand character and plot better – but especially character – we can make our plots stronger. 'When you begin to dwell on why he or she acted in this particular way,' William Kennedy says, '– that is what moves you forward to the next page.'

A further aspect of the symbiotic relationship between character and plot is the dramatic quality of your characters. If you're aiming to prioritise drama in your fiction, when you come to revise you may want to check that your characters are somewhat exaggerated for dramatic effect. 'Are your major characters bigger than life?' is Jack Bickham's challenge. 'Are you sure you haven't fallen into the trap of writing about average people in average situations? That can be deadly dull.'[11] I've been criticised for burying both character and plot in domesticity. You may be guilty of the same.

Relationships Between Characters

You might find your fiction benefits from looking at the dynamics of the relationships in it. Are your characters sufficiently different from one another? Watson's plodding consistency and placid nature acts as the perfect foil for Holmes' mercurial genius. Have you failed to use one character as a counterpoint to the other when the opportunity was there? If so, it's not too late. As you redraft and grow in your knowledge of your characters, you can delineate them more boldly, differentiating one from the other ever more clearly, and, ideally, make what distinguishes one character from the other a source of conflict. Jo is good with money to the point of being tight-fisted, whereas her partner Dan is open-handed, extravagant in every way. The tension between these two personality types will generate useful conflict, which is something that can be developed as you revise. It may even be introduced at the revising stage.

Dialogue

As you know, dialogue is close to being the best opportunity you have to reveal character. What characters say and the way they say it, and, indeed, what they don't say, all show the reader who they are and generate the conflict that makes a story. When you come to revise, there are a few aspects of your dialogue writing that may need checking.

Less is more (I've said it before). Many writers, once they learn that it is a thing you can use in fiction and that using it is a good idea, fall into the trap of writing dialogue that is baggy and overlong, so part of the job when you're looking at early-draft dialogue is to see how much of it you can manage without. In fact, whether we're starting out or have been at it for years, it's all too easy to include too much dialogue in a first draft; often too much first-draft dialogue is chaff that you will need to remove.

I hope Chapter 12: 'Dialogue' will help you redraft, but here are a few suggestions about how to hone your dialogue. Look especially for speeches with insufficient dramatic tension. The central purpose of dialogue – the central purpose of everything in fiction – is to move the story on. For a start on this, you can lose all the dead things we say, greetings and salutations, those phrases when the dialogue is simply treading water. Keep an eye out, too, for dialogue that is too direct. It's potent and effective when characters say one thing which readers clearly understand to mean another.

Avoid speeches designed to deliver background information, or characters explaining a situation or explaining what just happened. Dialogue that explains or is weighed down with exposition will lose you readers, for all the reasons that exposition can be damaging. (See Chapter 13: 'Scenes'.)

Make sure that what your characters say to each other communicates who they are. A handy tip when redrafting dialogue is to see if a given speech could have been said by another character. If it could, then it isn't revealing character as much as it might. In revising your dialogue, you will regularly find speeches you've given to one character which would be more appropriate for another character to say. When you spot these, move them and sharpen your dialogue. Half of the readers' pleasure in any narrative is gaining such an understanding of character that they can think, 'Yes, that's exactly what that character would say.'

Finally, remember what it is that you want the reader to take in: that which is said. So make sure as far as it is possible that you remove everything around speech that clutters and distracts. Lose any speech tags readers can manage without. Remove speech tags where the verb you've chosen will draw attention to itself ('I'm here,' she proclaimed). Revise any speech tags where you've used a verb that isn't a speaking one

('I know,' she smirked). Or when the speech tag isn't possible ('Get out of here,' she frowned). Or, in almost any instance, when the speech tag is used with an adverb to try to convey to the reader the tone of the speech ('I'll have that, thank you,' she said sardonically).

Openings

Whether they are of stories, sections or scenes, openings are crucial. (Remember that sections and scenes are not necessarily the same thing.) Walk into Waterstones, Angus & Robertson or Barnes & Noble and you will see the fiction section heaving with new releases. In the UK alone, 4,000 new books are published *each week*. Not all of them are short story collections, not by any means, but the short story is an increasingly popular form. As well as reading collections and anthologies, lovers of the short story (you) will read online literary magazines. For readers, the sea is not short of fish, so if you fail to snare them early on, they will simply go elsewhere. I know I do. Spend some time getting your openings right. (Chapter 13: 'Scenes' has some advice about this.)

Conflict and Drama

One constant consideration when you revise should be examining the quality of the drama. 'Never forget, something must happen!' Barnaby Conrad warns. 'A lot of beginning writers – and too many advanced ones – often forget that there is no drama without conflict.'[12] Drama is life with the dull parts left out. It's all too easy to leave them in. Remember Scott Fitzgerald and chewing with no gum? If so, you can in your second draft remove the dull parts, cut the dreariness that hangs like a millstone on the neck of your story and find some gum to chew with.

But maybe neither of these is your problem. Maybe you have left the dull parts out and you have achieved the conflict necessary to drama. Is it the right kind of conflict, though? Remember James N. Frey's breakdown of the three kinds of conflict (in Chapter 11: 'Plot')? As you revise your story, you will want to make sure that your conflict isn't static or jumping. Steadily rising conflict, brothers and sisters. Steadily rising conflict.

Is the conflict clear? It's easy for you to convey to your readers something different from your own understanding of it. Your intention may be that the source of conflict in your story is Mary's distrust of Archie – he has a wandering eye – but the reader is left with the impression that it has to do with their differing views on parenting. As far as you are able to, it's worth making sure you have communicated with sufficient boldness just what the conflict is and whom it's between. I say 'as far as you're able to' because the big problem in writing fiction is putting yourself in the reader's shoes. It's impossible. (I have a colleague who says he can, but I think he's fooling himself.) You might want to have a friend look at your story and tell you what they think the conflict is.

Action

Through characters and situations, you've managed to build in conflict, but does it result in action? In any story, however short, action is essential. You may be writing an old-fashioned story with a beginning, middle and end. You may be writing a story in which character and situation are revealed, where there's a middle, but not necessarily a beginning or an ending. Whatever kind of story you write, things have to happen.

If we think in terms of the simple linear plot, has your character kept pursuing her goal, has she taken action to overcome the obstacles impeding her progress to that goal? In this respect, there are a couple of ways you can go wrong.

If you have made readers spend any length of time in interior monologue mode, you will have frozen the action. Not only that, but living inside the character's consciousness for any length of time deprives readers of oxygen and eventually makes them lose the will to live, let alone continue reading. You can also impede the action through static description: stopping to describe someone or something.

In *Annie Hall*, Woody Allen tells Diane Keaton that a relationship is like a shark: it dies if it doesn't constantly move forward. 'I think what we've got on our hands', he adds, 'is a dead shark.' A story, like a shark, should always be moving forward. Your description needs to be on the hoof, incorporated into action and dialogue. Describe during action and dialogue – within the same sentence. Your story can and will pause some of the time, but if you want to retain the reader engagement you've built up, it won't pause for long. 'Time has to move,' says Paul Magrs. 'Keep it moving and fold all the info we need into the mix.'[13] When you come to revise, make sure your shark isn't floating face up in the water.

Characters act. In Chekhov's 'The Lady with the Lapdog', which you might classify as a story where a character and a situation are revealed, a story that lacks the drama and plotting of, say, one of Stephen King's, the characters still act, and in dramatic ways. Gurov seduces Anna Sergeyevna. She leaves him, intending never to see him again. Later in the story, they run into each other and again she intends never to see him. But then she gives in and they carry on with their affair. Whether your story is Chekhovian (and almost every literary story in the past hundred years is) or a miniature thriller, characters act. Given that, when you revise the characters in your story you might ask yourself if they are sufficiently proactive.

Writing Burst
- They made us wait in this shabby little room.

Foreshadowing

As you redraft, you may find an important element late in the story which it would be effective to foreshadow earlier – and you may choose to do that.

In *The Artful Edit*, Susan Bell identifies four separate points in *Gatsby* where Fitzgerald foreshadows the final, fatal car crash. Readers will barely register them at a conscious level, but these plants will have had an unconscious effect that makes what they foreshadow more potent.

The four points in the story that foreshadow the crash at the end of *Gatsby* are:

- when a car drives into a ditch at the end of the first party at Gatsby's
- the conversation between Nick and Jordan soon afterwards in which he tells her she's a rotten driver
- the party-goer who was so drunk at the party that somebody drove right over his hand

* Nick, bantering with Daisy early in the book and telling her that people in Chicago miss her so much that all the cars have the left rear wheel painted black as a sign of their mourning.

It's likely that one or two of these plants about what is to come were there at first-draft stage – the unconscious has a way of creating patterns like that – but you can bet that Fitzgerald spotted the pattern and developed it by writing in further foreshadowing.

Redrafting at Surface Level

At this point, you have for the moment finished with the aspects of a story that are beneath the words on the page. You've looked at the infrastructure, the chassis, the engine – whatever image you want to use for redrafting beneath the story's surface. You'll come back to it, of course, with each successive draft, but now you can set it aside as you look at the story at paragraph, line and word level. And remember Jenn Ashworth's advice, summarised above. If you've got something wrong at the macro level, the likelihood is that many sentences and whole paragraphs will end up in the bin. Beneath the surface first, on the surface second.

Before we look at some aspects of micro-editing, here's a strategy for it that helps no end. More writers commend this than actually practise it, I suspect, but hearing your work will facilitate line-level redrafting. You may have a friend who will read your work out for you, or listen to you read it out. Either way, when listening to it read or hearing yourself read it you will notice much that you won't see on the page. Rhythm and syntax, for example. Another way to achieve this is to record yourself reading the draft and then listen carefully to it. You will notice details that need work that you never would if all you did when revising was to look at the words.

Editing

'Every word is there for a reason,' according to Jerzy Kosinski, author of *Being There*, 'and if not, I cut it out.' Like Kosinski, when you edit you may well be stripping the clutter from your sentences so that the information you are communicating can go directly from your mind to the readers. An awful lot of what you do when you edit is remove the extraneous – words, phrases, sentences, passages. (See Chapter 16: 'Style'.) In my own work, the lion's share of editing has to do with cutting flab and altering syntax. In first drafts, I have a tendency to write baggy sentences and assemble them in the wrong order. I also go all around the houses to make my point. If you do too, your job as editor is to find and remove the flab, the botched syntax and the rambling.

Another perennial problem for me is almost the opposite: telescoping in on detail that doesn't warrant it. In cinematic terms, what I'm talking about is the close-up on something insufficiently significant. Every good writer is born with or develops the gift of noticing the world in the smallest detail – of paying close attention – but in my own work and in a lot of the student work I read, the author sometimes zooms in on details that don't merit it. When you edit, you will need to remove any focus on the insignificant.

Pruning

A key redrafting task is removing filler and flab, excising the words your sentences don't need, avoiding throwing in everything and the kitchen sink. When you've packed too much information into a sentence, remove the clutter. Why? Because when you overload your writing, readers won't know what they are meant to notice. But if you decide that you do need everything in the potentially cumbersome sentence, break it up into shorter, simpler ones. (For a more in-depth rationale of this, and a perfect example take a look at Chekhov's illustration in Chapter 16: 'Style'.)

Refining

Some editing tasks have to do with honing the language so that the meaning is clearer, but that isn't the only surface-level redrafting task.

Jonathan Swift's definition – 'Proper words in proper places make the true definition of style' – includes the refining and reordering, but it may also indicate that we refine and reorder not just to make the language effective, but also to make it more stylish. Style is a matter of fitness for purpose. If you redraft, as Hemingway claimed to, 'to get the words right', to ensure accurate usage, in editing you also shape your sentences for rhythm, music and *feel*, for style. (See also Chapter 16: 'Style'.)

To a large extent, style is an expression of the author; style comes from who you are. We absorb the beauty language is capable of in everything we read and hear, and we emulate this when we write. What you consume is inextricably linked with what you produce. All artistic endeavour has to do with absorbing influences, synthesising them and making them your own. Because of this, when you refine your work to make it beautiful, the stylistic flourishes and tics you have admired in your reading (and in your listening, if, like me, the cadences of song lyrics have influenced your writing) will emerge. What goes in comes out. What you focus on is what you will reflect.

Writers have, in their feel for language, an ear for a tune. If you want to develop this ear, read more and read better. Read ambitiously as well as voraciously. Write poetry, too. In any kind of poetry, language has to be distilled and, yes, *refined*. 'Delmore Schwartz wrote a sonnet every day. He didn't really like sonnets, but he wrote them for discipline.'[14] In a sonnet, you have fourteen lines to say what you need to say. Working to achieve that level of compression is bound to improve your prose.

Editing your sentences may be about getting the words right and making sure that the rhythm is appealing, but refining the language of a story is also about the voice. (See also Chapter 8: 'What Is a Short Story?' and Chapter 17: 'Voice'.) The voice partly derives from the author. We all write in particular ways, and our writing is shaped by the habits of syntax and vocabulary that we have. Voice should also emerge from who the viewpoint character is. (Voice creates character, too, and may be the key that unlocks the story. Again, study what Jenny Newman says in Chapter 17.)

There's yet more. When you're line-editing, you need to consider the tone of a story and whether or not it is consistent throughout, as Susan Bell proposes: 'Continuity of tone means that if we're writing a naturalistic novel, we don't suddenly and for no reason employ Gothic mannerism … Continuity of tone generally holds a text together and helps it move forward.'[15]

Sharpening

Another task you will perform in editing is sharpening your vocabulary to make the writing more effective. Sometimes this will mean replacing one word with another that is more accurate, sharper, more direct. Flaubert spoke of seeking *le mot just*, the right word. (Flaubert could spend a whole day working on one sentence, by the way.) You're rereading a draft and you suddenly realise that your comic character Billy Bob was not looking *vacant*; he was in fact looking *oblivious*. English has the largest vocabulary of any language. This means that you, as a writer in English, have more flexibility, more opportunity to be fluid and accurate, than writers in any other tongue.

Writing Burst
* People don't like me.

Verbs

One way of sharpening your fiction is to choose your verbs carefully for their dynamism. Rita Mae Brown suggests that your choice of verb can dictate the pace of your fiction: 'Any action verb will accelerate a sentence. Run, jump, shoot, ride, and so on.' Once you digest this piece of wisdom, it's not hard to propel your sentences through your choice of verb – when you want to propel them, that is. Sometimes you will want to slow down, to pause, to be gentle. Brown also recommends your choice of verb as a means of creating motion where there is none: 'If you've got characters sitting in a formal dining room, your verbs better reflect some inner motion or the reader will be bored by the characters' physical inactivity. So you might have a character steaming, seething, writhing.'[16]

Writing Exercise: Edit, Refine and Sharpen
Use the last four sub-sections of this chapter to redraft your 1,000-word story project.

Filtering

In *The Art of Fiction*, John Gardner warns against 'needless filtering of the image through some observing consciousness',[17] which is better demonstrated than explained.

Filtered	Unfiltered
He noticed the fly trapped in the web.	The fly was trapped in the web.
She heard the cat purring.	The cat purred.

The Active Voice

Choosing the passive voice will make your sentences flaccid and circuitous. If you use the active voice, your sentences will be energetic and direct. The passive voice goes round the houses to make its point, whereas the active voice drives forward in a straight line, making its meaning immediately clear. *This was a mistake that she had always regretted* is an example of the passive voice. *She had always regretted this mistake* is in the active voice, and consequently more straightforward and therefore more potent.

Cutting Good Writing

In redrafting you will sometimes replace words with better ones, but there will be occasions, all too many of them, when you will need to cut perfectly concise, even exquisite, writing. Some of the time, editing is going to mean chucking out work that is beautifully expressed and artfully realised: Samuel Johnson, G.K. Chesterton and Kurt Vonnegut have all in their time suggested that you will need to cut parts of your work that you think are particularly fine.

Spelling, Punctuation and Grammar

If you're using Microsoft Word, the Grammar and Spelling checker will highlight most of your spelling and grammar mistakes and should most of the time indicate to you when your sentences aren't sentences. However, to get a real understanding of what is and what is not grammatical in sentence construction, there is no better way than immersing yourself in good writing – reading your head off. In any case, Word's Grammar and Spelling checker is by no means 100 per cent reliable. It has a limited vocabulary and there are quite a few reasonably common English words that it will not recognise. And although the checker often makes helpful grammatical suggestions – such as making passive phrases active – it will sometimes suggest bizarre alterations or highlight grammar errors that are perfectly fine, idiomatic English. So you will have to supplement the spelling checks your computer offers with dictionary use, and you will have to take quite a bit of the grammatical advice it offers with a pinch of salt.

Nobody has perfect spelling or punctuation, but correcting the former is much easier than correcting the latter. I've spent my career marking written work and my experience is that many writers can't punctuate. If you have a problem with punctuation, I recommend you study it. There are several simple primers around and it won't take you long to find out how to use apostrophes, colons and semi-colons and how to punctuate direct speech. The truth is this: using an apostrophe or a full stop correctly is as important as any other aspect of fiction writing. Punctuation is fundamental, and poor use of it undermines your credibility as a writer.

Other Tasks

Line-level editing involves more fine-tuning than I know about, and more than can be covered here – as I say elsewhere, it's easy to devote a whole book to redrafting, and many have done – but let me offer you a few more micro-editing considerations.

* Vocabulary repeats! This is when you're sloppy enough to use the same word twice (or more) in swift succession. We all do it in early drafts, but if you don't eliminate them by your final draft you will just look sloppy. (See what I did there?)

- Use concrete rather than abstract nouns. (See the material on sensory writing in Chapter 13: 'Scenes'.)
- Beware of writing sentences or paragraphs in the wrong sequence. (See Chapter 22: 'Some Notes on Handling Time in Fiction'.)
- Watch out for sentences that lack variety. These may be all of the same length or structure (e.g. subject, verb, object), or start with the same word or have the same rhythm. (See Chapter 16: 'Style'.)
- Hunt down clichés. Instead, look for ways to make your writing fresh.
- Eliminate the present participle.

  - Typing up her notes, she turned and saw the door open.
  - Lying down, he set his head on the pillow

Used this way, the present participle makes your sentences flaccid, whereas simple perfect tense is tight:

  - She typed up her notes, turned and saw the door open.
  - He lay down and set his head on the pillow.

In Summary

Redrafting is perhaps the greater part of a writer's work, and many books have been written about it. I've only covered a few aspects of the subject here, but I'll conclude by reiterating a few key points:

- Pay attention to the story.
- Step away and leave the story alone for a while.
- Reflect in writing, tapping your unconscious.
- Record every thought about your draft that comes your way.
- Act on the ones that seem right.
- Come back and repeat the cycle (and repeat and repeat).

Look at the story, listen to it, act on what it says about itself and keep doing that until it becomes what it was always meant to be. If you want to distil water, you remove its impurities. That's redrafting. In the production of iron, you refine the rock by heating it in a blast furnace until the iron ore is extracted. That's redrafting.

Notes

1 Tom Wolfe in Plimpton (ed.), *The Writer's Chapbook*, p 137.
2 From a letter by Gustave Flaubert, quoted in Conrad, *The Complete Guide to Writing Fiction*, p 204.
3 W.G. Sebald, *The Rings of Saturn* (London: Vintage, 2002), p 19.
4 Raymond Carver, in Charters, *The Story and Its Writer*, p 1418.
5 Frey, *How to Write a Damned Good Novel*, p 151.
6 Higgins, *On Writing*, p 85.
7 Gardner, *The Art of Fiction*, p 70.
8 Roddy Doyle, interviewed by Pat Wheeler and Jenny Newman in Monteith, Newman & Wheeler (eds), *Contemporary British and Irish Fiction*, p 64.
9 Quoted in Plimpton (ed.), *The Writer's Chapbook*, p 195.
10 Andre Dubus, 'The Habit of Writing' in Bailey, *A Short Story Writer's Companion*, pp 138–9.
11 Jack M. Bickham, *Writing the Short Story: A Hands-On Guide for Creating Captivating Short Fiction* (Cincinnati: Writer's Digest Books, 1994), p 177.
12 Conrad, *The Complete Guide to Writing Fiction*, p 207.
13 Paul Magrs, 'Thoughts About Writing Fiction, at the End of Term' in Vanessa Gebbie (ed.), *Short Circuit: A Guide to the Art of the Short Story* (London: Salt Publishing, 2009), p 205.
14 James Laughlin quoted in Plimpton (ed.), *The Writer's Chapbook*, p 60.
15 Susan Bell, *The Artful Edit: On the Practice of Editing Yourself* (New York: W.W. Norton, 2007), pp 86–7.
16 Rita Mae Brown, *Starting From Scratch: A Different Kind of Writers' Manual* (New York: Bantam, 1989), p 69.
17 Gardner, *The Art of Fiction*, p 98.

19

Page Design

If your work is poorly presented, it won't stay long on the desk of an agent or editor. Since you don't want that, your page should be double-spaced (1.5 line spacing is also acceptable) and you should format it with an inoffensive, professional-looking font. Courier will indicate that you're a screenwriter, which, when you're writing short stories, you aren't. **Chalkboard** will suggest that you're eight years old, **Playbill** that you're putting together a Wanted poster for Billy the Kid. Curlz MT just says 'I design greeting cards for Hallmark.' Arial and Times New Roman are perhaps the most commonly used fonts in fiction writing and will demonstrate that you are interested in being published. A point size that will be easily read (for instance, 11 in Arial, 12 in Times New Roman) is essential. As is **numbering** pages.

Up at the top of the first page, the titles of stories and chapters are usually in bold. When you mention them in the story, you'll need italics for the titles of books, films, CDs, magazines and newspapers. The convention for a long time has been to put the titles of articles, short stories and songs in single speech marks, but the music press has begun to italicise song titles in recent years, so you'll have to play that one by ear.

Page design is an aesthetic rather than a technical consideration, and it relates mainly to the use of white space on the page. It's a crucial element in readers' perception of your fiction. White space can be used to make the page accessible and inviting. With this in mind, at both the composing and the revising stages, it may be helpful to use short paragraphs and, in dialogue, speeches that are generally no more than a few lines long.

In its day, Fay Weldon's use of the page was innovative. She was influenced in this by her background in advertising, where the most effective work carries a minimal amount of text (see, for instance, almost any print advertisement for a car). The logic behind this awareness of white space is that we live in a visual society. Just as description in nearly all contemporary fiction acknowledges the fact that most readers will know what most things look like, so intelligent use of white space works on the understanding that contemporary readers aren't nearly as text-friendly as their nineteenth-century forebears. Fay Weldon theorises this approach here: 'Designers and topographers actually teach you to look upon the page. Words are given resonance by their positions, they must be displayed properly. If you wish to give something emphasis, you surround it by space.'[1]

Some basic strategies will maximise white space on a page. Here are a few suggestions.

Dialogue

As I've just said, when you use dialogue the length of the speeches is a factor to consider. A useful rule of thumb is that longer speeches are harder to pull off. If you look, you will find that in most contemporary fiction, speeches are often only a few lines long. In the Amy Hempel passage below, only one speech is longer than that – and it consists of just three lines. Once a speech rises above five or six lines, it threatens to becomes a monologue, and, to my mind, monologues risk losing readers.

Paragraphs

One-paragraph pages might have been accessible in the nineteenth century, even in the first half of the twentieth. However, today's reader may find such a monolith of text uninviting. On a page without dialogue, two to three paragraphs will admit a little white space, but more than three paragraphs a page will make your fiction easier on the eye and more engaging for the reader. If you want to increase the pace of a passage in your fiction, short paragraphs will do the trick. Look at this extract from Amy Hempel's 'In the Cemetery Where Al Jolson Is Buried'.

> She introduces me to a nurse as 'the Best Friend.' The impersonal article is more intimate. It tells me that *they* are intimate, my friend and her nurse.
>
> 'I was telling her we used to drink Canada Dry Ginger Ale and pretend we were in Canada.'
>
> 'That's how dumb *we* were,' I say.
>
> 'You could be sisters,' the nurse says.
>
> So how come, I'll bet they are wondering, it took me so long to get to such a glamorous place? But do they ask?
>
> They do not ask.
>
> Two months, and how long is the drive?
>
> The best I can explain is this – I have a friend who worked one summer in a mortuary. He used to tell me stories. The one that really got me was not the grisliest, but it's the one that did. A man wrecked his car on 101 going south. He did not lose consciousness. But his arm was taken down to the wet bone – and when he looked at it – it scared him to death. I mean, he died.
>
> So I didn't dare look any closer. But now I'm doing it – and hoping I won't be scared to death.[2]

This is fast-paced, and in its short speeches and paragraphs it's representative of much contemporary fiction. Is all fiction published today like this? No. But if you flick through a short story published recently you will find that fewer than three paragraphs a page is rare, and that scenes can often resemble the shape on the page of the above extract. If you design your page differently, you may have good reasons for it, but you won't make your work as accessible as it might be for the reader.

Section Breaks

Shorter speeches and paragraphs in today's fiction recognises how much more impatient we now are as readers, as does the development over the past fifty years of short stories that are broken up through the use of section breaks. Ann Beattie's 'Tuesday Night' is eight pages long and has been broken into six sections. The longest runs to just under two pages, while the shortest is only half a page. David Foster Wallace, whom Zadie Smith has called 'the greatest contemporary innovator in the form',[3] can be found dividing a nine-page story into eight sections.

I'm not recommending without good reason that you model your work on that of these writers. Beyond the fact that we all live fast and busy lives, and that our culture is highly visual, there's a simple rationale behind this aesthetic of economy and division of the longer into the shorter. Life operates that way. We begin work at a certain time and, after an hour or two, have a break. An hour or so later, we break for lunch, and so on. Beyond the way we divide the day, the week has its divisions too: we rest from our labours in the evenings and at weekends, and those fortunate enough not to be on zero-hours contracts have annual leave. The human mind needs regular refreshment. In fact, never mind days and weeks, it's widely accepted that most of us have an attention span of forty-five minutes. It's advisable to include breathing spaces in your fiction. (For more on this, see Chapter 24: 'Transitions'.)

Layout Conventions

The way a page in fiction is laid out alters over time. If you went back to the 1980s, you would find subtly different fashions pertaining. However, as things stand, most of what you need to know about layout is listed here. This is how pages in fiction today look. If you are planning to submit your work, it's desirable that it should resemble today's published fiction.

In section and story beginnings, the first line of the first paragraph is not indented. Thus, a story beginning will look like this:

He answered the phone and tried to switch off the radio at the same time. First he clicked *Pause* on the BBC iPlayer, but, not being very alert, he also pressed the on-off button on the radio beside his computer. So as he paused the virtual radio he inadvertently switched on the actual radio set.
'Sorry,' he said.

And you will denote the end of one section and the beginning of another like this:

The building shook. She turned to stone where she lay in the bath. It wasn't long before the water turned cold.

Not having experienced bereavement, she was a bit shocked when Interflora delivered a bouquet with an 'In Sympathy' card attached.

Writing Burst
- A situation: sleeping rough.

The Focus of the Story

You can easily find advice on the theory of paragraphing – what a paragraph is and how you can best judge when to start a new one. It may be to do with a shift in an argument or a change of subject. Separate from that is how you paragraph your story to help the reader. A new paragraph for a new speaker is a good idea. Which of the following is easier for the reader to follow?

'I've never managed to read *Finnegan's Wake*,' William said.
    'Are you kidding?' Jacqui said.

or

'I've never managed to read *Finnegan's Wake*,' William said. 'Are you kidding?' Jacqui said.

A longer passage of dialogue in the manner of the second version would look like this:

'I've never managed to read *Finnegan's Wake*,' William said. 'Are you kidding?' Jacqui said. 'I couldn't even manage *Ulysses*.' 'Oh, I've read that.' 'Hasn't everyone?' Emma said. 'I don't think so,' Jacqui said. 'I've read it,' Jon said. 'But you've read everything,' William said.

That will definitely make it harder for the reader to engage with the story. It's optional, but I would say most of the time essential, to take a new paragraph when the focus of the story shifts from one character to another.

Getting the layout right is essential too, where there are actions and dialogue coming hot on the heels of each other.

> 'What do you think you're doing?' George asked. Jeff looked dumbfounded.
> 'What's it to you?'
> Kevin burst through the door. Ellie's jaw dropped.
> 'Ask Kevin.'
> George bristled. 'I said, What's it to him?'

The meaning of this would be more clearly indicated by the following layout:

> 'What do you think you're doing?' George asked.
> Jeff looked dumbfounded. 'What's it to you?'
> Kevin burst through the door.
> Ellie's jaw dropped. 'Ask Kevin.'
> George bristled.
> 'I said, What's it to him?'

Readers have no problem following where the focus is in the second version. In the first, they could be confused at least twice. It seems like Ellie has not said 'Ask Kevin,' when in fact she has. They would also assume that it was George, not Jerry, who said, 'I said, What's it to him?' When the action and the speech pertain to one character, they need to go in the same paragraph. If they don't, either your intended meaning will be ambiguous or readers will completely misunderstand it.

It's been said that stories are just ink on a page. There's no denying that ink on a page is the vehicle which delivers the story to the reader. If that's all you've got, you should design it to be as effective as possible.

Notes

1   John Haffenden (ed.), 'Fay Weldon' in *Novelists in Interview* (London: Methuen, 1985), pp 305–20.

2   Amy Hempel, 'In the Cemetery Where Al Jolson Is Buried' in *The Collected Stories of Amy Hempel* (London: Quercus, 2008), pp 30–1.

3   Zadie Smith, in the introduction to her micro short story collection *Martha and Hanwell* (London: Penguin Books, 2005), p vii.

20

Peer Appraisal

One of the key learning and teaching strategies in university Creative Writing is informal peer appraisal. Apart from the many good reasons for engaging in peer appraisal, which will follow in a moment, this is a useful stepping-stone to workshopping, which can be daunting in the early stages of learning your craft. When I talk about peer appraisal, what I mean is asking a small group of your friends or fellow students to read a draft of your work in progress and give you feedback on it-and vice versa.

Peer appraisal allows you to write for an audience wider than the tutor. This is important in building confidence and eliciting feedback for the redrafting process. Feedback is motivating for writers, and peer appraisal extends the feedback you can get. Without peer appraisal, you are writing for an audience of one: the tutor. In a Creative Writing degree you may depend on the expert tuition of individual tutors and on their informed assessment and commentary on coursework, but the addition of other, increasingly informed readers has a vital role to play in your development as a mature, autonomous writer.

Peer appraisal builds confidence and is a significant tool in redrafting. As a writer, you depend on being able to estimate an understanding of readers' responses to your work; with peer appraisal, you have the means of making this estimate a little more evidence-based.

I can't recommend too highly the practice of offering first or second draft work to a small group of your peers, and few professional writers would disagree with me on this. You don't have to be a student in further or higher education to acquire the habit. If you belong to a writers' group, for instance, what would stop you occasionally breaking into groups of three or four and peer-appraising work?

Modus Operandi

Four is the ideal size for a peer appraisal group, and each member will need a copy of the draft. The author, obviously, should not be in the same peer appraisal group as his or her work. The group members first of all read the draft, and then discuss it. When they have reached some agreement about the story's strengths, and perhaps about an area in need of development, they should complete something like the form below. (Adapt as you think best.)

As appraisers, the object of this exercise is for you to help your peers with their work. Think about how best to achieve that. A bland comment that glosses over significant flaws isn't doing anyone any favours; neither is a destructive comment that discourages the author. Your aim is to encourage improvements and to increase, not decrease, the author's confidence in his or her writing. If you stick to the requirements of the exercise, you should achieve that.

Remember that you are examining the story on its own merits; you're aiming to make this story as good as it can be, never to turn it into a different story, into your idea of what it should be.

Different tutors will suggest different parameters for the exercise, and I alter the details of the exercise every year or so, but try this.

First, the group of four that you're in reads and annotates the draft. Next, you discuss the work and each of you decides on one aspect of it that you admire or enjoy and one area that in your view needs more work. Make sure that there is no repetition here; by the end of that stage you should have four individual strengths and four distinct areas that need more work. After that, agree between you just one area that is strikingly good and one that needs more work. So now you have the strength and the weakness that the group has agreed on plus the individuals' original responses. Quite a bit of feedback.

When the peer appraisal group has completed the task and filled in the form below, it should invite the author over to discuss its responses to his or her work. This is important: it means that, as appraisers, you have to take responsibility for your comments.

Afterwards, the author retains the completed peer appraisal form and the annotated print-offs.

Peer Appraisal Form

Title ....

Author ....

Comments

Appraiser 1
A strength

An area in need of more work

Appraiser 2
A strength

An area in need of more work

Appraiser 3
A strength

An area in need of more work

Appraiser 4
A strength

An area in need of more work

(Each appraiser should sign his or her remarks.)

Appraisal Group
A strength the group has agreed on

An improvement the group suggests

21

Writers' Workshops

I've mentioned my visit to Iowa more than once, haven't I? On day two, I was a guest in Frank Conroy's MFA class, which was recognisable as the form of writers' workshop used in universities throughout the world. For a summary of this modus operandi, read my guidelines in 'How It Works' later in this chapter.

When I sat in on Frank Conroy's MFA workshop, students were asked, one at a time, going clockwise around the room, to comment briefly on the tabled piece. Once this was out of the way – it didn't take long, and students offered their observations with much trepidation – Frank launched into a line-by-line analysis of the story.

First up was a former medic wearing a neck brace, which came to seem like a metaphor for his ordeal. Frank held forth on many aspects of the fiction-writer's craft. He cited Flannery O'Connor, perhaps Iowa's most illustrious graduate, on the necessity of creating a sense of immediacy. (You remember: 'The reader isn't going to believe anything just because you tell them.') He demonstrated the difficulty of achieving 'meaning, sense and clarity'. He discussed choice of verb, choice of action; there was a lengthy debate about the best way to convey a character pinning underfoot a paper napkin that has blown off a table. Much of what was said pertained to the failings of Neck-Brace's story.

'We of course spend 95 per cent of our time finding out what is wrong,' Frank said, and then, of a particular aspect of the story: 'This is bad writing.'

Although Frank was a hard taskmaster, and I felt for Neck-Brace, the two-and-a-half-hour session was filled with wisdom about the writer's craft. For example, Conroy noted one of the fundamental truths about art, one that goes right back to Michelangelo's observation that the sculpture is already in the stone before a sculptor lifts a chisel to it: 'The text can be thought of as having a manifest destiny and it's our duty to find out what that destiny is. It's as if the story already exists and it's our duty to uncover it.'

By the end of this workshop, I was in no doubt that anyone passing through the semester each MFA cohort spends with Frank Conroy would emerge a better writer – as long as they survived. All the writer's wisdom notwithstanding, this class never once ran counter to Madison Smartt Bell's argument (again in *Narrative Design*) that the workshop process amounts to an autopsy: 'The attitude of the group toward the work is surgical. A process of dissection is going on. The text is handled as a machine in need of repair.'[1]

Neck-Brace's firm jaw appeared to recede a little with each flaw analysed, tucking further and further behind his brace. This was more masterclass than workshop. The criticism was indisputably valid, but students evidently need to be thick-skinned. The fortunate author of that day's second story was praised, amongst other things, for his characterisation – 'Creating a character', Frank said, 'is like building one layer of filo pastry on the next' – and stumbled from the workshop exuding the glee of a man who has passed his driving test.

Frank Conroy's philosophy seemed to centre on drumming into his students the strictures of good writing, so that when they were pushed out of the nest they might stand a chance of surviving as writers. If I picked up anything from his impressive, if savage, class, it was the value of rigour.

Writing Burst
- Put 'Bruce Gilden' in your search engine and choose one of his photographs as your prompt.

The Limitations of Workshops

Later in the week, one MFA student told me that Conroy believes he isn't doing his job unless the occasional student bursts into tears or faints. This, along with the intense competition there is to gain a place at Iowa, makes for a charged atmosphere.

The short story author Lan Samantha Chang, a former member of the Workshop, was Visiting Writer at Iowa when I was there. Over a raspberry soda in a downtown coffee shop, she was very positive about the benefits of the Iowa Workshop, but admitted that at a certain point she had had enough of the workshop experience and just wanted to get on with writing. This was corroborated by Brett Johnston, another student of the Writers' Workshop I spoke to: 'There comes a time when the benefits of the workshop will certainly dissolve.'

Madison Smartt Bell's misgiving about the value of the writers' workshop – that it doesn't recognise success – rings true. As he suggests, 'Fiction workshops are inherently incapable of recognising *success*.'[2] Having done my fair share of tabling texts in such workshops, and having led them on a weekly basis over the past twenty years, I know for sure that tutors and students alike enter the workshop with one question uppermost in their minds: *What's wrong with this piece?* That, and *How can we make it better?* This is the mindset of the workshopper, and it often has a reductive effect on the way the work is perceived. But my own experience is that, imperfect though it may be, a writers' workshop is a useful means of developing work in progress. As Brett Johnston said, 'The job of the workshop is to find the things that five or ten years down the road would embarrass the writer. Hopefully the workshop enables the writer to see that whatever it is is not doing the job he or she wants it to do.'

In order to develop, all creative work needs such responses from readers – in order to reach its 'manifest destiny', to use Frank Conroy's apposite term. In an article called 'The Rocky Road to Paper Heaven', Margaret Atwood describes the process of eliciting feedback from friendly readers:

> The work is shown to a few knowledgeable friends, if the writer is lucky enough to have some. Suggestions may be made, which the writer is free to accept or reject.

Pitfall 1: If s/he savages the friends for giving the suggestions, they are unlikely to make any more in future.

Pitfall 2: The friends may be wrong.

Pitfall 3: If all the writer wants from these people is an encouraging 'reaction,' i.e. not real suggestions but a 'Hey, that's great,' it would help matters to say so at the outset. There is nothing illegitimate about such a wish. Everyone needs morale uplift.[3]

If Atwood, one of the most distinguished fiction writers of our era, needs this kind of feedback to produce her finished work, it's a no-brainer that the rest of us do, too.

The Benefits of Workshops

Since workshops will require you to table pieces of creative work reasonably often, perhaps the first and most obvious benefit of being a member of a workshop is that it will provide you with a deadline. To illustrate: if you are in a weekly meeting of twelve students, where two texts are tabled each session, you will have to produce two pieces of work each term. Clearly this means that you will have a readership, which you may never have had before. Not only that, but an increasingly informed readership, who will add to your understanding of what you are doing. Membership of a workshop also puts you in regular contact with other writers, people who share your goals and anxieties, people who are trying to learn the same things as you are. Together, you will have the chance to discuss and compare working methods. Being passionate about reading and writing, you will no doubt recommend books to one another: collections, anthologies and books on craft.

In Chapter 5, you may have learned one or two things about how to read as a writer. What you do in workshops (as in peer appraisal groups) will help you grow ever more proficient in this discipline. Furthermore, in having your work appreciated and criticised by other writers, you will grow in self-awareness, self-criticism and, let's hope, self-esteem. Which leads me to my next points. Workshops that are worth their salt have two vital components.

First, they build mutual trust amongst their members. By offering your work to others, you are inviting them not to savage you: you are showing that you trust them. This in turn prompts a reciprocal response, so that, as the weeks go by, writers who are offering up their own work for critical reaction and responding constructively to the work of others learn increasingly to trust one another.

Second, workshops enhance the confidence of their members. In my experience, many learning writers undervalue their own work. In workshops, they usually come to see that, rather than being worse than everyone else's, their writing is as good as most of the work being tabled, and may in fact be better than that of some. The corollary of this is that writers who have an over-inflated view of their work will, when they see what everyone else in the group is producing, perhaps arrive at a more realistic view of its merits. In terms of confidence-building, though, perhaps the greatest achievement of the workshop is one I've already mentioned: the fact that here you have a group of people who are expecting to read and comment on your work. This, in the experience of every writer I know, is a strange and marvellous thing.

How It Works

Liz Allen says that 'The work you are expected to produce in workshops is first draft raw material for reworking and extending in your own time; a workshop is more about process than product.'[4] That process extends beyond receiving critical feedback; writers learn as much from reading work by other members of the workshop as they do from hearing their own work discussed.

The procedure begins the week before the workshop, with every member receiving copies of the work to be discussed and spending some time studying and annotating it in preparation for the discussion that will take place in the workshop. After that discussion, everyone hands over their annotated copy of the tabled work so that the author can see all the detail of the group's feedback. Some Creative Writing tutors – Frank Conroy, for instance – ask everyone to write a letter or critique to the author, in which they formally address the strengths and weaknesses of the piece.

In a workshop, you will need a leader or facilitator. In universities, this may well be your tutor, but by Year 3 of your degree, each student should be capable of fulfilling this role. The primary task of the leader is to keep the discussion aloft and moving forward. Another responsibility is to ensure that each member of the workshop is contributing and to prevent any one member of the group from dominating the discussion. The aim is to have a group discussion, not a monologue or dialogue, so if you are facilitating, you will have to do whatever is necessary to achieve this aim. A key part of this will be to ensure that the authors don't pipe up until you want them to. The positive reason for this is to ensure that as good a group discussion as possible takes place – and this discussion is a creative process in its own right; for one thing, in response to what others are saying, spurred by the debate, you will often find yourself having new things to say about the tabled work, insights that hadn't come when you were annotating the piece. The more negative reason for being strict about keeping the author out of the discussion at this stage is that author interjections quickly replace group discussion with a dialogue and destroy any possibility of a vibrant debate. It may help authors keep silent if the facilitator invites them to take notes during the discussion of any points to which they may wish to respond at the end. In recent years, because the tabler's attention may not always be on making notes, I've given someone the job of taking minutes of the discussion. This leaves the author free to give their whole attention to what is being said.

As facilitator, you may want to give the discussion some basic structure. It's helpful to begin with broad general statements, and it eases the author's passage through what some will see as a bit of an ordeal if this general stage of the proceedings can begin with examining the virtues of the tabled work. An added virtue of keeping it general and positive to begin with is that this allows the readers, through making simple statements, to warm up their engines before developing a full-blown discussion.

After these opening, general and more positive statements, it may be effective for the facilitator to encourage the discussion to go through two separate stages. In *The Fiction Editor, the Novel, and the Novelist*, Thomas McCormack identifies two fundamental shortcomings a piece of fiction may suffer from: 'the dermal flaw' and 'the internal flaw'.[5] The dermal flaw is much easier to deal with, and examples of it would include grammar or syntax errors, typos, inelegant phrases, repetitions of vocabulary and redundancies ('six a.m. in the morning …'). The internal flaw has to do with the inner workings of the text, and functions at the level of viewpoint, character, narrative and so on. Perhaps the tension fails to rise, or questions that the plot raises have not been answered, or at a most basic level, there is not enough at stake. Internal flaws may well occur at the beginning or end of the narrative. They may concern the quality of the characterisation as much as the efficacy of the narrative. In my experience, it makes most sense for a workshop discussion to begin by looking at the internal and deal with the dermal towards the end of the discussion. Internal flaws are more grievous and take more work to fix, while dermal flaws will be recorded in the annotations that members of the workshop write on copies of the text – which the author can absorb later. Whether looking at the dermal or the internal, though, it's helpful to try to keep a balance by examining the achievements as well as the inadequacies.

When the debate seems to have run its course, the facilitator invites the author to respond to what has been said. Here the author may counter criticisms that have been levelled at the work (or welcome them), clear up any aspects of the text that mystified readers, and perhaps discuss the difference between authorial intentions and readers' responses.

I've tried to maintain a balance here between the virtues and vices of the workshop's. Every writer should ideally be part of a workshop that meets regularly and reasonably formally. In redrafting your work, as Margaret Atwood's experience shows, you will always need a small readership on which you may road-test your prototypes before putting them into production, but this may mean nothing more formal than sending your story out to three or four friends and asking them to read and respond to it.

2,000-Word Story Project

Literary Revision

You may have come across the term 'literary revision'. Put simply, a work of fiction by one writer is used by another as the starting point for a new, related work of fiction. It's most commonly used in the novel. Jean Rhys's *Wide Sargasso Sea* is born out of Charlotte Brontë's *Jane Eyre*. In it, the central character is Antoinette, Rochester's first wife – the celebrated madwoman in the attic. Valerie Martin's *Mary Reilly* is a revision of Robert Louis Stevenson's *The Strange Case of Dr Jekyll and Mr Hyde*; Mary Reilly, the point-of-view character, is one of the maids in the house of Dr Jekyll. J.M. Coetzee's *Foe* has a similar relationship to Daniel Defoe's *Robinson Crusoe*, and *Ahab's Wife* by Sena Jeter Naslund has been inspired by one of the characters in Herman Melville's *Moby Dick*.

This exercise will require you to do a bit of extra reading, but it's reading which I hope will appeal to you. Choose one of the following short stories available online and read it carefully.

Kevin Barry, 'Atlantic City': http://thresholds.chi.ac.uk/story-atlantic-city-by-kevin-barry/

Ann Beattie, 'For the Best': www.newyorker.com/magazine/2016/03/14/for-the-best

Raymond Carver, 'Cathedral': www.ndsu.edu/pubweb/~cinichol/Creative Writing/423/Cathedral.docx

Junot Diaz, 'Miss Lora': www.newyorker.com/magazine/2012/04/23/miss-lora

Katherine Mansfield, 'Bliss': http://digital.library.upenn.edu/women/mansfield/bliss/story.html

Adam Marek, 'Remember the Bride Who Got Stung': http://thresholds.chi.ac.uk/story-remember-the-bride-who-got-stung/

Lorrie Moore, 'Debarking': www.newyorker.com/magazine/2003/12/22/debarking

Once you've read the story of your choice, choose one of the other characters as your viewpoint character and write a story of your own from that perspective. To make it easier for you, stick with the same storyline; all you have to do is see it from another character's point of view and find out how the whole will change as a result. Afterwards, don't forget to write a reflection, with an annotated bibliography.

Notes

1   Bell, *Narrative Design*, p 9.
2   Bell, *Narrative Design*, pp 6–9.
3   Margaret Atwood, 'The Rocky Road to Paper Heaven', Margaret Atwood Information Site, www.web.net/owtoad/road.html (accessed 27 February 2006).
4   Liz Allen, 'The Workshop Way' in John Singleton & Mary Luckhurst (eds), *The Creative Writing Handbook* (Basingstoke: Palgrave, 1996), p 18.
5   Thomas McCormack, *The Fiction Editor, the Novel, and the Novelist* (New York: St. Martin's Press, 1988), pp 16–17.

Part IV

How to Manage Fictional Time

22

Some Notes on Handling Time in Fiction

James Friel

Henry James observed that 'the eternal time question is … really a business to terrify all but stout hearts'.[1] Every writer of fiction must confront the question of how to handle time.

In a short story a writer might have to make time pause, accelerate, fall back, leap forward or go in circles. A sentence in a story might distil a decade or even an entire life ('In the end his misfortunes touched her; she grew to love him': Chekhov's 'The Darling'). A story might devote itself to the pivotal events of an hour as in Hemingway's 'Hills Like White Elephants', or an entire history of the world as in Italy Calvino's 'The Soft Moon'. A story, like Alice Munro's 'Friend of My Youth', might probe the past and how its secrets surface in the present. A story might plait the past and the present, as in Hemingway's 'The Snows of Kilimanjaro' with its feverous hero recalling his past as he dies in the African heat. A story might concern the passage of time very directly, as in Charles Dickens' *A Christmas Carol* with its visits from the Ghosts of Christmas Past, Present and Future. Tobias Wolff's 'Bullet in the Brain' manages to tell the story of man's whole life – often by detailing what he failed to do – in the seconds it takes for a bullet to enter his head during a bank robbery.[2] Liam O'Flaherty's 'The Wave' describes the impact of one wave on a cliff face: the work of a moment, but also several millennia.[3]

However else they deal with time, the stories mentioned so far also conform to a conventional structure: they have a beginning, middle and end, and in that order. Each follows the subjective experience of a character as it occurs to that character. However, simply following chronology does not answer or avoid the eternal time question.

For example, where – exactly – should one begin?

Before or After the Fall?

Take Humpty Dumpty. Round fellow? Sat on a wall, fell off, and was irremediably broken? What if your story was about him? What if you wanted to know why he climbed that wall? What desires provoked him to it? You might wish to probe the mind of such a reckless character. To do so, you might have to go back to the very beginning: his childhood, and the overly ambitious mother who had egged him on? Or you might just step back to the very start of the crucial action – the night before, and the drunken bet that leads to Humpty climbing the wall? Such a beginning is called *ab ovo* – literally 'from the egg'. The writer starts from the beginning, and provides all the *necessary* background events concerning the characters, their circumstances and conflicts.

The familiar nursery rhyme, however, cuts straight to the decisive act: *Humpty Dumpty sat on a wall*. We aren't even told that he climbs the wall – or why. The story begins in the middle of things – or *in media res*. No time is wasted. We jump right in without preamble or explanation. Action is all. Humpty is now in a thriller.

One might begin the story at the very end of things – or *in ultima res* – with one of the King's men (or one of his horses) studying Humpty's fragments and wondering how such an event had occurred. Humpty's tale has become a detective story.

A story can begin at any point in time, and, in consequence, its mood and intentions change.

Writing Exercise: Three Beginnings

Look more closely at these three types of beginnings:

Ab ovo At the age of five, when asked what he wanted to be when he grew up, Isaac said he wanted to be German.

Benedict Kiely, 'The Wild White Bronco'

In media res
The men were speaking in low voices in the kitchen.
V.S. Pritchett, 'Just a Little More'

In ultima res There was something strange, abnormal, about my bringing up; only now that my grandmother is dead am I prepared to face it.
Mary McCarthy, 'Ask Me Questions'

Now, take a familiar story like *Humpty Dumpty*, *Hamlet*, or, at random, a story or event reported in your local newspaper. Ponder how you might begin to tell the story *ab ovo*, *in media res* or *in ultima res*. For each one, write an opening sentence or even a paragraph.

You don't need to write the whole story. Just think – as storywriters do – in what ways might you begin to tell this story.

Summary or Scene

Summary (or telling) accelerates a narrative – events are being compressed. Summary, by its very nature, condenses time. One can summarise a novel in a sentence or even a title – *War and Peace*? But with this speed comes distance and detachment. It is much harder to make summary as vivid or immediate to a reader. Making a scene or dramatising an event (showing) decelerates a narrative. The narrative slows down for dialogue, for the description of a room or a gesture. Detail gives weight, and suggests to the reader that this moment or this exchange is significant. Too much scene-making, however, and the pace can be meandering or static. The story eventually stalls. This is why most fiction shifts between these two modes.

In fiction, although we often prize showing over telling, neither summary nor scene-making is an inherently better narrative method than the other. Both, ultimately, concern selection: choosing what to add or omit. What matters, always, is making the writing count.

This excerpt from Tim O'Brien's 'The Things They Carried' not only dramatises a crucial event in the story, but also summarises each of the main characters:

Until he was shot, Ted Lavender carried six or seven ounces of premium dope, which for him was a necessity. Mitchell Sanders, the RTO, carried condoms. Norman Bowker carried a diary. Pat Kiley carried comic books. Kiowa, a devout Baptist, carried an illustrated New Testament that had been presented to him by his father, who taught Sunday school in Oklahoma City, Oklahoma. When Ted Lavender was shot, they used his poncho to wrap him up, then to carry him across the paddy, then to lift him into the chopper that took him away.[4]

Except for the last sentence, this is summary. What these characters carry gives clues to their personalities and backgrounds. It is summary, but it is also a very condensed form of showing. For example, is Ted Lavender's dope for consumption or dealing?

But look, too, at those names – *Lavender, Norman Bowker, Kiowa* (a Native American name). O'Brien's choice of names deepens and complicates what we might guess about the characters.

Look at each word O'Brien has chosen. What if O'Brien had written that Bowker had a *journal*, not a *diary*? Bowker's character would subtly change, would it not? O'Brien could have given Kiowa a Bible, but Kiowa has a New Testament – an illustrated one. Every word matters here.

Notice the syntax, too. The shape of each sentence reveals character, too. That fifth sentence? Doesn't it imply that Kiowa is also likely to be rather long-winded and pedantic, repetitious even? And is Mitchell Sanders as curt in all his dealings as the sentence he inhabits?

There is a concentrated thought behind each of O'Brien's choices. These vivid summaries might be O'Brien's answer to the eternal time question.

Writing Exercise: The Things They Carried

Try something similar. Choose either a group of five children going to school, young people out clubbing, a family setting out on a long journey, or commuters in a traffic jam. Suggest their character and history – even their future – by the things they carried, their names, and the syntax and diction you employ to describe them.

Perhaps, also, as in the excerpt, you could write one more sentence that either moves the story on in time or concludes it.

Flashback/Forward

The use of flashbacks (or *analepsis*) in fiction is common enough – so many stories begin with a variant of *I remembered* – but flashbacks as a device within a story can seem clumsy if all a character is doing is remembering information that the writer can't fit in any other way. 'Plot', observed Eudora Welty, 'is not repetition – it is direction'.[5] If you are dealing in flashbacks, ask yourself if you are delaying your story or propelling it forward. Consider whether you need that flashback at all.

The flash-forward (or *prolepsis*), in which the plot or its outcome is given away, is less common but can be effective. In the excerpt from 'The Things They Carried', the author tells us immediately that Ted Lavender will be shot. An omniscient narrator can see a wider history his characters will never know or even live to see, as in William Faulkner's story 'Barn Burning':[6]

> His father mounted to the seat where the older brother already sat and struck the gaunt mules two savage blows with the peeled willow, but without heat. It was not even sadistic; it was exactly that same quality which in later years would cause his descendants to overrun the engine before putting a motorcar into motion, striking and reining back in the same movement.

Prolepsis does not destroy suspense: it can create a different and more sophisticated suspense. Rather than wondering how the story will end, the reader is encouraged to wonder how it reaches this point – and why.

Tenses

Tenses indicate time in a sentence. The present tense, for example, suggests that the events in a story are happening simultaneously with our reading it. Modishly, it is thought to be more 'immediate', but your prose will not be immediate or vivid in any tense if your writing is stiff and uninterested in pace. It is diction and syntax that make for pace and immediacy, not tense.

Errors in tense make a reader pause or stumble. Sometimes, notes Gerry Visco, the mechanics of the flashback technique can cause you to use cumbersome verb constructions.[7]

If you are writing the story in the past tense, you can begin the flash-back in past perfect. You can use 'had' plus the verb a couple of times. Then you can switch to the simple past. I gleaned this nugget from Janet Burroway in her helpful book on writing fiction. As she says (quoted in Visco's article), 'the reader will be with you'.

However, tense shifts can be very effective. Timothy J. Mason has noted how, in Angela Carter's 'The Company of Wolves', a young man's actions are reported in the past tense, but his metamorphosis into a wolf and when he kills and eats the grandmother is told largely in the present:

> He strips off his shirt. His skin is the colour and texture of vellum.
> A crisp stripe of hair runs down his belly, his nipples are ripe and dark as poison fruit, but he's so thin you could count the ribs under his skin if only he gave you the time.
> He strips off his trousers and she can see how hairy his legs are. His genitals, huge. Ah! huge.
> The last thing the old lady saw in all this world was a young man, eyes like cinders, naked as a stone, approaching her bed.
> The wolf is carnivore incarnate.[8]

In the penultimate sentence, the tense is changed to the past – the grand-mother is dead – and in the last sentence we return to the present tense and the triumphant wolf. Carter does this frequently in her stories. The effect is almost musical. It shapes and modulates her writing voice. The tense changes are deliberate, worked out, chosen. They may have been lucky accidents in the drafting, but they are not errors.

Pace: Get There Smoothly

Chronology matters in fiction because it is about control, a writer shaping the material. Take this piece of prose, for example:

> In a tight-ish tweed coat, un-tanned, ideally bald, and clean shaven, he began rather impressively with that great brown dome of his, tor-toiseshell glasses (masking an infantile absence of eyebrows), a thick

neck, an apish upper lip, and a strong-man torso, but he ended, somewhat disappointingly, in frail-looking, almost feminine feet and a pair of spindly legs.

It is cumbersome but syntactically correct. It has some pleasing phrases, but it reads lumpily. It fails to impact. There is a reason. It does not occur chronologically. The reader's eye must first take in a coat and then a bald head. A domed skull is described next and then we slip down to his glasses. We then zip down to his neck and back up again for his lips only to plummet past his torso to his feet and finish with a flick back to the legs. Dizzying, yes?

If this were written chronologically, if we followed as the eye would take in this sight or as a camera might – that is, as it occurs in time – then we would have this magisterial panning shot:

> Ideally bald, sun-tanned, and clean shaven, he began rather impressively with that great brown dome of his, tortoiseshell glasses (masking an infantile absence of eyebrows), an apish upper lip, thick neck, and strong-man torso in a tightish tweed coat, but he ended, somewhat disappointingly, in a pair of spindly legs and frail-looking, almost feminine feet.[9]

A great deal of writing commits the sins of the former passage. There is so much to do in writing that one gets flustered. In redrafting and shaping sentences, one can lose sight of common sense. Events occur in time. A description of a place or person is an event. Follow time.

This also applies to action. Graham Greene wrote that he learned never to interrupt an action; a man walks through a door with a gun and fires it. This is not a moment to describe the clouds.

Endings

Some stories reach a full stop, say with marriages or murders. Such endings are called *closed*. Others are called *open*. The story need not have reached its end in time, but arrives at a point where either what follows can be intuited – for example, the ending of James Joyce's 'The Dead' – or it would spoil the effect to spell it out.

In Chekhov's 'Sleepy', the climactic act is delivered as a devastating summary.

> Laughing and winking and shaking her fingers at the green patch, Varka steals up to the cradle and bends over the baby. When she has strangled him, she quickly lies down on the floor, laughs with delight that she can sleep, and in a minute is sleeping as sound as the dead.[10]

An even more brutal summary brings Raymond Carver's 'Popular Mechanics' to a dead halt:

> She would have it, this baby. She grabbed for the baby's other arm. She caught the baby around the wrist and leaned back.
>
> But he would not let go. He felt the baby slipping out of his hands and he pulled back very hard.
>
> In this manner, the issue was decided.[11]

In Elizabeth Bowen's 'The Demon Lover', a woman returns to a neglected and boarded-up house. The story builds up an eerie and threatening atmosphere. The house is chillingly evoked. We wait for the demon lover to appear before her, but, at the very close of the story, she leaves the house and climbs into a waiting taxi. There is almost relief, and then the driver turns and she recognises her dead lover:

> They remained for an eternity eye to eye … Mrs Drover's mouth hung open for some seconds before she could issue her first scream. After that she continued to scream freely and to beat with her gloved hands on the glass all around as the taxi, accelerating without mercy, made off with her into the hinterland of deserted streets.[12]

These stories work by creating scenes, but their real coup is to cut away to summary or a muffled silence – those *gloved hands*.

Writing Exercise: Suspense

In 'Sleepy', Chekhov conveys the poor maid's miserable life in such detail that we understand why she kills the child: it is one more dull and deadening task in a life filled with too many such tasks. The story appears to pay the child's death no more mind than she does and so we notice it all the more. In 'The Demon Lover', the house looks at Mrs Drover with 'a damaged glare'. Inside, the wallpaper looks 'bruised'. A piano has left 'claw marks' on a carpet. These details threaten. Something terrible *will* happen. It does – a woman is dragged off to a hell all the worse for it not being presented to us.

Take a simple or mundane event:

a trip round a supermarket
the cleaning of a kitchen
taking a bath
making a bed.

Imagine at the end of each of these events something terrible occurs:

an accident happens
a lie is told
a murder is committed
the world ends.

Try very hard not to announce this terrible conclusion. Show how it grows out of the event you described or cuts across it in a way only you as the writer could anticipate.

The eternal time question is one you must confront each time you tackle a story. We have only touched upon it here. I have had only 3,000 words and, for a writer, time is also space – and word counts.

I have not answered the question fully. I never will. Nor will you. That's one more reason why the question of time might terrify, but, if writing held no terrors, we would be uninterested in pursuing it. Love the questions. In the writing of fiction, a question takes you further than any answer.

Notes

1   Henry James, 'Preface to Roderick Hudson', at www.henryjames.org.uk/prefaces/text01.htm (accessed 27 March 2017).
2   Tobias Wolff, *Collected Stories* (London: Bloomsbury, 1997).
3   Tim Akers & Jerry Moore (eds), *Short Stories for Students*, Vol. 5 Detroit: Gale, 1999).
4   Tim O'Brien, *The Things They Carried* (New York: Broadway, 1998).
5   Eudora Welty, *The Eye of the Story* (New York: Random House, 1978).
6   William Faulkner, *Selected Short Stories* (New York: Modern Library, 1993).
7   Gerry Visco, 'Pacing in Writing Techniques You Need to Know', Writers Store, www.writersstore.com/article.php?articles_id=7 (accessed 27 March 2017).
8   Angela Carter, *Burning Your Boats* (London: Penguin, 1997).
9   Vladimir Nabokov, *Pnin* (New York: Vintage, 1989).
10 Anton Chekhov (trans. by Robert Payne), *Forty Stories* (New York: Vintage, 1991).
11 Raymond Carver, *What We Talk About When We Talk About Love* (New York: Vintage, 1989).
12 Elizabeth Bowen, *Collected Stories* (London: Cape, 1980).

23

Crossing Timelines and Breaking Rules

Heather Leach

How fast or slowly does time go? Most people will answer 'It depends' because we are all very well aware that time seems to go too fast when we are doing things we enjoy and extremely slowly when we're bored. The writer can simply *describe* this experience:

The long afternoons I spent in the Maths class nearly drove me mad with boredom

or

I was so much in love with Jenny that the hours I spent with her went by in a flash and were over far too soon.

But it is much more challenging and interesting for the writer to try to *show* the subjective experience of time in a story.

In David Foster Wallace's 'Forever Overhead', the protagonist is a boy on his thirteenth birthday. The story is told in the second person, an unusual point of view that enables the writer to add another time-shift: that of the boy narrator himself and of the omniscient narrator/writer remembering. The boy is rapidly turning from child to adolescent and is both thrilled and alarmed by his new sexual awareness and his changing body. On this special day he decides to make his first dive into the swimming pool from the top board. As he climbs the ladder, things get scary and time begins to shift:

There's wind. It's windier the higher you get. The wind is thin; through the shadow it's cold on your wet skin. On the ladder in the shadow your skin looks very white. The wind makes a thin whistle in your ears. Four more rungs to the top of the tower. The rungs hurt your feet. They are thin and let you know just how much you weigh. You have real weight on the ladder. The ground wants you back.

Now you can see just over the top of the ladder. You can see the board. The woman is there. There are two ridges of red, hurt-looking callus on the backs of her ankles. She stands at the start of the board, your eyes on her ankles. Now you're up above the tower's shadow. The solid man under you is looking through the rungs into the contained space the woman will look through ...

Time slows. It thickens around you as your heart gets more and more beats out of each second. [...] No time is passing outside you at all. It is amazing. If you wanted you could really stay here forever, vibrating inside so fast you float motionless in time, like a bee over something sweet.[1]

As the line of swimmers move forward and up the ladder, rung by rung with a machine-like regularity, the boy's perceptions of time are transformed by fear and adrenaline. He shifts out of 'normal' time into something close to timelessness. The story is told using short sentences, with many repetitions. Notice how often the words 'thin', 'wind' and 'rungs' are used in the first small paragraph alone. And also, even though this is prose, there are a number of rhymes and half-rhymes – thin/skin/wind; ladder/shadow – which work to reinforce the anxiety the boy feels about his own weakness and vulnerability, and also to add a lyrical, mythical quality. The boy notes the smallest detail: *the red, hurt-looking callus on the backs of her ankles.* These precise observations, along with the patterned, rhythmic texture of the language, slow down the action into a series of small, almost meditative moments.

I guess that this story is based on experience. It would be difficult to write in this way without having some subjective knowledge of how it feels. For the first part of the next exercise, dig down into your own experience to find the precise quality of your own time-shifting memory, its taste and texture, its colours and patterns. Then, in the second part of the exercise, you will have the materials to begin to reframe these qualities into a fictional story.

Writing Exercise: Slowing Down Time

1. Bring to mind an event in your life when your normal experience of time was altered and your perceptions changed. Try to re-enter the experience, to reimagine how it felt, using all your senses.
2. Imagine two people: any age or gender. One person is in life-threatening danger; the other is trying to rescue them. The endangered person could be someone who has fallen over a cliff, is balanced precariously on the ledge of a building, or has their foot trapped in a railway line, etc. Write a page of the story, plunging straight into the action, no preliminaries. Try to create a powerful sense of immediacy. Experiment with some of David Foster Wallace's methods: staccato sentences; repetition; tiny details. Time is tick-tocking somewhere in the background, but in this place, for the two of you, time has almost stopped.

Travelling in Time

Time travelling has long been a popular fictional theme. 'Rip Van Winkle', a short story by Washington Irving, published in 1819,[2] depicts a man sleeping his way into the future and waking to find the world transformed. H.G. Wells' novel *The Time Machine*[3] is another classic example and was one of the first to reach a mass audience. Published in 1895, it pre-dated Einstein's theories by ten years and has inspired two film versions. Today's most well-known time fictions are probably television series: *Star Trek* and *Doctor Who*, for example, both of which translate scientific observation and theory (black holes, relativity) into fantastic fact, allowing characters to jump back and forth in time as if the universe were a dog and they were its fleas.

Martin Amis's *Time's Arrow* uses a reversed chronology to disrupt the way we normally perceive events. The main theme of the book is the Holocaust, a period in history, *Time's Arrow* implies, when human progress was reversed. The novel also draws on semi-scientific speculation that if the Big Bang were to reach its limit the universe might implode and time, including human time, would go backwards. Amis uses these ideas to create very odd effects. A doctor speaks of what happens in a hospital:

> Some guy comes in with a bandage around his head. We don't mess about. We'll soon have that off. He's got a hole in his head. So what do we do? We stick a nail in it. Get the nail – a good rusty one – from the trash or wherever. And lead him out to the Waiting Room where he's allowed to linger and holler for a while before we ferry him back to the night.[4]

This passage summarises (in reverse) the way a person is treated in hospital and is both shocking and funny. The key to this, I think, is that Amis takes us through each step of a familiar time structure – person coming into the hospital from outside, yelling in the waiting room, rusty nail taken out of his head and thrown in the trash, hole in his head bandaged – and then carefully reverses them. It doesn't work perfectly, of course, but there is a strange logic to this inverted world, as if we are looking through the writing to another dimension, through a quantum looking-glass.

Stuart: A Life Backwards by Alexander Masters[5] is the story of an actual person described on the book cover as 'a chaotic, knife-wielding beggar'. Masters collaborates with Stuart to recount his crazy, violent life story, which has involved many spells in prison, drug addiction, alcoholism and life on the street. The added twist is that this story, as the title says, is told backwards. It begins at the end, as Stuart and Alexander meet,[6] and works its way through to the beginning of Stuart's life.

Masters' book uses reversal to trace some of the possible causes of Stuart's chaotic and unhappy life. It leads the reader back from half-deranged and threatening man, step by worsening step, to small and vulnerable child.

The key point is that both texts use time reversal as a method of exploring meaning and character in greater depth, not simply as clever but empty experimentation. They also work by being grounded in the real world and by focusing carefully on the 'normal' order of events. Try it for yourself, but don't force every detail into reversal and don't comment on the strangeness. Let the writing speak for itself.

Time Loops and Jump Cuts

One of the most well-known time-loop stories is the film *Groundhog Day*, directed by Harold Ramis, in which the central character, a bored and cynical television reporter, is forced to repeat the same day over and over until he learns the value and meaning of his life. Margaret Atwood also uses this relentless repetition in her short story 'Happy Endings'.[7] A number of alternative boy-meets-girl romantic scenarios are set out in a series of blocks. Each block is labelled: A, B, C, etc., beginning with the happy-ever-after version:

> A. John and Mary fall in love and get married. They both have worthwhile and remunerative jobs which they find stimulating and challenging. They buy a charming house.

Atwood, of course, has her tongue firmly in cheek here, in order to critique idealised relationships. The use of the formulaic names and short sentences, the repetition of the corporate-speak words, 'stimulating' and 'challenging', make John and Mary appear robotic and unreal. In the other versions, things don't always turn out so well:

> B. Mary falls in love with John but John doesn't fall in love with Mary. He merely uses her body for selfish pleasure and ego gratification of a tepid kind. He comes to her apartment twice a week and she cooks him dinner, you'll notice that he doesn't even consider her worth the price of a dinner out and after he's eaten the dinner he fucks her and after that he falls asleep, while she does the dishes so he won't think she's untidy.

Note how this block begins with a similar tone to version A, but within a sentence or two the story slips into something more painfully human, more real; and the language becomes richer, sentences running on without full stops, like a voice speaking. In Block C the power struggle is reversed:

> John, who is an older man, falls in love with Mary, and Mary, who is only twenty-two, feels sorry for him because he's worried about his hair falling out.

Atwood's method gives us a series of mini-sagas, each one entertaining in its own right, but with the repeating form also echoing and resonating with deeper patterns and meanings: the universality of love and sex; expectations and experience; the patterns we find ourselves stuck in; and the truth that we all must eventually learn – that all stories, even love stories, will come to an end.

Writing Exercise: Writing in Pieces

Create two characters in a relationship (not a romantic one).
    e.g.: Human/Pet; Teacher/Pupil; Parent/Child.
    Tell the story of this relationship in ten sections – number the sections one to ten. Think of possible permutations from the familiar to the bizarre and unexpected. Start formally but then let the stories take off, allowing characters and events to develop. Use the final section to draw a conclusion – to make some kind of fictional statement about the nature of such relationships. However, this statement should be implicit, not explicit: *shown, not told*.
    Remember that, although there is repetition, there still needs to be narrative development – something must always change in a story. But the change can be in the reader's mind.

There are many other ways of playing with time and form which you may be interested in finding for yourself. The important thing is to be aware that not all writing follows, or needs to follow, the classical linear time narrative. There are as many ways of telling stories, of writing the world, as there are writers. If you are someone who finds the traditional forms difficult and restrictive, this is an opportunity for you to try out some of the alternatives for yourself. Learn the rules first. Then learn to break them.

Reflection Project

Your Work

Here are some prompts to help you reflect about your work. Write a paragraph or two in response to each of them.

Reading

* What is the relationship between your reading and your writing?
* How do you see to it that your reading informs your writing?
* Which short story writers have particularly inspired you? Why?

Writing

* What is your idea of a short story?
* What is your philosophy of writing?
* Are you more self-critical than you were? If so, how did that happen?
* Has your confidence grown? If so, how did that happen?

Craft

* Reflect on what you have learned about craft from the stories you have studied in the last year.
* Consider any aspects of craft that you have struggled with.
* Which elements of craft do you now feel more confident with?
* What have you learned about reader engagement?

Redrafting

* What do you like about redrafting and what do you find difficult about it?
* What consideration have you given to the larger structural aspects of your work?
* What consideration have you given to your work line by line?
* What problems have you had with crafting your last short story? What were your strategies for overcoming these problems?

Notes

1   David Foster Wallace, 'Forever Overhead' in *Brief Interviews with Hideous Men* (London: Abacus, 2001), pp 10–12.

2 Washington Irving, *Rip Van Winkle* (London: Puffin Books, 1996).

3 You can read a free online version at www.online-literature.com/wellshg/ timemachine/ (accessed 27 March 2017) – but be warned that the story takes until the third chapter to get into the time travel journey.

4 Martin Amis, *Time's Arrow* (London: Vintage, 1991), p 76.

5 Alexander Masters, *Stuart: A Life Backwards* (London: Fourth Estate, 2005).

6 Although this isn't the true end, which is given to us in the introduction, to say anymore would be to give it away.

7 Margaret Atwood, 'Happy Endings' in Hermione Lee (ed.), *The Secret Self* (London: J.M. Dent, 1985), pp 370–1.

24

Transitions

One aspect of the pressure to maintain reader engagement is the need for movement. I've said already that a story has more in common with a movie than a photograph: it ought to involve movement almost all the time. In attempting to keep your story in motion, you will need a variety of means for a variety of purposes to move your reader around.

Perhaps the most obvious movement – and it is prompted by wanting to leave the dull parts out – is moving through time watch how Amy Tan. In this passage from one of the stories in *The Joy Luck Club*, achieves the most elementary moving through time:

> When Harold returns from the store, he starts the charcoal. I unload the groceries, marinate the steaks, cook the rice, and set the table. My mother sits on a stool at the granite counter, drinking a mug of coffee I've poured for her. Every few minutes she wipes the bottom of the mug with a tissue she keeps stuffed in her sweater sleeve.
>
> During dinner, Harold keeps the conversation going. He talks about the plans for the house: the skylights, expanding the deck, planting flower beds of tulips and crocuses, clearing the poison oak, adding another wing, building a Japanese-style bathroom. And then he clears the table and starts stacking the plates in the dishwasher … [A dialogue passage follows and then this:]
>
> After dinner, I put clean towels on the bed in the guest room. My mother is sitting on the bed.[1]

The opening line is the beginning of a new section within the chapter and follows an extra space on the page, so the reader has been moved from an earlier scene, on a previous day, to Harold returning from the store.

However, Tan shunts us through time again at the beginning of the second paragraph. We had been at some earlier point in the day and now we are in the evening: 'During dinner, Harold ...'. The following sentence, beginning 'He talks about the plans for the house ...', includes a summary of the conversation while the family are eating, so that moves us along again. In the last sentence of the second paragraph ('And then he clears ...'), Tan uses ellipsis once more: she cuts out another piece of time. In the first sentence of the final paragraph, we have moved from the conversations while clearing up after dinner to a later point in the evening, and then Tan moves us on to a little later in the day ('My mother is sitting on the bed.')

This means that in this very short passage, Amy Tan has moved the reader through time or space five times (if we count the plans for the house summary as one movement), which has several beneficial effects for readers. Number one, it's a moving picture, skipping through time and space and omitting less-interesting business. Movement, as you know, is desirable. Clearly it creates pace, since motion and pace are interrelated. By leaving out the inconsequential, it also gives air to the scene and helps it get off the ground. (If you have young children whose comprehensive summary of their escapades, or of a film's storyline, leaves nothing out, you will know how desperately long a complete account of any series of actions can feel.) You register consciously or unconsciously the author editing the fictional reality into a palatable narrative, removing the irrelevant to help you focus on the pertinent, and this must at some level reassure you that you are in competent hands, that this story is being crafted for your reading pleasure.

Writing Burst

- Put 'Arctic Monkeys, Cornerstone' in your search engine and use the song as your prompt. Listen without any visuals – the official video or anything else. You just want the experience of hearing the lyrics and the music.

Transitions Between Sentences

The same effects can be achieved at sentence level, as William Boyd does in this passage from 'Bethany-next-the-Sea':

> The next day, keen for it to pass as quickly as possible, Bethany takes a bus from Faith-next-the-Sea along the coast to Hunstanton. 'Hunston,' the bus driver corrects her pronunciation when she pays for her ticket, 'Sunny Hunny.' She wanders around the town and buys herself a sandwich and can of Coke. She takes a photograph of the curious striped cliffs with their horizontal bands of white and red chalk making them look like some kind of giant cake. It is a cool, hazy day and she peers across vainly at the Wash, failing to make out the Lincolnshire shore. Given the weather conditions, she decides against the boat trips to Sea Island to seal-watch and finds herself a sheltered corner, where she sends texts to various people. To her mother; to her father and stepmother, Chen-Chi, in Los Angeles ('Movie going great!'); to her girl friends – Moxy, Jez and Arabella. She also sends a blunt text to her so-called boyfriend, Kasimierz, who has promised to come and visit her on set but seems to be the busiest man in London. She has been looking forward to them playing house (and making love) in the tilting Faith-next-the-Sea caravan but he seems determined to disappoint her. 'Two days left. The clock is ticking. B.' is all she sends him. Everyone else replies over the course of the afternoon except Kasimierz – which casts her down somewhat. It's drizzling when she reaches the bus stop and she smokes two cigarettes as she waits with four old ladies for the bus back along the coast. They stare at her as if she's some kind of alien.[2]

The first sentence includes Bethany's decision to take a bus to Hunstanton. In the second, she's on the bus. In the third, she's in the town and busy with lunch. In the fourth, she's at the cliffs. By the sixth, she has found a sheltered corner and is busily texting. In the tenth, we are moving swiftly through the afternoon, and in the sentence after that, Bethany is back at the bus stop.

In the 270 words quoted here, William Boyd has moved the reader through time or space five times. One way of seeing it is as summary, of course, which increases the pace, but that summary is achieved by transitioning from one sentence to the next, and its purpose is the same as the movement in the Tan extract: to omit unnecessary content in order to increase the pace.

These movements are all forms of transition, which Jack M. Bickham defines as 'passages that get a character from one place to another, or from one time to another'.[3] These particular transitions were between one sentence and the next, or between paragraphs.

Transitions Between Sections

Transitions may also be between one scene and another. (Scenes and sections are not quite the same thing, though: one scene may take place over two sections; three may be in one.) We see such transitions in these examples from Margaret Atwood's story 'The Sin Eater', which concerns the death of the unnamed narrator's therapist, Joseph.

The end of the first section quoted below is from a scene where Karen, one of Joseph's ex-wives, has come to let the narrator know that Joseph has died. The scene after the section break happens later, and in it the narrator is preparing for Joseph's funeral.

> I was furious with him. It was an act of desertion. What made him think he had the right to go climbing up to the top of a sixty-foot tree, risking all our lives? Did his flowerbeds mean more to him than we did?
>
> 'What are we going to do?' said Karen.
>
> *What am I going to do?* is one question. It can always be replaced by *What am I going to wear?* For some people it's the same thing.[4]

Why use this sort of transition, which requires a break between two scenes? It gives readers some breathing space, allows a pause and perhaps gives their unconscious a chance to process the information that has gone before the break. The alternative is a monolithic text without breaks of any kind. It's preferable to cut your fiction up into sections which have some relation to the attention span of the human mind. If pushed, I can concentrate pretty well for up to forty-five minutes, but not much more than that. The same is probably true of you. And your readers – so make some allowances.

In the extract above, the earlier section ends with Karen saying, 'What are we going to do?' and the later one begins with almost exactly the same line, 'What am I going to do?' As a result, the relationship between the two scenes is established. In these two consecutive sections, Atwood illustrates one of the characteristics of transitions between sections of scenes. They are bridges, with feet on both sides of the divide, which lead from one scene to the next. In this example, though, there is more than one kind of bridge. The first is created by the repeated questions, the second by the emotion of the characters: both Karen and the narrator feel lost without Joseph. The emotions and the repeated question are the markers which signal the bridge, the connection between the end of one scene and the beginning of the succeeding one.

Markers

Using markers is effective because it lets the reader know that these scenes are closely related. This way you can fight against losing or confusing your reader. You don't always have to insert those markers to help readers along, though. They are as smart as you and maybe smarter. They've read postmodern novels with fragmented chronologies and can leap from here to there without you holding their hand. But some of the time, as we've just seen in the Atwood transition, using markers to help the reader is desirable: because both women are asking the same questions, the two sections are shown to be related. Even when successive sections aren't directly related, you may want to plant markers on either side of the transition just to be elegant, to show that you have given some thought to the construction of the fiction, as Margaret Atwood does in the story's next transition. Towards the end of the first of the two sections I'm talking about, the narrator is looking for 'the blackest thing I can find' to wear to the funeral. The next section begins with her saying, 'I needn't have bothered with the black.' The two markers serve to demonstrate that the author has carefully designed the story.

In all three stories, a transition, whether it's between sentences, paragraphs or section breaks, has been used to show that the narrative has moved through time or space (the Atwood) or has omitted some irrelevant action (the Tan and the Boyd).

Markers and Changes of Viewpoint

Another form of transition is used when one viewpoint changes to another – as in George Saunders' 'The Falls'. The viewpoint character at the start of the story is Morse. We know this because the first word of the opening line identifies him as such: 'Morse found it nerve-racking to cross the St Jude grounds just as the school was being dismissed.' The change of viewpoint, when it comes, to that of another character, Cummings, is flagged up in precisely the same way – by naming him in the first word of the first sentence of the new section:

> … he pictured himself weeping on the shore, and to eradicate this thought started manically whistling 'The Stars and The Stripes Forever', while slapping his hands against his sides.
>
> Cummings bobbed past the restored gristmill, pleased at having so decisively snubbed Morse, a smug member of the power elite in the conspiratorial Village …[5]

'The Falls' has very few viewpoint shifts. Even though there are many in Bernard MacLaverty's 'Father and Son',[6] he indicates them in the same way. The two viewpoints are – guess what – that of a father and his son, and most of the changes are indicated by the father making a reference to his son, usually in the first line or two and mostly by using the word 'son'.

A transition is like anything that connects two separate objects – a hinge holding door and frame together, or a stitch holding the arm of a shirt to the body: it's functional. Transitions are useful, elegant and sometimes necessary (necessary because you have to omit and you have to leave spaces). On the face of it, using them might look like one of the slighter fiction-writing techniques, but it won't take much time or effort, and the effect on the reader is usually significant, even if it's at an unconscious level.

Writing Exercise: Transitions

Using an existing draft of a piece of fiction, see if you can't make it more cohesive and engaging by introducing transitions between sentences and paragraphs. Then introduce more breathing space for the reader by introducing transitions between scenes which move from one place to another, from one time to another or from one viewpoint to another.

Notes

1   Amy Tan, *The Joy Luck Club* (London: Minerva, 1991), pp 162–3.
2   William Boyd, 'Bethany-next-the-Sea' in *Ox Tales: Water* (London: Profile, 2009).
3   Bickham, *Writing the Short Story*, p 39.
4   Margaret Atwood, 'The Sin Eater' in *Bluebeard's Egg* (London: Vintage, 1980), pp 216–17.
5   George Saunders, 'The Falls' in *Pastoralia* (London: Bloomsbury, 2001), p 178.
6   Bernard MacLaverty, 'Father and Son' in *A Time to Dance* (London: Vintage, 1999).

25

Foreshadowing

According to James N. Frey, 'Foreshadowing is the art of raising story questions.'[1] Every time you raise a question in the reader's mind, you are foreshadowing and – not just because it is central to raising questions in the reader's mind – this is a key storytelling technique.

In a way, foreshadowing is connected to cause and effect: because this happens, that should follow. Chekhov observed that the gun in the first act should go off in the third. If Raymond Chandler's Philip Marlowe is shown taking a gun with him at the start of one of his adventures, we expect a follow-through. The expected effect of this private eye setting out with a gun is that he will use it later. And he'd better use it. In *Words Fail Me,* Patricia T. O'Conner sees foreshadowing as a promise the author makes to the reader, and warns of the dangers in unfulfilled promises:

> A careless hint or a subject that's raised and then dropped is a gun left in plain view but never fired. It's a promise to the audience – 'Trust me to deliver the goods' – that's never kept.[2]

Another way of looking at it is Frank Conroy's. At that Iowa Writers' Workshop I sat in on, he likened broken promises such as this to equipping readers for a stiff uphill walk. If you give them things they will need later in the journey (a compass, a pen-knife, water, a packed lunch), fine. But if you make them carry a lot of things up the hill that they find out later they didn't need (a laptop, thermal clothes, a walkie-talkie with heavy battery pack, etc.), not so good. In other words, don't annoy your readers by burdening them with superfluous things to carry.

Foreshadowing may also act like an omen – or at least what will come to seem like an omen later on. A minor action at the start of a story may suggest a major action at the end. For example, Pip's dramatic encounter with the convict Magwitch at the start of *Great Expectations* foreshadows the novel's climax. In the minor action, our first impression that the child Pip is kind-hearted and brave is formed when Magwitch, a frightening escaped convict, orders him to bring him food. In the major action, the climax of the novel, the adult Pip almost loses his life while attempting, once again, to help Magwitch escape. Dickens underlines the relation between these two scenes by setting both of them on murky marshland. But there's another level to foreshadowing in this example. Yes, the minor action foreshadows the major one, but the way Pip is characterised in it is confirmed in the major action. We were initially led to believe that he was brave and noble, which the major action confirms for us: he's so much so, he almost gets himself killed. 'What a character does under a little stress,' says Frey, 'is very telling about what he might do under a lot of stress.'[3]

The screenplay guru Robert McKee has a lovely definition of foreshadowing: he says it is 'the arrangement of early events to prepare for later events'.[4]

Writing Burst

- This was turning out to be a huge mistake.

Plants

'Some promises', Patricia T. O'Conner advises, 'are subtle; the reader recognizes them only in retrospect. They may be as unobtrusive as a recurring image.'[5] These subtle promises may be seen as plants, little seeds the author sows and which the reader unconsciously stores away for future use.

Adam Marek's 'Remember the Bride Who Got Stung?' (which you can read by following the link on p. 234) has as much foreshadowing as could be expected in a 3,500-word short story. Below are the examples I found in it, in the order they appear. If you want to analyse it along with me, it's available via the Thresholds website.[6]

1. Its title is the first hint of the climax of the story. Readers may well fail to register it as such, but after they finish the story it becomes evident that the title is an unglossed plant for the dramatic pay-off when the conflicts peak close to the end.
2. The characters, Victor and Tara and Nate, their young son, are slogging towards a picnic spot. Victor is struggling to carry their picnic hamper. It's too heavy and too uncomfortable, and before long one of its 'pointy wicker corners' stabs him in the shin, leaving a bloody scrape. Another plant, as you'll see: stabbing will become significant.
3. On the second page, Nate tells his mother that his imaginary friend has died. More foreshadowing: a death is threatened later in the story.
4. A few pages later, Victor's phone buzzes. Bees, buzzes – right? A page or two later and it buzzes again.
5. Several times Victor complains about how far Tara is making them walk: 'Honey, remember we're going to have to walk the whole way back, too.' Foreshadowing: the distance back to their car becomes crucial.
6. They discover that they've forgotten to pack a knife in the hamper, but Victor saves the day: he has his Leatherman pocket-knife with him. More foreshadowing, big plant. The knife is Chekhov's gun.
7. Victor's phone appears to be buzzing again – although as it turns out moments later, it isn't the phone. Three references to buzzing so far, and of course there's the bee in the title, which makes four.
8. Tara says of the phone, 'It sounds like a bee.' Two direct references to bees now, and then, right away, an actual bee, flying at each one of them as it patrols 'the whole airspace above the blanket'. It stings Nate. (As the words 'got stung' are there in the title, it has to sting someone.) The drama deepens, for it now emerges that Nate is allergic to bee stings and although they usually pack a syringe to deal with this, today they've forgotten to.

9. Victor tries to calm Tara down by telling her the story of the bride who got stung on her way to church. She was 'allergic and she didn't have her shot with her, but she was so nervous about the wedding she had pumped herself full of adrenaline, so she survived'. This – the fact that the bride's adrenaline saved her life – is yet another plant.

Here's the run-up to the story's climax:

> 'You're allergic to stings,' Victor said. '*Very* allergic. So we've got two choices. We can make a run for the car together and try to get to the nearest hospital, but there's a good chance we won't get there in time, or ...'
>
> 'Good God, Victor! Shut up! Here, I'll pick him up.' Tara bent low to scoop her hands under his legs, but Victor barred the way with his outstretched hand.
>
> 'There isn't time,' he said. 'Our other option, poppet, is to deal with the poison in your leg before it gets any further into your body. If we do it now we might just catch it.'
>
> 'You can't suck out bee poison!' Tara said.
>
> 'No, we can't suck it out. We're going to have to do something more drastic, and you're going to have to be brave, Nate, because this is going to hurt.'
>
> Tightening his right arm around Nate's waist to hold him firm, Victor reached down with his left hand and picked up the Leatherman knife from the blanket.'
>
> 'No way! *No* way!' Nate yelled, using both hands to push against the side of Victor's face.

Remember Chekhov's gun. Here it's Victor's Leatherman. So one of the most potent plants has now been paid off, but almost immediately the point of the story about the bride who got stung is paid off, too.

> Something sharp jabbed into Victor's right eye and it filled with tears. 'I can't see!' he yelled. 'You've fucking blinded me!' Victor dropped the knife and put his hand to his eye.
>
> Nate pummelled Victor with his knees, elbows and knuckles, scrambling to get free of his father's weight. Tara grabbed Nate's wrists and helped him out, lifting him to his feet. Together they fled through the long grass.
>
> 'I'm pretending you stupid fuck! I'm pretending.'

The plant was the fact that the bride's anxiety about her wedding had pumped her full of adrenaline, thus saving her life when she got stung. The pay-off has been delivered when it turns out that Victor didn't mean to cut into his son's sting; he only intended to scare him enough to flood him with adrenaline, and so save his life.

As you've seen, 'The Bride Who Got Stung' is generously supplied with foreshadowing. You can learn at least three lessons from it.

One, plant sufficiently for the information being planted to register, as Barnaby Conrad recommends: 'If the fact that a character is left-handed is vital to the plot, show the reader in Chapter One or possibly Chapter Five or Six, but well before Chapter Thirteen when that fact becomes important.'[7]

Two, you want the reader to register the plant without noticing they are registering it. An efficient way of achieving that is to disguise it by making it seem like something else. For example, when the Leatherman is first mentioned, it appears to be nothing more than the solution to the problem of not having a knife with which to cut the bread.

The third lesson is a subtle one. The planted Leatherman seems to prepare us for it being used to cut, stab or even kill someone – or will seem to have done so once Victor picks it up as he struggles with Nate, but that's sleight of hand on Marek's part. At the pay-off, the knife isn't used for anything more than trying to scare Nate enough to – in theory, at least – save his life. Even if it's only in a small way, Marek has created an expectation which he then thwarts.

Most of the time, however, planting is simply a matter of creating an expectation and satisfying it. 'With each line of dialogue or image or action,' Robert McKee says, 'you guide the audience to anticipate certain possibilities, so that when events arrive, they somehow satisfy the expectation you've created.'[8]

Finally, remember this: handling foreshadowing correctly will achieve two things. Readers will spot the pay-off and remember the plant and be pretty impressed with themselves for doing so. Even better, they will be equally impressed that you have been artful enough to execute that little trick.

> **Writing Exercise: Foreshadowing**
>
> Like many writers, I only ever have a vague idea of where I'm going with a story, so thinking about plants and pay-offs in advance isn't an option. What I have found, though, is that when I discover a pay-off in a first or second draft, it's quite simple and fun to go back afterwards and insert the plants for it. In its most basic form, this may be a case of realising at the end of a short story that your protagonist needs, for dramatic purposes, to be asthmatic. So you go back and show him being asthmatic a couple of times earlier in the story.
>
> This is an exercise to use with an existing draft of a story. Read it carefully and see if you can find a pay-off looking for a plant; see if you can find something it will be helpful to go back and foreshadow. Say the story ends with your protagonist heroically rescuing his fellow passengers after an air crash: you could foreshadow that by going back and inserting an opening scene where he takes a risk to help somebody in some minor difficulty – the minor action that will prepare your readers for the major action.
>
> When you have the first draft of a story, study it and see if you can find a plant for a pay-off that's already there.

3,000-Word Story Project

Dental Surgery

Your next Story Project is set in a dental surgery. Your protagonist is the vivacious, slightly zany receptionist. She has fallen for the new dentist at the practice, whose surgery is the one closest to reception, and your story is about what she does to try to win him over.

You are allowed to use the waiting room, the reception desk and the small storage area just behind it. Your characters might include receptionists, dental nurses, dental hygienists, dentists and patients. People might come in to collect or deliver dentures. Repairmen might call.

Write a 3,000-word short story, as either comedy or drama, particularly incorporating what you have learned recently about managing time and about style. There's also an opportunity here for you to research data relating to dental surgeries.

Write a 500-word reflection, and include a bibliography of any texts that have informed the creative work.

Notes

1   Frey, *How to Write a Damn Good Novel*, p 116.
2   O'Conner, *Words Fail Me*, p 165.
3   Frey, *How to Write a Damn Good Novel*, p 119.
4   McKee, *Story*, p 200.
5   O'Conner, *Words Fail Me*, p 169.
6   Adam Marek, 'Remember the Bride Who Got Stung?' in his collection *The Stone Thrower* (Manchester: Comma Press, 2012), available at http:// thresholds.chi.ac.uk/wp-content/uploads/2012/07/REMEMBER-THE-BRIDE-WHO-GOT-STUNG_Adam-Marek.pdf (accessed 19 April 2017).
7   Conrad, *The Complete Guide to Writing Fiction*, p 186.
8   McKee, *Story*, p 200.

Part V

How to Go the Distance

26

Finding an Audience

Rodge Glass

A Sideways Look at the Landscape

The first story I read by the great Chilean writer Roberto Bolaño was in *Last Evenings on Earth*. The book is a randomly ordered hotchpotch from two different Spanish-language collections. Context is everything, and I knew nothing about how or why this book was put together. As far as I was concerned, *Last Evenings on Earth* was what the author intended. For me to read this particular story first. And, given the content, it seemed a deliberate statement, which comes back to me each time I ask myself: how do short story writers find readers? Let me explain the connection.

The story in question is called 'Sensini'. It focuses on the relationship between a young Bolaño and the eponymous, exiled Argentinian writer Luis Antonio Sensini. Set in late-1970s Spain, with Bolaño in his twenties, our narrator is isolated and suffering from insomnia. Recently unemployed, all he does is write and go for night walks, which leave him 'with a feeling like jet lag'. But there is a sliver of artistic hope. He's just come fourth in the Alcoy Literary Competition and discovered Sensini has come third. Bolaño asks the organisers if they'll put him in touch with his fellow nominee. The younger man writes of his admiration, not expecting a reply – he gets a warm one, quickly.

Bolaño has mixed feelings about their burgeoning friendship. As a Sensini admirer, it's depressing that he, a nobody, is in the same territory as his hero. But he also sees an opportunity, and an ally. Throughout their correspondence, Sensini's advice to Bolaño remains consistent: keep sending your work off. Keep trying. Not because competitions are a barometer of quality: on the contrary, the story foregrounds the random nature of who wins what.[1] What gets published, where. Why does Sensini advise perseverance? Not because he desires praise or believes in judges. Rather, it's about finding ways to keep yourself going. And competitions are part of that process – the place in Sensini's 'little world of letters' where they find their first readers. They're something many writers have in common. Sensini writes to Bolaño 'as if the pair of us were on our marks for a race'. The sentence that stands out to the younger man is, 'Pen to paper now, no shirking!' Bolaño muses on that sentence for days. And I remembered it too, because that's how I felt once. Like literature was a race which was won and lost not by talent, but by graft. And I didn't want to be straining to catch up.

For both writers here, writing is an essential way not just to communicate, but to exist. And to this reader at least, now a fully paid-up Bolaño convert, the subtext in this story seems clear. A writer without at least the prospect of readers will struggle to survive. Your stories can only truly live if you find those readers. So (virtual) pen to paper, no shirking! Which, yes, means the writing itself. Without quality writing, you've got nothing. (Hence every other chapter in this book.) But 'no shirking' also means taking that writing into the world. Finding places to publish. Entering into the literary race. Which, despite appearances, is not too different now to how it was for Sensini and a young Bolaño in Spain, or Alice Munro starting out in Canada, or Kafka in Austria-Hungary. Survey the landscape, try to make sense of it, then set about engaging with it. Now, all this talk of dead Latin American exiles and literary races is fine, as far as it goes – but what does it mean for us in the here and now?

A Head-On Look at the Landscape

I'm convinced the world of the short story is morphing in positive ways, and that for new writers this represents a land of genuine opportunity. The old cliché, so often repeated, is what the curator of the Short

Stops website, Tania Hershman, exposes as the 'myth about the poor old, beleaguered and unloved short story'. And it is a myth. Publishers don't want short stories! Readers don't buy them! The short story is maligned! Ignored! Worthless! Nothing could be further from the truth. And whether it's Munro's Nobel Prize, the explosion of interest within academia, or the mushrooming of live literature events, the last decade provides plenty of evidence for this. We've taken a sideways look at the landscape with Roberto. Now let's look head on.

The internet has much to answer for, but the short story world should be grateful for it. No longer do we need to scour newspaper adverts with a magnifying glass, looking for openings. All is available, immediately. The internet has opened our fictional universe, democratised it, and multiplied the ways writers and readers can find each other, engage, learn from each other and find an audience. When the Edge Hill Prize was set up in 2007, with £10,000 awarded to a single-author collection from the UK and Ireland, the landscape was radically different. This year we at Edge Hill celebrate ten years of the Prize, and I've been struck by the transformation that last decade has seen. This year's competition has seen more entries than ever, more independent publishers, more new ones investing in the form, as well as traditional houses supporting more high-quality work. The short story world isn't perfect. None is. But don't let anyone tell you there's no point in this. In practical terms, what does this culture change mean? Well, potential breakthroughs at every stage of your career – from entry-level newbies taking a punt on an online call-out, to Premier League professionals who already live by their writing, have reputations to defend and have major book deals already in their back pocket. There's encouragement to be found everywhere, if you have the patience for detail. That's the abstract. Now the detail.

The Prizes

Amongst the bigger competitions, the BBC National Short Story Award is one of the most prestigious, with a £15,000 prize for a single story. Yes, winners have included household names such as Lionel Shriver and nominees like Hilary Mantel, but newer writers have broken through too. In 2012, the BBC prize was won by the then-unknown Bulgarian Miroslav Penkov, beating off competition from Deborah Levy and M.J. Hyland. (Four years later, Penkov's debut novel *Stork Mountain* was published on both sides of the Atlantic. He's no longer unknown.) Then there's the *Sunday Times* EFG Short Story Award, putting the BBC's prize money in the shade – that's £30,000 for one story, won by Jonathan Tel in 2016, also a winner of the £5,000 Commonwealth Writers' Short Story Prize in 2015. He must be an optimist, having also entered and been shortlisted for multiple awards elsewhere too. Tel has lived all over the world; many fields are international. As long as the guidelines permit it, there's no reason why you can't apply in every country on earth. And because most competitions are anonymous, favouritism is rare.

As well as being fairly clean, the evidence shows that the competition process often leads directly or indirectly to publication. The two are intrinsically linked. Two examples. When James Rice (author of Chapter 6: 'Research') won the Pulp Idol new writers' competition in Liverpool, a judge gave him his card and said, 'When you've finished your novel, let me know.' Rice's novel was published by Hodder in 2015 and a follow-up is on the way. Meanwhile, Anne Donovan famously got signed up by Canongate Books because the MD of the company, Jamie Byng, had only judged two competitions and she'd won them both, so he said, 'I thought I'd better publish her!' Those early stories of Donovan's were written in Glaswegian Scots, and might otherwise have found it difficult to find a home. But her winning stories went into her Canongate collection and three novels followed, one of which, *Buddha Da*, is now a set text in Scottish schools. Without those competitions, who knows where she would be now? So competitions aren't everything, but they are something. That's because publishers are always looking for new writers. And always looking for a shorthand they can rely on.

It's often said that there's no money in writing short stories, no way to sustain yourself. For some that may be true, but according to the 'Do You Love Your Publisher?' survey, as cited in *The Bookseller*[2] in 2015, the median advance per book (novel, short stories, non-fiction etc.) for traditionally published authors in the UK is under £6,600. Some professional writers reading this may see that figure and think it's surprisingly high.[3] But, seen in that context, the sums on offer for single stories, as detailed above, look generous indeed. And they keep multiplying. To list every literary opening here is impossible – the landscape is always evolving, and by the time you read this, there will be something new out there – but it's worth taking a moment to appreciate how much there is in terms of opportunity for aspiring writers.

If you survey the landscape a while, you begin to notice the same literary names popping up across the world of the short story, from the shortlists of the Bridport Prize (£5,000 first prize) to the Bristol Short Story Prize (£5,000) to the V.S. Pritchett Memorial Prize (£1,000), from the likes of The Moth Short Story Prize in Ireland (£3,000) to *Carve Magazine*'s Raymond Carver Short Story Contest in the US. (Remember, you don't need to stick to this country. Since we moved online, the English-speaking world is the market for any writer in English.) And many of these are judged by agents or, as with The Novella Award – run jointly by Manchester Metropolitan University and Liverpool John Moores University – are actually tied to a publication.[4] There are also many different types for different kinds of writers. If you're a flash fiction writer, for instance, the thrice-yearly, rolling Bath Flash Fiction Award is a good one (£1,000). Flash fiction prizes may have smaller prize money, but are more reachable for new writers – an example of that is the quarterly Flash500 competition (£300). Many of the higher profile prizes do charge for entry, so learn to be selective or go bankrupt fast. For example, the Bridport costs £10 to enter, the Bristol prize costs £8 per story – but the prices are not prohibitive, and for entry-level writers there are also a plethora of online competitions and publishing opportunities that are free. When I'm teaching 'Introduction to Fiction' to undergraduates, I tell them all about the *New Yorker, Granta* and the *Paris Review* – and I applaud those with the chutzpah to pitch high. But then I usher them towards something achievable in the short term. The happiest I've ever seen a young writer is when she sent a story to the free-to-enter Postcard Shorts (stories which fit on a postcard), which was accepted and published online within days. Suddenly confident, after that there was no stopping her. If she'd gone straight to the *New Yorker*, she'd never have got that buzz.

So think carefully about what level suits you best. The highest prize money tends to attract the most acclaimed writers, but there are prizes out there which are less popular but still prestigious. Search these out. Look at past shortlists and see which accept stories anonymously. Which have a history of rewarding unknowns as well as Premier Leaguers. Always read the 'About Us' section on every website. See what the history of each competition or magazine is. See what their taste is. And when submitting, stick to what they ask for. If they want stories 12 point, 1.5 line spaced, justified to the left, that's what you need to do, or you're wasting your time. Oh, and also: perseverance is essential, as is savvy. Building up a writer's CV takes time. There's no point throwing up your hands because the first set of judges doesn't understand your genius. Get organised. Draw up a list of what's open, and what the guidelines are. All this detail can be dizzying. So try to find yourself a shortcut that suits you – a website you trust that can help you navigate the landscape, perhaps somewhere which hosts regular content which will help you learn about that landscape. There are several excellent short story sites out there, and they're easy to find.

Websites and Apps

One of the most well respected of these is Thresholds, the International Short Story Forum run by the University of Chichester. User-friendly and well researched, this has a clear section with ongoing deadlines, along with discussion forums; articles and essays on the work of great short story writers; author profiles; and a Resources section broken down into Markets & Magazines, Funding Sources, Writing Exercises, Agents and so on. Any writer who wishes to make a genuine breakthrough raises their chances hugely by engaging with this kind of material. Meanwhile, good writers are of course good readers, so if you're one of those who doesn't read much, that needs to change, and now. Thresholds also has an archive of free-to-view short stories from the UK & Ireland's foremost short story practitioners like Helen Simpson and Kevin Barry (if you don't know who they are, find out), and also up-and-coming, distinctive story writers like Stuart Evers and Adam Marek. They are the landscape too. And we can all improve as writers by broadening our reading habits. The most common mistake new writers make is arrogance – what could I possibly learn from others? The ones that do well are almost always humble and keen to learn. That doesn't mean you have to be conventional. The radical writer is often the most likely to stand out. But know and understand the rules before you set about breaking them. Thresholds is just one of the online resources that are now essential for new writers of stories. Each organisation has a different market. You've just got to find the one that suits you.

A fantastic new resource is MacGuffin, Comma Press's highly acclaimed self-publishing platform, where writers can upload audio which is then transferred via an archive to their app for listeners to access. You can then search for stories based on your literary tastes, or listening time desired. You can tag stories: 'feminist', 'artifice', 'classics'. The *Times Literary Supplement* calls MacGuffin 'a democratic approach to writing'; it's also been called 'a Spotify for books'. As a reader, and a fan of the *Granta, Guardian* and *New Yorker* books podcasts, I find MacGuffin another liberating development – because it returns us to the writing itself, and allows readers to navigate the landscape for themselves. It's a genuinely dynamic, free resource, which is shaped by its users, and it's different for every person. Comma Press is an internationally minded publisher which specialises in the short story. It's not surprising they're interested in developing technology which will help sustain the form.

Personally, I subscribe to Tania Hershman's Short Stops site. It sends me a fortnightly round-up with magazine call-outs, workshops, upcoming festivals from international to local, and a useful 'Last Minutes & Gentle Reminders' section for those who might be about to hear the sound of deadlines whooshing past their ears. Short Stops also has an author archive, giving information about writers and their collections, reviews of the best literary magazines available (useful, as a bewildering number come and go fast), and also a hugely active, well-connected Twitter account, which doesn't miss a thing. Essentially, it's a useful way of disseminating information. Still, when pursuing the opportunities on or via these sites, be careful. Read the guidelines closely. It's wonderful, for example, that BBC Radio 4 commissions so much short fiction, but if you've no idea of the process for pitching that work, never mind how to present it, how can you hope to have any success?

If you've been getting to know the landscape as laid out in this chapter, the chances are you'll have come across the most comprehensive writer's story website at the moment, that of Paul McVeigh. The Director of the London Short Story Festival and most recently the author of *The Good Son*, what marks McVeigh out is his determination to populate his site with useful material for other writers. Interviews with writers. Resources. Competition deadlines. Events. If you're reading his site, you're likely to have come across his blog post on getting a short story commissioned – which covers everything from the advice he received from a BBC radio producer right up to the recording of the story he wrote and eventually got accepted. The article points readers to the essential BBC Writers' Room. This is just one example of many, but it shows what all aspiring writers need to know: the rules of engagement. If you're subscribed to Thresholds, Short Stops, Paul McVeigh and Word Factory (who run literary salons and masterclasses), the chances you'll miss any opportunities are very small indeed. And along the way, you'll learn a great deal by reading articles, following the news, and familiarising yourself with that landscape.

Online Profile

The example of Paul McVeigh takes me onto the issue of online profile. Though ten years ago it was rare for writers, especially ones who were not well known, to engage directly, it is now increasingly expected by publishers and readers alike. If ever there was a time where you could sit in the corner of your garret, collar up, rocking back and forth, waiting for cult status to come along, I'm afraid those days are gone. Writers build up Facebook followings as standard, starting from nothing. They answer direct questions from readers on Twitter. Writers run their own websites and their own blogs, and have to learn to shout about their own work or else risk sinking. This much is obvious.

But what seems less obvious to many is that what matters is how you bring readers to you. If you have a novel coming out, or a short story in an anthology, that's great – and you can post about it. But you can only post about it so many times, and readers will soon tire of you talking about how great you are. The Edinburgh-based Laura Hird (author of the excellent collection *Born Free*) was one of the first to realise this. In 2006, she began publishing stories and poems by other writers on her own site – which brought web traffic. Other writers. More traffic. Paul McVeigh is now working on a similar principle, making his site somewhere that writers and readers want to come even if they've not heard of his writing. Not everyone that visits your site will buy your book, but they might read your interview with Carys Bray (novelist and short story writer), with Cathy Galvin (of Word Factory) or with Kevin Barry. You become part of the landscape, which you begin to recognise more fully. You make a contribution. Which leads to opportunity. My advice to writers who want to build a profile for themselves is: find a space in the literary world, fill it, and don't bore everyone with emotional blog posts about how much you always wanted to be a writer and it's a dream come true to feature in *Vampire Writers of Birmingham 9*. That may well be an exciting development, but a little restraint, a little control, goes a long way in terms of perception.

There are many great examples of how writers are doing this smartly. Jenn Ashworth is a good model – one of a minority who keeps her site fresh with her various projects, collaborations such as the northern-based Curious Tales, and a design which is clear, clean and professional. (Too many are messy and amateur.) Then there's Sarah Jasmon, a first-time novelist who has already made a name for herself by doing several things well: (a) not taking herself too seriously, (b) making her site personal (she writes about living on a boat) and (c) talking with enthusiasm about the writing of others. As I visited the site just now to check for updates on her book reviews, I noticed that she has a new interview with Carys Bray (another name that keeps coming up), discussing her new novel *The Museum of You* (Windmill, 2016). Bray is a popular writer, and she'll bring readers to Jasmon's website. Equally, it makes sense for her to be interviewed by a fellow writer who she knows will be sympathetic and read her work closely, before posting the interview in a place where, increasingly, writers and readers are going to get recommendations. This also goes for Jasmon's recent interview with Claire Fuller, author of the breakout success *Our Endless Numbered Days* (Fig Tree, 2015). Some readers might think this all sounds like a lot of hard work: and it is. But it's one of the ways to get afloat, and keep afloat.

Offline Profile

Still, there's only so much you can do at your laptop. Nothing replaces human interaction, and many of the writers who succeed in getting themselves on the literary ladder do so by good old-fashioned meetings with human beings. I got my agent by attending a talk and asking if I could send her my work. I ended up collaborating with the award-winning Bad Language in Manchester after attending their events and getting chatting to the organisers. Live Literature is an area which is essential for the new writer who wishes to hone their craft, and do so amongst other writers. In London there's the Faber Social. There's the globetrotting Literary Death Match. But you don't have to go to one of the high-profile nights. Most cities and towns have equivalents – and many have literary festivals now too. It's true that some of these have a short shelf life (alas, Edinburgh's glorious Rally & Broad is no longer), but there's little excuse any more for not being able to find a place where you can see authors giving readings or test out new work in public, amongst others who truly care about the form. And while you're there, you'll meet other writers, who will help you, a little like Sensini helped Bolaño, find new opportunities. That doesn't mean shouting desperately about your own talent. It doesn't mean being aggressive or openly, nakedly networking. But it does mean not hiding.

There are many examples out there of up-and-coming writers who are also excellent performers. I'm thinking of Anneliese Mackintosh, whose *Any Other Mouth* won 2015's Green Carnation Prize for LGBT writers and acts out her voice-led work with power; or the deadpan comedy of Kevin Barry (there's that name again), who has gained a live reputation for performance all over the world. These are some favourites of mine, but there are thousands out there, and they're not confined to the short story form. As we learn from other story writers, we can also learn from poets, performers, musicians, film-makers. Many of the most dynamic literary live nights in the UK are multi-arts. The difference between success and failure isn't talent, it's concentration. In this case, concentrating on how to get noticed. So see how others do it, then forge your own path.

Roberto's Happy Ending

Roberto Bolaño's life radically changed in the final ten years of his life. After several decades of obscurity, exile, failure, and being both ignored and laughed at by the establishment in his adopted Spain and entirely forgotten in Chile, after lengthy periods of poverty, and after giving up on poetry in favour of prose, he became an overnight success. All this started, arguably, with that fourth prize at Alcoy, which encouraged him to 'keep trying'.

In 1981–2 he wrote a novella, *The Elephant Walk*, and entered it into the Félix Surabaya Prize, which it won.

In 1984 the City Council of Toledo, Spain, published it – that was Bolaño's first published small-run book.

A mere fifteen years later, and with the author's final title, *Monsieur Pain*, it was republished.

Another eleven years after that, the highly respected New York-based New Directions publisher commissioned a translation into English.

By that time, Bolaño was widely acknowledged as the premier Spanish-language writer of his generation, one of the finest of the twentieth century, and perhaps the most influential from that continent since Gabriel Garcia Marquez emerged forty years earlier – a bestseller in North as well as South America. One of the pre-eminent short story writers on Planet Earth. All of which is a pretty unlikely story, no? Something the alter-ago in 'Sensini', 'twenty-something and poor as a church mouse', would have assumed to be a bad joke in poor taste if we'd told him that was his future. We all take circuitous routes. No two writers have the same story. And most of us won't become Bolaño. None of us aspiring writers can afford to be precious, but all of us can afford to be optimistic. Get organised. Keep trying. Now, if that isn't a happy ending to the story, I don't know what is.

Notes

1 Sensini supplements his living as a translator by submitting the same stories to multiple places simultaneously. A story might win first prize in a high-profile professional competition with one title, shortly before failing to be commended in a small amateur field the following week with another title.

2 Philip Jones, 'Median Author Advance Under £6,600', *The Bookseller*, 25 March 2015, www.thebookseller.com/news/average-author-advance-under-6600 (accessed 27 March 2017).

3 That number is affected by the handful of very high advances which do still happen, post-economic crash of 2008, and are possible – but which most writers will never experience.

4 Since 2014, the winners of The Novella Award have been published by Sandstone Press, the official partners of the award.

References

Short Story Prizes

Bath Flash Fiction Award.
BBC National Short Story Award.
Bridport Prize.
Commonwealth Writers' Short Story Prize.
Postcard Shorts.
Sunday Times EFG Short Story Award.

Indicative List of Websites

Flash500: www.flash500.com/index.htm
MacGuffin – via Comma Press: http://commapress.co.uk/macguffin/
Postcard Shorts: www.postcardshorts.com/
Paul McVeigh: http://paulmcveigh.blogspot.co.uk/
Short Stops: https://shortstops.info/
Thresholds: http://blogs.chi.ac.uk/shortstoryforum/
Word Factory: www.thewordfactory.tv/

Stories and Resources to Read (And Think About)

More short stories to read and resources to use exist than I could ever list here. The following – which includes texts recommended by contributors to this book – is a subjective set of suggestions which, although limited, ought to lead you in many further directions. As you can see, I've leaned heavily towards the American short story. I would argue that it isn't bias; it's just a flat fact that in the past seventy years the USA has led the world in the short story form.

Ten Anthologies

Ann Charters, *The Story and Its Writer*, 5th Edition (Bedford Books of St Martin's Press, 1997).*

Junot Diaz (ed.), *The Best American Short Stories 2016* (Houghton Mifflin, 2016). (At the time of writing, this is the latest edition of an anthology which, since 1978, has been published each year and is always guest-edited by an esteemed short story writer.)

Dave Eggers (ed.), *The Best of McSweeney's* Vol. 1 (Penguin, 2005).

Richard Ford (ed.), *The New Granta Book of the American Short Story*, Vols 1 and 2 (Granta, 2008).

Phillip Hensher (ed.), *The Penguin Book of the British Short Story*, Vols 1 and 2 (Penguin Classics, 2001).

Nicholas Royle (ed.), *The Best British Short Stories* (Salt Publications, annually since 2011).

Tobias Wolff (ed.), *The Vintage Book of Contemporary American Short Stories* (Vintage, 1995).

---

*The Bible of the form, more or less, this 1,500-page doorstop spans three centuries of short stories from around the world, and includes a host of essays by one author about another. Although it's expensive new, you can buy second-hand copies of earlier editions for next to nothing.

Twenty Collections

Kevin Barry, *Dark Lies the Island* (Vintage Classics, 2014).

Ann Beattie, *The Burning House* (Vintage, 1998).

Ray Bradbury, *The Golden Apples of the Sun* (New York: William Morrow, 1997).

Angela Carter, *The Bloody Chamber and Other Stories* (Penguin, 1990).

Raymond Carver, *What We Talk About When We Talk About Love* (Vintage, 2009).

John Cheever, *Collected Stories* (Vintage Classics, 2010).

Anton Chekhov, *About Love and Other Stories* (Oxford's World Classics, 2008).

Junot Diaz, *This Is How You Lose Her* (Faber & Faber, 2013).

F. Scott Fitzgerald, *Flappers and Philosophers: The Collected Short Stories* (Penguin Classics, 2010).

Ernest Hemingway, *The Essential Hemingway* (Penguin, 1995).

Amy Hempel, *Reasons to Live* (Harper Perennial, 1995).

Denis Johnson, *Jesus' Son* (Granta, 2012).

James Joyce, *Dubliners* (Wordsworth Classics, 1993).

Katherine Mansfield, *Bliss and Other Stories* (Various publishers, many in cheap editions).

Lorrie Moore, *Birds of America* (Faber & Faber, 2010).

Alice Munro, *Runaway* (Vintage, 2006).

Flannery O'Connor, *A Good Man Is Hard to Find* (Faber & Faber, 2016).

George Saunders, *Tenth of December* (Bloomsbury, 2014).

Wells Tower, *Everything Ravaged, Everything Burned* (Granta, 2009).

William Trevor, *The Children of Dynmouth* (Penguin, 2014).

(The publication dates above are for the latest editions; the Flannery O'Connor collection, for example, wasn't first published in 2016. The collected or selected stories of several of these writers are available, but, for the same reason that it's preferable to listen to a single album than a box set, I've tried to avoid sending you in the direction of the bumper book. My choices in that respect are subjective: who can say which is the one Alice Munro collection to read? Lastly, before you protest, Franz Kafka's 'The Metamorphosis' isn't here because (a) I got hung up on limiting the list to twenty titles and (b) you can find it (alongside 123 other timeless short stories) in Ann Charters' *The Story and Its Writer*.)

Seven Craft Texts

Tom Bailey, *A Short Story Writer's Companion* (Oxford University Press, 2001).

Susan Bell, *The Artful Edit: On the Practice of Editing Yourself* (W.W. Norton, 2007).

Dorothea Brande, *Becoming a Writer* (Jeremy P. Tarcher, 1999).

Janet Burroway, *Writing Fiction: A Guide to Narrative Craft*, 6th edition (Longman, 2003).

John Gardner, *The Art of Fiction: Notes on Craft for Young Writers* (Vintage, 1991).

Vanessa Gebbie (ed.), *Short Circuit: A Guide to the Art of the Short Story* (Salt, 2009).

Rust Hills, *Writing in General and the Short Story in Particular* (Houghton Mifflin, 2000).

Seven Websites

Duotrope

www.duotrope.com

A conduit to the whole world of submitting fiction (and poetry, memoir etc.) anywhere in the English-speaking world.

MacGuffin

http://commapress.co.uk/digital/macguffin/

Spotify for books, as Rodge Glass puts it in Chapter 26: 'Finding an Audience'. It has a hint of Wikipedia, too, as it's a collaboratively built platform. Anyone can upload a story, and via the app you'll find an archive you can search in a number of ways and stories to listen to on your mobile device. Work by unknown writers appears alongside names many will recognise – Frank Cottrell Boyce, Rose Tremain and Hilary Mantel, for instance.

The *New Yorker* Fiction Podcast

www.newyorker.com/series/fiction-podcast

Each month a distinguished writer reads out a short story he or she particularly admires (for example, Jhumpa Lahiri reads a story by William Trevor). Following that, Deborah Treisman (the *New Yorker's* fiction editor) and the guest discuss it.

The *New Yorker*: Fiction

www.newyorker.com/magazine/fiction

The *New Yorker* is the world's premier publisher of short stories. If they accept a story of yours, you can die happy, possibly on the spot, when you receive the good news. Consequently, the enormous treasure trove of stories on this site is second to none.

The *Paris Review*: Interviews

www.theparisreview.org/interviews

Interviews with writers: it's that simple. The contents of this archive go back to the 1950s, and you can search by author or decade. Here's Ray Bradbury, from an interview in 2010: 'A book has got to smell. You have to hold it in your hand and pray to it.'

Story

www.theshortstory.org.uk/

A site that celebrates the short story and includes stores to download, reviews of short stories, essays on writing them (for example, Raymond Carver's 'Principles of A Story') and abundant information on where to submit.

Thresholds

http://thresholds.chi.ac.uk/

Features, stories, discussion forums, writers' resources, short stories, essays about the short story, ongoing deadlines – plenty for you to devour. Have a listen to the Short Story Masterclass podcasts, which include interviews with the likes of Sarah Hall, Deborah Levy and Michel Faber.

(For more websites, take another look at Rodge Glass's chapter, and of course all of the sites above will lead you to further sites.)

Bibliography: The Short Story

Kate Atkinson, *Not the End of the World* (Black Swan, 2003).

Elizabeth Bowen, *Collected Stories* (Cape, 1980).

Ray Bradbury, *The Golden Apples of the Sun* (New York: William Morrow, 1997).

Anton Chekhov, *Forty Stories* (Vintage 1991).

Angela Carter, *Burning Your Boats* (Penguin, 1997).

Raymond Carver, *What We Talk About When We Talk About Love* (Vintage, 1989).

Sandra Cisneros, *The House on Mango Street* (Bloomsbury, 2004).

William Faulkner, *Selected Short Stories* (Modern Library, 1993).

Ernest Hemingway, *Death in the Afternoon* (Vintage, 2000).

Amy Hempel, *The Collected Stories of Amy Hempel* (Quercus, 2008).

Bernard MacLaverty, *A Time to Dance* (Vintage, 1999).

Adam Marek, *The Stone Thrower* (Comma Press, 2012).

Guy de Maupassant, *A Parisian Affair and Other Stories* (Penguin Classics, 2004).

Tim O'Brien, *The Things They Carried* (Broadway, 1998).

Flannery O'Connor, *Everything That Rises Must Converge* (Penguin, 1975).

Ian Rankin, *The Beat Goes On* (Orion, 2014).

J.D. Salinger, *Nine Stories* (Little, Brown, 1970).

James Salter, *Burning the Days* (Vintage, 2003).

George Saunders, *Pastoralia* (Bloomsbury, 2001).

Amy Tan, *The Joy Luck Club* (Minerva, 1991).

William Trevor, *The Stories of William Trevor* (Penguin, 1983).

David Foster Wallace, *Brief Interviews with Hideous Men* (Abacus, 2001).

Tobias Wolff, *Collected Stories* (Bloomsbury, 1997).

V.S. Pritchett, Collected Stories (London: Penguin Books, 1984).

Bibliography: Craft

Tom Bailey, *A Short Story Writer's Companion* (Oxford University Press, 2001).

Michael Baldwin, *The Way to Write Short Stories* (Elm Tree Books, 1996).

Julia Bell & Paul Magrs (eds), *The Creative Writing Coursebook* (Macmillan, 2001).

Madison Smartt Bell, *Narrative Design: A Writer's Guide to Structure* (W.W. Norton, 1997).

Susan Bell, *The Artful Edit: On the Practice of Editing Yourself* (W.W. Norton, 2007).

Jack M. Bickham, *Writing the Short Story: A Hands-On Guide for Creating Captivating Short Fiction* (Writer's Digest Books, 1994).

Will Blythe (ed.), *Why I Write: Thoughts on the Craft of Fiction* (Little, Brown, 1998).

Dorothea Brande, *Becoming a Writer* (Jeremy P. Tarcher, 1999).

Rita Mae Brown, *Starting from Scratch: A Different Kind of Writers' Manual* (Bantam, 1989).

Janet Burroway, *Writing Fiction: A Guide to Narrative Craft*, 6th Edition (Longman, 2003).

Robert Olen Butler, *From Where You Dream: The Process of Writing Fiction* (Grove Press, 2005).

Julia Cameron, *The Artist's Way* (Macmillan, 2016).

Orson Scott Card, *Characters and Viewpoint* (Robinson Publishing, 1990).

Guy Claxton, *Hare Brain, Tortoise Mind: Why Intelligence Increases When You Think Less* (4th Estate, 1998).

Barnaby Conrad, *The Complete Guide to Writing Fiction* (Writer's Digest Books, 1990).

Mason Correy, *Daily Rituals* (Picador, 2014).

Jonathan Culpeper, *Language and Characterisation* (Routledge, 2014).

Ansen Dibell, *Plot* (Robinson Publishing, 1990).

Joan Didion, *Slouching Towards Bethlehem* (Flamingo, 2001).

Richard Ford, *The Granta Book of the American Long Story* (Granta Books, 1998).

Jonathan Franzen, *How to Be Alone* (4th Estate, 2002).

James N. Frey, *How to Write a Damned Good Novel* (Macmillan, 1988).

John Gardner, *The Art of Fiction: Notes on Craft for Young Writers* (Vintage, 1991).

Vanessa Gebbie (ed.), *Short Circuit: A Guide to the Art of the Short Story* (Salt Publishing, 2009).

Natalie Goldberg, *Wild Mind: Living the Writer's Life* (Rider, 1991).

Josip Novakovich, Fiction Writer's Workshop (Cincinnati: Story Press, 1995).

Oscar Wilde, The Critic as Artist: With Some Remarks on the Importance of Doing Nothing and Discussing Everything (Los Angeles: Sun & Moon Books, 1997).

Harry Levin (ed.), The Essential James Joyce (London: Triad Grafton, 1988).

Frank O'Connor, The Lonely Voice: A Study of the Short Story (London: Macmillan, 1993).

Robert Graham et al. (eds), *The Road to Somewhere: A Creative Writing Companion*, 2nd Edition (Palgrave Macmillan, 2013).

John Haffenden (ed.), *Novelists in Interview* (Methuen, 1985).

Oakley Hall, *The Art and Craft of Novel Writing* (Story Press, 1989).

George V. Higgins, *On Writing* (Bloomsbury, 1991).

Stephen King, *On Writing* (Hodder and Stoughton, 2000).

Nancy Kress, *Write Great Fiction – Characters, Emotion & Viewpoint: Techniques and Exercises for Crafting Dynamic Characters and Effective Viewpoints* (Readers Digest Books, 2005).

Anne Lamott, *Bird by Bird: Some Instructions on Writing and Life* (Anchor Books, 1995).

Bonnie Lyons & Bill Oliver (eds), *Passion and Craft: Conversations with Notable Writers* (University of Illinois Press, 1998).

Thomas McCormack, *The Fiction Editor, the Novel, and the Novelist* (St Martin's Press, 1998).

Jay McInerney (ed.), *The Penguin Book of New American Voices* (Penguin, 1995).

Robert McKee, *Story: Substance, Structure, Style, and the Principles of Screenwriting* (Methuen Publishing, 1999).

Sara Maitland, *The Writer's Way* (Capella, 2005).

Susan Garland Mann, *The Short Story Cycle: A Genre Companion and Reference Guide* (Greenwood, 1989).

Sharon Monteith, Jenny Newman & Pat Wheeler (eds), *Contemporary British and Irish Fiction: An Introduction Through Interviews* (Arnold, 2004).

Jennifer Moon, *Learning Journals: A Handbook for Academics, Students and Professional Development* (Kogan Page, 1999).

Jenny Newman et al., *The Writer's Workbook*, 2nd Edition (Arnold, 2004).

Joyce Carol Oates, *Telling Stories* (W.W. Norton, 1997).

Patricia T. O'Conner, *Words Fail Me: What Everyone Who Writes Should Know About Writing* (Harcourt, 1999).

George Plimpton (ed.), *The Writer's Chapbook* (Penguin Books, 1992).

Daniel Price, *How to Make a Journal of Your Life* (Ten Speed Press, 1999).

Tristine Rainer, *The New Diary* (Jeremy P. Tarcher, 1981).

John Singleton & Mary Luckhurst (eds), *The Creative Writing Handbook* (Basingstoke: Palgrave, 1996).

Zadie Smith, [Introduction to] *Martha and Hanwell* (Penguin Books, 2005).

John Updike, *More Matter: Essays and Criticism* (Fawcett Books, 2000).

Eudora Welty, Eudora, *The Eye of the Story* (Random House, 1978).

Writing Bursts Collection

For those who like all their eggs in one basket, here are the writing bursts you've seen in individual chapters, niftily collected together.

Opening Lines

* She didn't want to go to London.
* The next day was better.
* As far as she could see, it was over.
* They went to school together, in different classes.
* Things were dead, but now they're picking up.
* It made me smile when the others began to believe that she had done it.
* Everyone knows someone who has it, but not everyone who has it knows they've got it.
* I wish you had told me this before.
* Things could have been very different.
* Everything begins with a question, and not all questions have answers.
* Five pints, right.
* A lot of people leave this town and sooner or later most of them come back.
* That was the moment when I wished I could remember what we had been taught.
* 'I feel so pathetic crying,' he said.
* They made us wait in this shabby little room.
* People don't like me.
* This was turning out to be a huge mistake.

Situations

* A situation: any relevant app notwithstanding, a young couple can't find their destination walk round and round for a long time, getting increasingly frustrated.
* A situation: sleeping rough.
* A situation: your protagonist is entering a room and meant to be giving a speech to a large crowd. He hasn't a single idea about what to say.

Images

Put any of the following in your search engine and use the image as your prompt.

* Henri Cartier-Bresson: Puddle.
* Sam Walsh, 'The Dinner Party'.
* Andrew Wyeth, 'Christina's World'
* Henri Fantin-Latour 'White cup and saucer'.
* Cy Twombly, Untitled Peonies.
* Bruce Gilden.

Music

Put any of the following in your search engine and use the music as your prompt. Where it's a song, listen without any visuals – the official video or anything else. You just want the experience of hearing the lyrics and the music.

* Part, 'Spiegel im Spiegel'
* Arctic Monkeys, 'Cornerstone'
* 'Joni Mitchell, Chelsea Morning'

Video

Put any of the following in your search engine and use the film clip as your prompt.

* To Kill a Mockingbird Boo is a hero.
* Hail, Caesar! Would that it were so simple.
* Three Reasons: Three Colors: Blue.

Bonus Burst

* Search for the lyrics of Bob Dylan's 'Things Have Changed'. You'll find a prompt in almost every line.

Index